Christian
Ethics

Christian
Ethics

Norman L.
Geisler

APOLLOS
Leicester, England

APOLLOS (an imprint of Inter-Varsity Press),
38 De Montfort Street, Leicester LE1 7GP, England

Unless otherwise indicated, Scripture references are from the Holy Bible, New International Version. Copyright © 1973, 1978, 1984 International Bible Society. Used in USA by permission of Zondervan Bible Publishers, Grand Rapids, Michigan, and published in Great Britain by Hodder and Stoughton Ltd. Other translations cited are the American Standard Version (ASV), the King James Version (KJV), the New American Standard Bible (NASB), the New English Bible (NEB), and the Revised Standard Version (RSV).

First British edition 1990

British Library Cataloguing in Publication Data

Geisler, Norman L.
    Christian ethics.
    1. Christian ethics
    I. Title
    241

    ISBN 0-85111-418-0

Typeset and printed in the United States of America

To my children:
Ruth, David, Daniel, Rhoda, Paul, and **Rachel**

Contents

Tables

Acknowledgments

I wish to thank Professor J. P. Moreland, David Geisler, and Thomas Howe for reviewing this entire manuscript and making many helpful suggestions for improving it. I also appreciate the evaluation of the last section by Drs. Carl Haisch, Wayne House, and Daryl Bach. While deeply grateful for their contributions, I take responsibility for the contents.

Preface

This book is not a revision of previous works on ethics; it is a totally new work. Obviously there is a continuity with previous works, but the structure, content, and much of the thought are new. Part 1 supersedes *Options in Contemporary Christian Ethics,* and the book as a whole replaces *Christian Ethics: Alternatives and Issues.*

Several factors made this book necessary: changes in approach to certain topics; reorganization of topics; an updating of the material; emergence of new issues (such as bioethics); and a shift of viewpoint from earlier works on such issues as abortion. In the light of all of these factors, it seemed best to write a new book. I hope that it will be a usable textbook for those seeking a survey of basic ethical options and issues.

Much has happened in our world since I first wrote on ethics in 1971, and none of it has decreased the need for an analysis of the ethical problems facing Christians today. More than ever before, we need to bring the standard of God's revealed truth to bear on the multitudinous moral problems that confront a Christian in our contemporary culture.

Someone has said that we live in a strange world where the relativity of Einstein is considered absolute, and the absolutes of the Bible are considered relative. Be that as it may, in our relativistic culture Christians can ill afford to make an uncertain sound on our ethical trumpet. Rather, the need for a clear understanding of the issues and a courageous application of God's Word to them is pressing. It is my hope that in some small measure this book may contribute to these ends.

PART 1

Ethical Options

1

All the Options

Ethics deals with what is morally right and wrong. Christian ethics deals with what is morally right and wrong for a Christian. This is a book on Christian ethics. Since Christians base their beliefs on God's revelation in Scripture, the Bible will be cited as an authority for conclusions drawn here.

God has not limited himself to revelation in Scripture; he also has a general revelation in nature (Rom. 1:19–20; 2:12–14). Since God's moral character does not change, it should be expected that there will be similarities and overlaps between God's natural and supernatural revelations. However, the focus of this book is not God's natural law for all men, but his divine law for believers.

Definitions of Ethics

Numerous theories have been proposed concerning what is meant by a morally good action. Before we undertake to develop a Christian ethic, it will be helpful to discuss the various views that contrast with a Christian view of morality.

Might Is Right

The ancient Greek philosopher Thrasymachus is credited with holding that "justice is the interest of the stronger party." In other words, what is morally right is defined in terms of who has the power. Often this is understood as political power, as in the case of Machiavelli, though it could mean physical, psychological, or other kinds of power.

Although this is not a widely confessed view, nonetheless it is too often practiced. But the theory has several fatal flaws. First, it fails to note the difference between power and goodness. It is possible to be powerful without being good, and it is possible to be good without being powerful. Second, evil tyrants, from Nero to Stalin, are sufficient evidence to refute the theory that might makes right. The testimony of history is that power corrupts, and absolute power corrupts absolutely.

Morals Are Mores

Another ethical theory holds that what is morally right is determined by the group to which one belongs. Ethics is defined in terms of the ethnic. What is morally right is what the community says is right. Community demands are the ethical commands. Each society creates its own ethics. Whatever similarity may happen to exist between moral codes in different social groups is simply due to common needs and aspirations, not to any universal moral prescriptions.

The first problem with this position is what is called the "is-ought" fallacy. Just because someone is doing something does not mean he ought to be. Otherwise, rape, cruelty, and murder would automatically be morally right. Second, if each community's mores are right, then there is no way to adjudicate conflicts between different communities. For unless there are moral principles above all communities, then there is no moral way to solve conflicts between them. Third, if morals are relative to each social group, then even two opposite ethical principles are both right. But contradictories cannot both be true. Everything cannot be right, at least not opposites.

Man Is the Measure

Protagoras, an ancient Greek philosopher, claimed that "man is the measure of all things." Understood in the individual sense, this means that each person's own will is the standard for what is right and wrong. The morally right thing to do is what is morally right to me. What is right for me may be wrong for another and vice versa.

The most obvious criticism is that this view implies that an act is right for someone, even if it is cruel, hateful, or tyrannical. But this is morally unacceptable. Second, if this theory were put into practice, society would be rendered inoperative. There can be no true community (com-unity) where there is no unity. If everyone did as he pleased, chaos would result. Finally, this theory does not tell us which aspect of human nature should be taken as the measure of all things. It is simply begging the question to claim it is the "good aspects," for that implies some standard of good beyond humans by which we can tell what is good and what is evil in human nature or activity.

The Human Race Is the Basis of Right

One way to avoid the radical individualism and ethical solipsism of Protagoras' position is to use the human race as a whole as the standard for good. In this way the part does not determine what is right for the whole, but the whole determines what is right for the part. In brief, mankind is the measure of all things.

In response, it should be noted first that even the whole race could be wrong. Whole communities, like Jonestown, have committed mass suicide. What if the vast majority of the human race decides that suicide is the best "solution" to the world's problems? Should dissenters be forced to conform? Second, the human race is changing, as are ethical practices. Child sacrifice was once more commonly approved, as was slavery. Hence, we say the race has a better expression of values. But "better" implies a "best" by which the progress is measured. We cannot know that the human race is better or worse unless there is a perfect standard outside it by which it can be measured.

Right Is Moderation

According to Aristotle, morality is found in moderation. The right thing is the "golden mean" or moderate course of action. For example, Aristotle believed that temperance is the mean between indulgence and insensibility. And pride is the moderate course between vanity and humility. Likewise, courage is the halfway point between fear and aggression.

To be sure, moderation is often the wisest course. Even the Bible says, "Let your moderation be known unto all men" (Phil. 4:5 KJV). The question is not whether moderation is often the proper expression of morality, but whether it is the proper definition (or essence) of morality. There are several reasons for thinking that it is not the very nature of what is good. First of all, many times the right thing is the extreme thing to do. In emergencies, in self-defense, and in wars against aggression, moderate actions are not always the best ones. Even some virtues obviously should not be expressed in moderate amounts. One should not be moderately loving. Neither should we be moderately grateful, thankful, or generous. Second, there is no universal agreement on what is moderate. Aristotle, for example, considered humility a vice; Christians believe it is a virtue. Third, moderation is at best only a general guide for action, not a universal ethical law.

Right Is What Brings Pleasure

Springing from the Epicureans (fourth cent. B.C.), hedonists claim that what brings pleasure is morally right and what brings pain is morally wrong. But since few things are all pleasure or all pain, the formula for determining what is good is complicated. The good, they claim, is what brings the most pleasure and the least pain to the greatest number of people.

There are many difficulties with this definition of good. First, not all pleasures are good (e.g., sadism), and not all pain is bad (e.g., warning pain). Second, what kind of pleasure should be used as the basis of the test? There are physical, psychological, spiritual, and many other kinds of pleasure. Third, are we to use immediate pleasure or ultimate pleasure as the test? Pleasures in this life or the next? Fourth, should it be pleasure for the individual, the group, or the race?

Right Is the Greatest Good
for the Greatest Number

Reflecting on the problems just mentioned, some utilitarians have defined moral rightness in terms of what brings the greatest good for the greatest number of persons in the long run. Some understand the meaning of good quantitatively (Jeremy Bentham [1748–1832]). Others understand it qualitatively (John Stuart Mill [1806–1873]).

The problems with this kind of utilitarian definition of good are multiple. First, there is no agreement on how good should be understood (i.e., quantitatively or qualitatively). Second, it begs the question to say that moral right is what brings the greatest good, for then we must ask what is "good." Either right and good are defined in terms of each other, which is circular reasoning, or good must be determined by some standard beyond the utilitarian process. Third, no human being can accurately predict what will happen in the long run. Hence, for all practical purposes a utilitarian definition of good is useless. It must still fall back on something else to determine what is good now, in the short run.

Right Is What Is Desirable for Its Own Sake

Following Aristotle, some have defined the good as that which is desirable for its own sake, in and of itself. That is, moral value is an end but not a means. It is never to be desired for the sake of anything else. For example, no one should desire virtue as a means of getting something else (e.g., riches). Virtue should be desired for its own sake.

This view has some obvious merit, but it raises several questions nonetheless. First, it does not really define the content of a morally good act but simply designates the direction in which one finds good (namely, in ends). Second, it is easy to confuse what is desired and what is desirable (e.g., what ought to be desired). This leads to another criticism. Good cannot simply be that which is desired (as opposed to what is really desirable), since we often desire what is evil. Finally, what appears to be good in itself is not always really good. Suicide seems to be good to someone in distress but really is not good. It does not solve any problem; it is the final way to avoid solving the problem.

Right Is Indefinable

Despairing of any hope of specifying what is morally good, some simply insist that good is indefinable. In *Principia Ethica,* G. E. Moore (1873–1958) argued that every attempt to define good commits the "naturalistic fallacy" of assuming that since pleasure can be attributed to good, they are identical. Moore contended that all we can say is that "good is good," nothing more. Attempting to define good in terms of something else makes that something the intrinsic good.

Again, there is some merit in this view. There can be only one ultimate good and everything else must be subordinated to it. However, the view as such is inadequate. First of all, it provides no content for what good means. If there is no content to what is right or wrong, then there is no way to distinguish a good act from a bad one. Second, just because the good cannot be defined in terms of something more ultimate does not mean that it cannot be defined at all. A morally good God can create morally good creatures like himself. Although in such a case God is the ultimate moral good, nonetheless something of his goodness can be understood from the moral creatures he has willed to be like himself.

Good Is What God Wills

One final alternative is to define good in terms of what God wills. This, of course, is the Christian view of the nature of good. The good is what God wills is good. Whatever action God specifies is a good action is a good action. Conversely, if God wills an action to be evil, then it is evil. Thus, moral good is both ultimate and specifiable. It is ultimate because it comes from God. And it is specifiable since it can be found in his revelation to mankind.

Two objections are often raised. First, it is alleged that this view is a form of authoritarianism. This objection, however, is valid only if the authority is less than ultimate. That is, if any finite creature professed to have this ultimate authority, then we could rightly cry "authoritarianism." However, there is nothing wrong with considering the ultimate authority to be the ultimate authority. If an absolutely morally perfect God exists, then by his very nature he is the ultimate authority (or standard) for what is good and what is not.

The second objection is that defining good in terms of God's will is arbitrary. This objection applies, however, only to a voluntaristic, not to an essentialistic, view of good. A voluntarist believes that something is good simply because God wills it. An essentialist, on the other hand, holds that God wills something because it is good in accordance with his own nature. This form of the divine-command view of ethics escapes these criticisms and forms the basis for a Christian ethic.

A Christian View of Ethics

Now that we have discussed the various theories of ethics, we are in a better position to understand a Christian view of ethics. There are several distinguishing characteristics of Christian ethics, each of which will be briefly discussed here.

Christian Ethics Is Based on God's Will

As we have just seen, Christian ethics is a form of the divine-command position. An ethical duty is something we ought to do. It is a divine prescription. Of course, the ethical imperatives that God gives are in accord with his unchangeable moral character. That is, God wills what is right in accordance with his own moral attributes. "Be holy, because I am holy," the Lord commanded Israel (Lev. 11:45). "Be perfect, therefore, as your heavenly Father is perfect," Jesus said to his disciples (Matt. 5:48). "It is impossible for God to lie" (Heb. 6:18). So we should not lie either. "God is love" (1 John 4:16), and so Jesus said, "Love your neighbor as yourself" (Matt. 22:39). In brief, Christian ethics is based on God's will, but God never wills anything contrary to his unchanging moral character.

Christian Ethics Is Absolute

Since God's moral character does not change (Mal. 3:6; James 1:17), it follows that moral obligations flowing from his nature are absolute. That is, they are always binding everywhere on everyone. Of course, not everything God wills flows necessarily from his unchanging nature. Some things are merely in accord with his nature but flow freely from his will. For example, God chose to test Adam's and Eve's moral obedience by forbidding them to eat a specific fruit on a tree (Gen. 2:16–17). Although it was morally wrong for Adam and Eve to disobey that command, we are no longer bound by that command today. That command was based on God's will and did not flow necessarily from his nature.

On the other hand, God's command not to murder (Gen. 9:6) applied before the law was given to Moses, under the law of Moses (Exod. 20:13), and also since the time of Moses (Rom. 13:9). In brief, murder is wrong at all times and all places and for all people. This is true because humans are created in the "image of God" (Gen. 1:27; 9:6). This includes a moral likeness to God (Col. 3:10; James 3:9). And whatever is traceable to God's unchanging moral character is a moral absolute. This includes such moral obligations as holiness, justice, love, truthfulness, and mercy. Other commands flowing from God's will, but not necessarily from his nature, are equally binding on a believer, but they are not absolute. That is, they must be obeyed because God prescribed them, but he did not prescribe them for all people, times, and places. Absolute moral duties, on the contrary, are binding on all people at all times and in all places.

Christian Ethics Is Based on God's Revelation

Christian ethics is based on God's commands, the revelation of which is both general (Rom. 1:19–20; 2:12–15) and special (Rom. 2:18; 3:2). God has revealed himself both in nature (Ps. 19:1–6) and in Scripture (Ps. 19:7–14). General revelation contains God's commands for all people. Special revelation declares his will for believers. But in either case, the basis of human ethical responsibility is divine revelation.

Failure to recognize God as the source of moral duty does not exonerate anyone, even an atheist, from his or her moral duty. For "when Gentiles, who do not have the law [of Moses], do by nature things required by the law, they are a law for themselves, even though they do not have the law, since they show that the requirements of the law are written on their hearts" (Rom. 2:14–15). That is, even if unbelievers do not have the moral law in their minds, they still have it written on their hearts. Even if they do not know it by way of cognition, they show it by way of inclination.

Christian Ethics Is Prescriptive

Since moral rightness is prescribed by a moral God it is prescriptive. For there is no moral law without a moral Lawgiver; there is no moral legislation without a moral Legislator. So Christian ethics is by its very nature prescriptive, not descriptive. Ethics deals with what ought to be, not with what is. Christians do not find their ethical duties in the standard of Christians but in the standard for Christians—the Bible.

From a Christian point of view, a purely descriptive ethic is no ethic at all. Describing human behavior is sociology. But prescribing human behavior is the province of morality. The attempt to derive morals from mores is, as we have already noted, the "is-ought" fallacy. What people actually do is not the basis for what they ought to do. If it were, then people ought to lie, cheat, steal, and murder, since these things are done all the time.

Christian Ethics Is Deontological

Ethical systems can be broadly divided into two categories, deontological (duty-centered) and teleological (end-centered). Christian ethics is deontological. Utilitarianism is an example of a teleological ethic. The nature of a deontological ethic can be seen more clearly by contrast with a teleological view (see table 1.1).

A couple of illustrations will clarify this point. A man attempts to rescue a drowning person but fails. According to one form of teleological ethic, this was not a good act because it did not have good results. Since the results determine the goodness of the act, and the results were not good, then it follows that the attempted rescue was not a good act.

Of course, a more sophisticated form of teleological (utilitarian) ethic might argue that the attempt was good, even though it failed, because it had a good effect on society. People heard about it and were encouraged to help rescue others in the future. But even here the attempted act of rescue that failed was not good in itself. Rather, it would have been good if and only if it had brought some good results, either for the drowning person or for someone else.

By contrast, the Christian ethic is deontological and insists that even some acts that fail are good. Christians believe, for example, that it is better to have loved and to have lost than not to have loved at all. Christians believe that the cross was not a failure simply because only some will be saved. It was sufficient for all, even if it is efficient only for those who believe. The Christian ethic insists that it is good to work against bigotry and racism, even if one fails. This is so because

TABLE 1.1
Two Views of Ethics

Deontological Ethic	Teleological Ethic
Rule determines the result	Result determines the rule
Rule is the basis of the act	Result is the basis of the act
Rule is good regardless of result	Rule is good because of result
Result always calculated within the rules	Result sometimes used to break rules

moral actions that reflect God's nature are good whether they are successful or not. Good for the Christian is not determined in a lottery. In life the winner is not always right.

However, Christian ethics does not neglect results. Simply because results do not determine what is right does not mean that it is not right to consider results. Indeed, results of actions are important in Christian ethics. For example, a Christian should calculate in which direction a gun is pointing before he pulls the trigger. Drivers need to estimate the possible consequence of their speed in relation to other objects. Speakers are responsible for calculating the possible effects of their words on others. Christians have a duty to anticipate the results of not being immunized to serious disease, and so on.

However, in all the foregoing illustrations there is an important difference between the deontological use of results and a teleological use of them. In Christian ethics these results are all calculated within rules or norms. That is, no anticipated result as such can be used as a justification for breaking any God-given moral law. Utilitarians, on the other hand, use anticipated results to break moral rules. In fact, they use results to make the rules. Existing rules can be broken if the expected results call for it. For example, while Christian ethics allows for inoculation for disease, it does not allow for infanticide to purify the genetic stock of the human race; in this case the end result is used to justify the use of an evil means. In brief, the end may justify the use of good means, but it does not justify the use of any means, certainly not evil ones.

Various Views on Ethics

There are only six major ethical systems, each designated by its answer to the question, Are there any objective ethical laws? That is, are any moral laws not purely subjective but binding on humans in general?

In answer, *antinomianism* says there are no moral laws. *Situationism* affirms there is one absolute law. *Generalism* claims there are some general laws but no absolute ones. *Unqualified absolutism* believes in many absolute laws that never conflict. *Conflicting absolutism* contends there are many absolute norms that sometimes conflict, and we are obligated to do the lesser evil. *Graded absolutism* holds that many absolute laws sometimes conflict and we are responsible for obeying the higher law.

Differences Between Various Views

Of the six basic ethical views, two deny all objectively absolute moral laws. Of them, antinomianism denies all universal and general moral laws. Generalism, on the other hand, denies only universal moral laws but holds to general ones. That is, there are some objective moral laws that are binding most of the time but not necessarily all the time.

Four ethical views claim to be absolutisms. Of these, situationism believes in only one absolute, while the others believe in two or more absolutes. Of them, unqualified absolutism contends that these absolute moral principles never conflict, while the other two believe that they sometimes do conflict. Of the two that believe these moral principles sometimes conflict, conflicting absolutism contends that we are responsible to do the lesser evil but guilty for whichever one we break. On the other hand, graded absolutism holds that our responsibility is to obey the greater commandment. Consequently, we are not guilty for not following the lesser commandment in conflict with it.

Examples of the Six Major Ethical Views

Corrie ten Boom tells how she lied to save Jews from the Nazi death camps. During U.S. Senate hearings on the Iran-Contra issue, Lieutenant Colonel Oliver North testified that he had, in the process of performing his duties, lied to save innocent lives. North said, "I had to weigh lying and lives."

In a number of biblical stories, people lied to save lives. The Hebrew midwives lied to save the baby boys Pharaoh had commanded them to kill (Exod. 1:15–19). Rahab lied to save the lives of the Jewish spies in Jericho (Josh. 2).

Is it ever right to lie to save a life? This issue will serve to focus the differences among the six basic ethical positions.

Lying is neither right nor wrong: There are no laws. Antinomianism asserts that lying to save lives is neither right nor wrong. It affirms that there are no objective moral principles by which the issue can be judged right or wrong. The issue must be decided on subjective, personal, or pragmatic grounds, but not on any objective moral grounds. We are literally without a moral law to decide the issue.

Lying is generally wrong: There are no universal laws. Generalism claims that lying is generally wrong. As a rule, lying is wrong, but in specific cases this general rule can be broken. Since there are no universal moral laws, whether a given lie is right will depend on the results. If the results are good, then the lie is right. Most generalists believe that lying to save a life is right because in this case the end justifies the means necessary to attain it. However, lying in general is wrong.

Lying is sometimes right: There is only one universal law. Situationism claims that there is only one absolute moral law, and telling the truth is not it. Love is the only absolute, and lying may be the loving thing to do. In fact, lying to save a life is the loving thing to do.

Hence, lying is sometimes right. Indeed, any moral rule except love can and should be broken for love's sake. Everything else is relative; only one thing is absolute. Thus the situationist believes lying to save lives is morally justified.

Lying is always wrong: There are many nonconflicting laws. Unqualified absolutism believes that there are many absolute moral laws, and none of them should ever be broken. Truth is such a law. Therefore, one must always tell the truth, even if someone dies as a result of it. Truth is absolute, and absolutes cannot be broken. Therefore, there are no exceptions to telling the truth. Results are never used as a rationale to break rules, even if the results are desirable.

Lying is forgivable: There are many conflicting laws. Conflicting absolutism recognizes that we live in an evil world where absolute moral laws sometimes run into inevitable conflict. In such cases it is our moral duty to do the lesser evil. We must break the lesser law and plead mercy. For instance, we should lie to save the life and then ask for forgiveness for breaking God's absolute moral law. Our moral dilemmas are sometimes unavoidable, but we are culpable anyway. God cannot change his absolute moral prescriptions because of our moral predicaments.

Lying is sometimes right: There are higher laws. Graded absolutism holds that there are many moral absolutes and they sometimes conflict. However, some laws are higher than others, so when there is an unavoidable conflict, it is our duty to follow the higher moral law. God does not blame us for what we could not avoid. Thus he exempts us from responsibility to follow the lower law in view of the overriding obligation to obey the higher law. Many graded absolutists believe that mercy to the innocent is a greater moral duty than telling truth to the guilty. Hence, they are convinced that it is right in such cases to lie in order to save a life.

In summary, antinomianism sets forth its view to the exclusion of all objective moral laws. Generalism claims that there are exceptions to moral laws. Situationism holds one moral absolute to the exclusion of all others. Unqualified absolutism insists that there is always an escape from the apparent conflict in absolute moral laws. Conflicting absolutism contends that when moral laws conflict then doing the lesser evil is excusable. And graded absolutism holds that when moral laws conflict, God grants an exemption to the lower in view of our duty to obey the higher. Each of these views will be examined in the next six chapters.

Select Readings

Aristotle. *Nicomachean Ethics.* In *The Complete Works of Aristotle: The Revised Oxford Translation,* edited by Jonathan Barnes. 2 vols. Princeton, N.J.: Princeton University Press, 1984.

Bourke, Vernon. *History of Ethics.* New York: Doubleday, 1968.

Fletcher, Joseph. *Situation Ethics: The New Morality.* Philadelphia: Westminster, 1966.

Gula, Richard M. *What Are They Saying about Moral Norms?* Mahwah, N.J.: Paulist, 1982.

Hume, David. *Essays, Moral, Political, and Literary.* Edited by Eugene F. Miller. Indianapolis: Liberty Fund, 1985.

Kant, Immanuel. *Foundations of the Metaphysics of Morals: Text and Critical Essays.* Edited by Robert P. Wolff. New York: Bobbs-Merrill, 1969.

Plato. *The Republic.* New York: Oxford University Press, 1967.

2

Antinomianism

Broadly speaking, ethical systems fall into two categories: non-absolutisms and absolutisms. In the first category are antinomianism (chap. 2), situationism (chap. 3), and generalism (chap. 4). In the second category are unqualified absolutism (chap. 5), conflicting absolutism (chap. 6), and graded absolutism (chap. 7).

Since Christian ethics is firmly rooted in the unchanging moral character of God (Lev. 11:45; Mal. 3:6), the first three options are not for the Christian. Nonetheless, since they challenge Christian ethics, they must be addressed.

Background of Antinomianism

Antinomianism, which literally means "against or instead of law," holds that there are no binding moral laws, that everything is relative.

Antinomianism in the Ancient World

Ethical antinomianism has a long history. There were at least three movements in the ancient world that influenced the rise of antinomianism: processism, hedonism, and skepticism.

Processism. The ancient Greek philosopher Heraclitus said, "No man steps into the same river twice, for fresh waters are ever upon him." Everything in the world, he believed, is in a constant state of flux. A later Greek thinker, Cratylus, carried this philosophy one step further, contending that no one steps into the same river once. He argued that the river and everything else have no "sameness" or unchanging essence. So convinced was Cratylus that all is flux that he was not even sure that he existed. When asked about his existence, he would simply wiggle his finger, indicating that he too was in flux. It is clear that if this is applied to the realm of ethics, there can be no abiding moral laws. Every ethical value will change with the situation.

Hedonism. The ancient Epicureans gave impetus to a relativistic ethic, which makes pleasure the essence of good and pain the essence of evil, known as hedonism (from the Greek *hedone*—pleasure). But pleasures are relative to persons, places, and periods. An airplane ride is pure pleasure for some and sheer agony for others. Sometimes the same music is relaxing, and at other times annoying. Applied to the realm of morals, this view contends that what is morally good for one person may be evil for another.

Skepticism. The central thesis of skepticism is: Suspend judgment on all matters. Sextus Empiricus was a famous skeptic in the ancient world, as was David Hume in modern times. The skeptic insists that every issue has two sides and every question can be argued to a stalemate. Since no firm and final conclusion can be drawn, we must suspend judgment in all matters. In ethics this would mean that nothing should ever be considered absolutely right or wrong.

Antinomianism in the Medieval World

Although the medieval Western world was dominated by a Christian point of view, it still generated several strains of thought that contributed to antinomianism. The most notable among these were intentionalism, voluntarism, and nominalism.

Intentionalism. In the twelfth century, Peter Abelard argued that an act is right if it is done with good intention and wrong if done with bad intention. Hence, some acts that seem bad are really good. For example, someone who accidentally kills another is not morally culpable. Neither is giving money to the poor a good act, if it is done for the wrong motives (e.g., to be praised by others). This being the case, it would seem that the rightness or wrongness of an act is relative to a person's intentions.

Voluntarism. The fourteenth-century thinker William of Ockham argued that all moral principles are traceable to God's will. Thus God could have decided differently about what is right and what is wrong. Ockham believed that something is right because God wills it; God does not will it because it is right. If this is so, then what is morally right today may not be so tomorrow. Although Christian voluntarists took comfort in the belief that God would not change his will on basic moral issues, they could not be sure that morals would not change. In this way voluntarism helped pave the way for antinomianism.

Nominalism. Another aspect of Ockham's thought was called nominalism, or the denial of universals. Nominalists believe there are no universal forms or essences, that only particular things exist. Universals exist only in the mind, not in reality. The real world is radically individual. There is, for example, no such thing as the essence of "humanness." Individual humans exist in the real world, but "humanness" exists only as a concept in the mind. It is not difficult to see that if the same reasoning is applied to ethics, then there is no such thing as goodness or justice. There are only individual acts of justice that differ from others, but no such thing as justice itself.

Antinomianism in the Modern World

The growth of relativism in the modern world is manifest in three movements: utilitarianism, existentialism, and evolutionism. Each of these contributes in its own way to antinomianism.

Utilitarianism. Building on ancient hedonism, Jeremy Bentham (1748–1832) laid down the principle that one should act so as to produce the greatest good for the greatest number of persons in the long run. This is sometimes called the "utilitarian calculus." This he understood in the quantitative sense of what brings the greatest amount of pleasure and the least amount of pain.

John Stuart Mill used the same utilitarian calculus, only he understood it in a qualitative sense. He believed that some pleasures were of higher quality than others. He even went so far as to say it would be better to be an unhappy man than a happy pig, for the intellectual and aesthetic qualities of human life are qualitatively superior to the mere physical pleasures of an animal. In any event, there are no absolute moral laws. It all depends on what brings about the greatest pleasure. And this may differ from person to person and place to place.

Existentialism. Søren Kierkegaard (1813–1855) is the father of modern existentialism. Although he was a Christian thinker, many believe that he opened the door for antinomianism by claiming that our highest duty goes beyond moral law. Even though Kierkegaard earnestly believed the moral law which says "thou shalt not kill," he also believed that God told Abraham to kill his son Isaac (Gen. 22). He believed there was no moral reason or justification for such an act, but that it was necessary in this case to transcend the ethical by "a leap of faith."

Following Kierkegaard, non-Christian thinkers such as Jean-Paul Sartre (1905–1980) took existentialism a step closer to antinomianism. Sartre argued that no ethical acts have any real meaning. He concluded *Being and Nothingness* by saying, "It amounts to the same thing whether one gets drunk alone or is a leader of nations."[1]

Evolutionism. After Darwin, men like Herbert Spencer (1820–1903) expanded evolution into a cosmic theory. Others, such as T. H. Huxley (1825–1895) and Julian Huxley (1887–1975), worked out an evolutionary ethic. The central tenet is that whatever aids the evolutionary process is right and whatever hinders it is wrong. Julian Huxley laid down three principles of evolutionary ethics: it is right to realize ever-new possibilities in evolution; it is right to respect human individuality and to encourage its fullest development; it is right to construct a mechanism for further social evolution.

Adolf Hitler worked out an evolutionary ethic in *Mein Kampf* (1924). Applying Darwin's principle of natural selection or survival of the fittest to human ethnic groups, Hitler concluded that since evolution has produced the superior (Aryan) stock, we must work to preserve it. Likewise, he believed that inferior breeds must be weeded out. On this basis he killed six million Jews and six million other non-Aryans.

Antinomianism in the Contemporary World

Several movements in the contemporary world contribute to a lawless morality. Three that stand out are emotivism, nihilism, and situationism. In their extreme forms, all of these are antinomian.

Emotivism. A. J. Ayer (1910–1970) argued that all ethical statements are emotive. That is, they are really only an expression of our feeling. Thus statements like "thou shalt not kill" really mean "I dislike killing" or "I feel killing is wrong." Ethical statements are merely expostulations of our subjective feelings. There are no divine imperatives. Everything is relative to one's individual feelings. Hence, there are no objective moral laws which are binding on all persons everywhere.

Nihilism. The famous German atheist Friedrich Nietzsche (1844–1900) said, "God is dead and we have killed him." When God died all objective values died with him.[2] The Russian novelist Fyodor Dostoevsky (1821–1881) noted correctly that if God is dead, then anything goes. For Nietzsche, the death of God meant not only the death of God-given values, but also the need for man to create his own values. In doing so, he argued, we must go "beyond good and evil." Since

1. Jean-Paul Sartre, *Being and Nothingness,* trans. Hazel E. Barnes (New York: Philosophical Library, 1956), p. 767.

2. Friedrich Nietzsche, *The Gay Science,* in *The Portable Nietzsche,* trans. Walter Kaufmann (New York: Viking, 1968), p. 95.

there is no God to will what is good, we must will our own good. And since there is no eternal value, we must will the eternal recurrence of the same state of affairs. Nietzsche said, in the last line of *The Genealogy of Morals,* that he would rather will nothingness than not to will at all. This willing of nothingness is what is called nihilism (nothingness-ism).

Situationism. According to this view, everything is relative to the situation in which one finds oneself. Although the contemporary ethicist Joseph Fletcher claims to believe in one absolute ethical norm (see chap. 3), he has no absolute moral principles with substantive content. In this sense, his view contributes heavily to antinomianism. Fletcher says we should avoid words such as "never" and "always." There are no moral principles that apply to all people at all times. All ethical decisions are expedient and circumstantial.

Basic Beliefs of Antinomians

Antinomians are without moral law. This can be understood in an absolute or in a limited sense. In an absolute sense, they are without any moral law whatsoever, though few claim to hold this view. This is usually something said of ethical relativism by way of critique. It is a view that they are charged with holding by way of reduction, not by their explicit confession.

Limited antinomianism is more widely held. This is a form of ethical relativism that denies any objective, absolute, or God-given laws. It does not deny all moral law, but does deny all laws anyone might impose on others. Let us examine some of the basic beliefs of antinomianism in more detail.

There Are No God-given Moral Laws

Antinomians are either theoretical or practical atheists because they do not believe that any moral principles have divine sanctions. Either there is no God or else there is none that has enjoined universal moral laws on us.

There Are No Objective Moral Laws

Most antinomians do not deny that persons can choose to live by some moral standards. They simply refuse to accept that these are more than the subjective choices of the individual. Whatever moral laws there may be are relative to individuals who choose to live by them. There are no objective moral laws binding on all human beings.

There Are No Timeless Moral Laws

Antinomians are also opposed to any timeless moral laws, whether they derive from some God or are just there. Whatever moral laws there may be are temporal, not eternal. Mankind is literally without any abiding laws. Morals are simply mores, and they change from place to place as well as from time to time.

There Are No Laws Against Laws

Most antinomians are not against law but simply without law. They are not necessarily opposed to laws but feel that there are not any objective moral laws. This does not mean that they are without any kind of law. Most antinomians accept the need for family rules as well as civil laws. They realize that without some kinds of laws society cannot operate. But while they accept positive social law, they insist that it is not based on any divine or natural law. It is this kind of moral law behind the civil law that they believe human beings are without. And it is in this sense that they are antinomian, or without law.

Positive Contributions of Antinomianism

Few positions are totally without any merit. There is usually enough truth in any false view to make it hold water. Hence, even the antinomian view contains some fragments of truth. Different forms of antinomianism make different contributions, but all of them make some contribution. These positive aspects of antinomianism include those which follow.

It Stresses Individual Responsibility

In taking their focus off the universal, antinomians often place emphasis on the individual. This points out the truth that ethics is ultimately a matter of personal responsibility. No reference to God as the source of moral principles can be used to excuse humans from taking responsibility for their own actions.

Likewise, stress on the individual avoids absolving personal responsibility in a collectivity. The individual cannot escape into the group. The individual cannot hide in the crowd. No one can rightfully blame society for his moral actions.

It Recognizes an Emotive Element

Some antinomians rightfully point to an emotive dimension in much of what passes as a moral prescription. Not everything that takes the linguistic form of "thou shalt not" or "you ought not" is really a divine imperative. Many such statements are merely expressions of some individual's feelings. Not all alleged imperatives are really prescriptive; some are merely emotive. We often couch our own personal feelings in the more powerful language of divine injunctions. The antinomians can be thanked for helping us to be conscious of such abuses.

It Stresses Personal Relations

Some forms of antinomianism, existentialism for example, stress personal relations instead of mere prescriptive regulations. In so doing, they focus on an important dimension of morality. After all, our primary ethical responsibility is to persons, not to mere laws. Jesus made this point when he said, "The Sabbath was made for man, not man for the Sabbath" (Mark 2:27). Persons are ends, not means to an end. By putting the focus on persons rather than on mere prescriptions for persons, the antinomian has served to refocus an important aspect of moral responsibility.

It Stresses the Finite Dimensions of Ethics

Absolutists often overstate their case, acting as though they have an absolute understanding of absolutes. Antinomians make a contribution to ethics by stressing the relative dimension. Finite man does not have an infinite understanding of the infinite. Paul said, "now I know in part" (1 Cor. 13:12). The basic ethical principles are absolute, but our human perspective on them is less than absolute. In pointing to our changing understanding of God's unchanging moral law, antinomians have rendered an unwitting service to Christian ethics.

Some Criticisms of Antinomianism

Although many antinomians are not necessarily irresponsible in their actions, there are nonetheless some irredeemable difficulties with the view as a whole. A number of views from ancient times to the present gave rise to antinomianism. Each was discussed earlier, and a brief response will be made to each here.

A Response to Processism

Two points can be made in response to the view, springing from Heraclitus, that all is in flux. First, Heraclitus himself did not believe that everything is relative. In fact, he held that there was an unchanging *logos* beneath all change by which change could be measured. He saw this as an absolute law by which all men should live.

Second, if one carries the idea of change all the way, as Cratylus tried, then he uses change to destroy change. For if everything is changing and nothing is constant, then there is no way to measure the change. Everything cannot be changing or we would not be able to know it.

A Response to Hedonism

Claiming that pleasure is the essence of good is subject to several criticisms. First of all, not all pleasures are good. For example, the sadistic pleasure some deranged individuals get from torturing little children is not good; in fact, it is grossly evil. Second, not all pain is bad. Pains that warn of impending disease or damage, for instance, are good pains. Third, it is a confusion of categories to reduce good to pleasure. A person is not virtuous because he is feeling good, nor is he necessarily sinful because he is suffering pain. Finally, personal happiness may be relative to happenings, but values are not. Many martyrs have suffered adversely for their values. Hence, the good cannot be equated with the pleasurable.

A Response to Skepticism

There are numerous problems with skepticism. First, consistent skepticism is self-defeating. If the skeptic were really skeptical about everything, then he would be skeptical about skepticism. If he does not doubt his own doubting, then he is really not a skeptic but is dogmatic and wants us to suspend judgment on everything except his skeptical views. Second, some things ought not to be doubted. Why, for example, should I doubt my own existence? Some things are obvious, and it is frivolous to deny the obvious. Third, ethics has to do with the way we live, but no skeptic can consistently live his skepticism. He cannot suspend judgment on whether he needs food and water—at least not for long. And if he is married, he dare not suspend judgment on whether he loves his wife!

A Response to Intentionalism

Perhaps the easiest way to state the fundamental objection to intentionalism is to point out that "the road to hell is paved with good intentions." Furthermore, even Hitler had what he considered good intentions for the Holocaust: he wanted to weed out "inferior" strains of the human species. In addition, intentionalism wrongly assumes that because bad intentions are always bad, good intentions are always good. Bad intentions are always bad, even if they do not result in bad actions. Attempting to kill an innocent person is of course bad, even if the attempt does not succeed. However, killing handicapped people to alleviate the financial burden on society is not good no matter how noble the intention may be.

A Response to Voluntarism

Contrary to voluntarism, an act is not good simply because God wills it. First of all, this would make God arbitrary and not essentially good. Second, it exalts God's will above his nature and allows it to operate independent of his nature. This is questionable theology at best. Third, voluntarism provides no security that God will remain constant in his ethical concerns, since he could change his mind at any time and will that hate is right rather than love. Fourth, an act is not good simply because it flows from the choice of some sovereign being. As we all know, sovereigns can be capricious about their will. Something is not good simply because someone else has the power to perform it. In order for it to be a good act, it must come from a good power. A will alone is not a sufficient basis for good; it must be a good will.

A Response to Nominalism

First of all, if nominalists are correct in saying there is no universal form or essence of meaning, then meaning could not be translated from one language to another. But translation of meaning from language to language occurs daily around the world. Thus there must be some universal basis for meaning that transcends any given language. Second, when applied to ethics this means that all good acts must participate in some universal goodness by which they are designated good acts. So there must be some universal good that is common to all good acts. Third, for the Christian this universal good is the moral character of God. To deny that God has such a transcendently good nature that it is the basis of all creaturely good is contrary to the Christian view of God.

A Response to Utilitarianism

The first problem with utilitarianism is that it implies that the end justifies any means necessary to attain it. If this were so, then Stalin's slaughter of some eighteen million could be justified in view of the communist utopia he hoped would eventually be achieved. Second, results alone do not justify an action. When the results come, we must still ask whether they are good results or bad ones. The end does not justify the means; the means must justify themselves. Forced infanticide of all children thought to be carriers of genetic "impurities" is not justified by the goal of a purified genetic stock. Third, even utilitarians take the end as a universal good, showing that they cannot avoid a universal good. Otherwise from whence do they derive the concept of a good that should be desired for its own sake? Finally, desired results alone do not make something good. Often we desire what is wrong. Even desires for ends thought to be good are subject to the question, Are they good desires? So even here there must be some standard outside the desires by which they are measured.

A Response to Existentialism

Many criticisms can be leveled at an existential ethic. First of all, if everyone literally "did their own thing," it would be chaos, which would hinder anyone from doing his own "thing." Second, even free choices need a context or structure. Absolute freedom for two or more persons is impossible, for if one person chooses to do to others what they choose not to have done to them, then an unavoidable conflict emerges. This is why law is necessary to structure free choice, thus maximizing the freedom of all without negating the freedom of any. Third, no free act is without justification; otherwise one is unjustified in performing it. No action escapes the first principle of justice any more than a thought can escape the first principle of noncontradiction. Both thought and action are justified by first principles, and he who breaks first principles will in the end be broken by first principles.

A Response to Evolutionism

The response to an evolutionary ethic is similar to the response to a process ethic. First, on what basis do we decide what the goal is? What is meant by "development"? Is this to be understood biologically, politically, culturally, or morally? Second, how do we know that the desired development is really good development? One can also develop in an evil direction. Third, who decides what will hinder or help the evolutionary process? Some standard outside the evolutionary process must be assumed in order to measure it. Otherwise, we could not know whether the change is for better or for worse. Since no stage in the process is final or perfect, there must be some standard beyond it by which we can measure the progress. Otherwise we do not know the difference between mere change and real progress.

A Response to Emotivism

The first difficulty with emotivism is that it attempts to prescribe that ethical statements are not prescriptive. It dictates that "ought" statements do not mean one ought to do such and such, but simply, "I feel it is wrong." This is legislating meaning rather than listening to meaning. It prescribes what an ethical statement should mean, rather than listening to what it does mean. Second, even emotivists do not really believe that everything is a matter of subjective feeling.

Like everyone else, emotivists believe some things are really wrong, such as robbing humans of their freedom of thought and expression. Third, the way emotivists react to being cheated, robbed, assaulted, or tortured reveals that they really believe these are wrong.

A Response to Nihilism

Nihilism is hard-core antinomianism. It negates all objective value. Such a view is subject to severe criticism. First of all, it is self-destructive, for the nihilist values his right to negate all value. He values his freedom to hold his view and not to be forced to hold another position. Second, even Nietzsche could not help making value judgments, both negative and positive. For example, he considered Christianity to be "the highest of all conceivable corruptions,"[3] but by what standard did he make this judgment?

A Response to Situationism

A situational ethic that denies all absolute norms is vulnerable to the same criticisms that all total relativisms are. First, a situationist has no place to stand to make his value judgments. He cannot relativize everything else unless he has some nonrelative place to stand himself. It is clearly self-destructive to make an absolute claim that there are no absolutes. Second, even situationists cannot avoid making such universal ethical statements as "no unwanted baby should ever be born" or "love only is always good."[4] Third, situationism is really a form of utilitarianism and as such is subject to the same criticisms.

Criticisms of Antinomianism in General

In addition to the criticisms which can be leveled at the particular views that have contributed to antinomianism, there are several general criticisms which can be made of antinomianism as a whole. Let us examine them in turn.

It Is Self-Defeating

The denial of all moral value is self-destructive. One cannot deny all value without presupposing some value. There is no way to be a consistent total relativist, for one cannot move the world unless he has some place to put his fulcrum. Relativists really stand upon their own

3. Friedrich Nietzsche, *The Anti-Christ,* in *The Portable Nietzsche,* trans. Walter Kaufmann (New York: Viking, 1968), p. 655.
4. Joseph Fletcher, *Situation Ethics: The New Morality* (Philadelphia: Westminster, 1966), pp. 39, 57.

absolutes in their attempts to relativize everything else. This becomes more obvious when one reduces to its common denominator their basic claim, which amounts to saying, "We should never use the word *never*," or "We should always avoid the word *always*." But if they are absolutely sure there are no absolutes, then there must be some. Moral absolutes cannot be denied unless they are implied. Everyone who denies all value believes there is value in his denial, or he would not take the trouble to make the denial.

It Is Too Subjective

There may be a subjective element in much of ethics, but this does not mean that all ethical statements are subjective. There is no doubt a subjective element in the application, but the principle itself is objective. For example, the understanding of love varies from person to person, but love itself does not change. There may be progress in a society's application of justice to its members, but justice is not purely subjective. A purely subjective ethic is like a game without rules. In fact, it is not a game at all; it is a free-for-all.

It Is Too Individualistic

Not only is an antinomian ethic like a ball game without rules, it is like a game without umpires. Everyone is really his or her own umpire, since there are no objective moral laws that bind everyone. Each individual is really his own authority because there is no binding external moral authority. Each person can literally do what is right in his own eyes, and there is nothing that everyone ought to do.

It is one thing to stress the value of each individual's responsibility but quite another to say there is no real responsibility for any individual. In such an atomistic ethic, each situation is distinct. There is no real community of value that transcends the individual, no meaningful moral milieu for interpersonal relations. Each individual lives in a hermetically sealed moral vacuum jar on his own isolated shelf.

It Is Ineffective

As long as there are two or more persons in the world, there will be conflicts. But if there are no objective moral laws, there are no ways to adjudicate these clashes. Moral laws regulate the ways in which persons relate to each other. Even antinomians want to be treated with respect. But why ought anyone else treat them with this respect, unless there is a moral law that says they ought to do so? Unless there is a moral standard outside of two individuals in conflict, there is no way to resolve their moral conflict. It is simply insufficient to appeal to a different standard within each individual in order to judge between them. Voluntarily assumed moral standards are no moral standards at all. A moral duty is an obligation, not an option. One cannot simply choose whether he will be just and loving; he is *obligated* to be just and loving.

It Is Irrational

Antinomianism does not make peace with such laws of rationality as, for example, the laws of noncontradiction. It makes no sense to say everything is right for people to do, even opposites. If love is right for one person, hate cannot be right for another person. If kindness to children is right in one culture, then cruelty to them cannot be right in another. These are contradictory actions, and contradictories cannot both be true. It is irrational to contend that opposite moral duties can both be equally binding.

Summary and Conclusion

Antinomianism is a radical form of ethical relativism. It denies not only that there are any valid ethical absolutes, but also that there are any binding moral laws whatsoever. It is literally "without law." This does not mean that it is without any value. Antinomians do stress the value of the individual in making ethical decisions, as well as the value of personal relations. Furthermore, they often point out an obviously emotive dimension in much of our ethical exhortation.

However, as an adequate ethical system, antinomianism falls far short of the mark for many reasons. First, it is self-defeating to deny all binding moral values. The one denying all values certainly values his right to deny them. Second, it is also purely subjective, providing no objective rules for the game of life. In fact, for antinomians life turns out not to be a serious game at all; it is a free-for-all. Third, it is too individualistic. Everyone does what is right in his own eyes. Fourth, it is ineffective, since two or more people cannot function in a society without objectively binding rules. Finally, it is irrational, since it entails the belief that opposing views are both right.

Select Readings

De Beauvoir, Simone. *The Ethics of Ambiguity.* New York: Citadel, 1962.

Fletcher, Joseph. *Situation Ethics: The New Morality.* Philadelphia: Westminster, 1966.

Heraclitus. *Cosmic Fragments.* Edited by G. S. Kirk. New York: Cambridge University Press, 1954.

Huxley, Julian S. *Essays of a Biologist*. Harmondsworth: Penguin, 1939.

Nietzsche, Friedrich. *The Birth of Tragedy and The Genealogy of Morals*. Translated by Francis Golffing. Garden City, N.Y.: Doubleday, 1956.

Sartre, Jean-Paul. *Being and Nothingness*. Translated by Hazel E. Barnes. New York: Philosophical Library, 1956.

Sextus Empiricus. *Against the Dogmatists*. In *Sextus Empiricus*. Translated by R. G. Bury. Cambridge: Harvard University Press, 1935–49.

3

Situationism

Contrary to what the word *situationism* might seem to imply, it is not a completely normless ethic. According to one of its most vigorous proponents, Joseph Fletcher, author of *Situation Ethics,* situationism is located between the extremes of legalism and antinomianism. The antinomians have no laws, the legalists have laws for everything, and Fletcher's situationism has only one law.

There are a number of situationists whose works might have been examined here, among them Emil Brunner (*The Divine Imperative*), Reinhold Niebuhr (*Moral Man and Immoral Society*), and John A. T. Robinson (*Honest to God*). But Fletcher's position is better known than these.

Situationism Explained

Since Fletcher's situationism claims allegiance to one unbreakable norm, it will be treated here as a one-norm absolutism. According to Fletcher, his position is neither a lawless relativism which says there is no law for anything, nor a legalistic absolutism which has laws for everything. Rather, he contends that there is one law for everything, the law of love.

Avoiding the Extremes of Legalism and Antinomianism

Fletcher fears both the radical right and the radical left in ethics. However, his position yields more readily to the criticism that it, too, is not distinguishable from antinomianism. Between these two poles, he attempts to firmly establish one absolute norm which can be applied to every ethical situation.

The legalist is one who enters every decision-making situation encumbered with a bundle of predetermined rules and regulations. For him the letter, not the spirit, of the law prevails. The post-Maccabean Pharisees can be singled out as classic examples of legalists. With their 613 (or 621) laws, they were prearmed for any moral predicament. They had a preset and prescribed manual for morality. Fletcher considers Judaism, along with both classical Catholicism and Protestantism, to be legalistic, though Judaism is less so than the latter two. The Jews stoned homosexuals and the church burned them, says Fletcher. Both put law over love. The legalist believes in the love of duty; the situationist holds to the duty of love.

At the other end of the ethical spectrum, Fletcher locates the antinomians, who are complete libertines with no norms whatsoever. Each of their moral decisions is spontaneous and unprincipled, based only on the situation of the moment. Some antinomians claim to have a clairvoyant conscience, a kind of direct moral insight into right and wrong. As examples of the antinomian view, Fletcher cites the New Testament Libertines with their lawlessness, the early Gnostics with their "special knowledge," the modern Moral Rearmament movement with its "spiritual power," and Jean-Paul Sartre's existentialism (discussed here in chapter 2). Common to all these views, says Fletcher, is the rejection of all moral rules, even any generally valid ones. No norm is accepted, not even a norm of love. From Fletcher's point of view, the antinomians throw out the ethical baby (love) with the legalistic bath water.

Between the polar opposites of legalism, with laws for everything, and antinomianism, with its lack of laws for anything, Fletcher posits his situational absolutism with its one law for everything. The situationist comes into every ethical battle armed with but one moral weapon—love: "Only the command to love is categorically good."[1] Every other decision is hypothetical: do this *if* it is loving. "We are 'obliged' to tell the truth, for example, only if the situation calls for it; if a would-be murderer asks his victim's whereabouts, our duty might be to lie."[2] As far as other moral rules are concerned, they are helpful but not unbreakable. The only ethical imperative one has is: "'Act responsibly in love.'" Literally "everything else without exception, all laws

1. Joseph Fletcher, *Situation Ethics: The New Morality* (Philadelphia: Westminster, 1966), p. 26.
2. Ibid., p. 27.

and rules and principles and ideals and norms, are only *contingent,* only valid *if they happen* to serve love in any situation."[3]

The situationist has the one law of love (*agape*), many general rules of wisdom (*sophia*) which are more or less reliable, and the particular moment of decision (*kairos*) "in which the *responsible self in the situation* decides whether the *sophia* can serve love there or not."[4] The "legalists make an idol of the *sophia,* antinomians repudiate it, situationists use it," writes Fletcher.[5] The solidification of these generally valid rules into absolute norms is legalism, and the rejection of all value in them is antinomianism.

There are at least two basic reasons for accepting only one universal norm. First, universals cannot be derived by deduction from other universals like "middle axioms"—one cannot derive an underived norm. Second, each situation is so different from every other situation that it is questionable whether a rule which applies to one situation can be applied to all situations like it, since the others may not really be like it. Only the single axiom or norm of love is broad enough to be applied to all circumstances and contexts.

Setting Forth the Presuppositions

According to Fletcher, there are four working principles of situationism: pragmatism, relativism, positivism, and personalism. He does not, however, intend that we should conclude that situationism is totally relativistic and nonnormative. He means, rather, that within the framework of this absolute norm of love, everything else is pragmatic, relativistic, positivistic, and personalistic.

Pragmatism—By a pragmatic approach Fletcher means that "the right is only the expedient in our way of our behaving." It is what "works" or "satisfies" for love's sake. He wants to put love to work in order to make it successful and to realize its "cash value."[6] The pragmatic approach disdains abstract, verbal solutions to ethical problems; it seeks, rather, concrete and practical answers.

Relativism—There is only one absolute; everything else is relative to it. "As the strategy is pragmatic, the tactics are relativistic."[7] The divine command of love is changeless in its why, but contingent in its specific what and how. "The situationist," writes Fletcher, "avoids words like 'never' and 'perfect' and 'always' and 'complete' as he avoids the

---

3. Ibid., pp. 28, 30.
4. Ibid., p. 33.
5. Ibid.
6. Ibid., pp. 41, 42.
7. Ibid., p. 43.

plague, as he avoids 'absolutely.' "[8] Of course, it is impossible to be "absolutely relative." "There must be an absolute or norm of some kind if there is to be any true relativity." "In *Christian* situationism the ultimate criterion, as we shall be seeing, 'agapic love.' "[9] But Christians should constantly remind themselves that everything else is relative to this one norm.

Positivism—A positivistic position, as opposed to a naturalistic view, holds that values are derived voluntaristically, not rationally. A man decides on his values; he does not deduce them from nature. This is also called "emotivism" because moral values are thought to be expressions of one's feelings rather than prescriptions for one's life. A positivistic or emotive ethic places art and morals in the same camp—both call for a decision or leap of faith. Ethical statements do not seek verification; they look for justification. And only in the one norm of Christian love do all other moral expressions find their ultimate justification.

Personalism—Moral values are not only what persons express; persons are the ultimate moral values. There are no inherently good things; only persons are inherently valuable. Value only "happens" to things. Things are of value only to persons. "Things are to be *used;* people are to be *loved.*"[10] The reverse of this—loving things and using people—is the perversion of morality. According to Fletcher, considering only persons to have intrinsic value is what Kant meant by treating persons always as ends and never as means. So this is the meaning of love: relating everything to the good of persons, who alone are good as such.

In brief, situationism is an ethic with a pragmatic strategy, a relativistic tactic, a positivistic attitude, and a personalistic value center. It is an ethic with one absolute to which everything else is relative and which is directed toward the pragmatic end of doing good to persons.

Explaining the Propositions

The situational position in ethics can be explained by six basic propositions. Each proposition is an elaboration of what it means to live situationally with only the one absolute norm of love. Let us examine them in the order in which they are presented by Fletcher.

"Only one thing is intrinsically good; namely, love: nothing else at all." The realist argues that God wills something because it is good. Fletcher follows the voluntarists like Scotus and Ockham who say that

8. Ibid., pp. 43, 44.
9. Ibid., p. 45.
10. Ibid., p. 51.

something is good because God wills it so. Nothing is good in and for itself. It is good only if it helps persons and bad if it hurts persons. The person "finding" the value may be divine or human, but only persons—God, self, neighbor—determine something to be valuable. No act has intrinsic value. It gains its value only as it relates to persons. Apart from helping or hurting persons, all ethical acts are meaningless. All value, worth, goodness, and rightness are predicates, not properties. They may be predicated about persons, but they are not real things in themselves. God is goodness and love; all other persons merely *have* or *do* good.

Love is an attitude, not an attribute. Love is something that persons give and something that persons should receive, because only persons have intrinsic value. In fact, according to Fletcher, the image of God in man is not reason but love. Love and personhood constitute mankind's characteristic similarity to God. This is why the only human thing with intrinsic value is love—it makes man like God.

The other side of the proposition that only benevolence (love) is inherently good is that only malevolence is intrinsically evil. However, for Fletcher the opposite of love is not hate, which is really a perverted form of love, but rather *indifference*. Hate at least treats the other as a *thou* or person. Indifference treats others as inanimate objects. To totally ignore another and his needs is to depersonalize him. It is worse than attacking him, for an attack presupposes at least that the attacker considers the other person worth attacking.

Fletcher is opposed to calling some acts lesser and, therefore, excusable evils. A spy's lie, for example, is not wrong at all. "If it [a lie] is told in love it is good, right." "It is not an excusable evil; it is a positive good." "If love vetoes the truth, so be it."[11] Whatever one must do for love's sake is good, for only love is intrinsically good; nothing else whatsoever is good. Whatever is the loving thing to do in a given situation is the right thing to do, even if it involves sacrificial suicide under torture to avoid betraying one's comrades to the enemy.

"The ruling norm of Christian decision is love; nothing else." Love replaces the law. The spirit replaces the letter. "We follow law, *if at all, for love's sake*."[12] One does not follow love for the law's sake; one follows the law only for love's sake. Traditionally, men believed that they kept love by obeying the law because the two were identical. But love and law sometimes conflict, and when they do, it is the Christian's obligation to put love over the law. It is not the love of the law but the law of love which one ought to follow.

11. Ibid., p. 65.
12. Ibid., p. 70.

According to Fletcher, Jesus summed up the Mosaic law and the Ten Commandments in one word—*love*. Indeed, there is no one of the commandments which may not be broken in some situation for love's sake. "There are no 'universal laws' held by all men everywhere at all times, no consensus of all men."[13] For "any precepts all men can agree to are platitudes such as 'do the good and avoid the evil' or 'to each according to his due.' "[14] There are no universal laws except love. Every other law is breakable by love. As Augustine put it, "Love with care and then what you will, do." He did not say, adds Fletcher, "Love with desire and do what you please."[15]

Christian love is a giving love. Christian love is neither romantic (erotic) love nor friendship (philic) love. Christian love is a sacrificial (agapic) love. And it is also a responsible love which is no more subject to exploitation than to the evasive motives of legalism. In fact, a legalistic refuge in the safety of universal laws can be a retreat from individual responsibility. One may wish for the security of absolutes rather than the responsibility of relatives. The classical pacifist is, for Fletcher, escaping the responsibility of deciding which wars are just. It is an easier ethic if someone else decides what is right or wrong and simply tells us what to do.

"Love and justice are the same, for justice is love distributed; nothing else." Love and justice are identical. Love does more than take justice into account; love becomes justice. Justice means to give others their due, and love is their due. Fletcher quotes the apostle Paul's injunction, "Owe no man anything except to love." Even if love and justice differed (and they do not), the least love could do would be to give justice to every man. In loving, in being just, one must be multidirectional, not just one-directional. The command is to love one's neighbors.

Love is not merely a present activity toward one's immediate neighbor. Love must have foresight. It must borrow the utilitarian principle and try to bring the greatest good (love) to the greatest number of men, for if love does not calculate the remote consequences, it becomes selfish. In short, justice is love using its head. Christian ethics welcomes law and order for love's sake and even foresees the need at times for a loving use of force to protect the innocent. It makes "rights" practical. Sometimes, one may have the moral (loving) responsibility to disobey unjust civil law. And on occasion love may demand a revolution against the state—if the state has gone beyond love's pale.

"Love wills the neighbor's good whether we like him or not." Fletcher's

13. Ibid., p. 76.
14. Ibid.
15. Ibid., p. 79.

fourth proposition stresses that love is an attitude and not a feeling, and in so doing it stresses the distinctive characteristics of Christian love. In *eros* desire is the cause of love, while in *agape* love is the cause of desire. Agapic love is not reciprocal. A comparison of the three kinds of love reveals what Fletcher has in mind here. Erotic love is egoistic. It says, "My first and last consideration is myself." Philic love is mutualistic. It says, "I will give as long as I receive." Agapic love, on the other hand, is altruistic, saying, "I will give, requiring nothing in return." It is this kind of love which is the ruling norm in situational ethics. Agapic love holds that one ought to love one's neighbor as oneself.

Fletcher sketches four interpretations of the command to love one's neighbor as oneself. First, some say it means to love your neighbor just *as much as* you love yourself. Second, it may mean to love others *in addition to* loving yourself. Third, thinkers such as Søren Kierkegaard hold that it means to love your neighbor in the way *you ought to* love yourself—rightly and honestly. Fourth, it is said that the command is to love your neighbor *instead of* loving yourself (as you have been doing but must now stop doing). Which is the true meaning of self-love?

Following the ladder of self-love suggested by Bernard of Clairvaux, which ascends from love of self for self's sake, to love of God for self's sake, to love of God for God's sake, to love of self for God's sake, Fletcher outlines his own understanding of loving one's neighbor as oneself. We move, he says, from love of ourselves for our own sake, to love of our neighbor for our own sake, to love of our neighbor for the neighbor's sake, to love of ourselves for the neighbor's sake. The last is the highest and the best. It is the right kind of self-love, namely, the love of oneself for the sake of loving others.

When self-love and neighbor-love conflict, "the logic of love is that self-concern is obligated to cancel neighbor-good whenever *more* neighbor-good will be served through serving the self."[16] A ship's captain or a plane's pilot, for example, is to keep himself alive, even at the expense of some passengers if need be, for the sake of the safety of the rest of the passengers. In actuality, there is no real conflict between self-love and neighbor-love. One is to love himself only to the degree that it maximizes neighbor-love.

All love is self-love, but it is the self loved for the sake of loving the most men possible. Love is one, but there are three objects: God, neighbor, and self. Self-love may be either right or wrong. "If we love ourselves for our own sakes, that is wrong. If we love ourselves for

16. Ibid., p. 113.

God's sake and the neighbor's, then it is right. For to love God and the neighbor is to love one's self in the right way . . . ; to love one's self in the right way is to love God and one's neighbors."[17] And in no case does loving one's neighbor imply that we must *like* him.

In fact, love does not even necessarily involve *pleasing* our neighbor. Love demands that we will our neighbor's good, whether or not he pleases us, and whether or not our love pleases him. Calculating the neighbor's good, even if it displeases him, is not cruel. A military nurse, for example, may lovingly treat patients roughly so as to hasten their recovery and return them to battle.

"Only the end justifies the means; nothing else." If this were not true, no act would be justified. There are no intrinsically good acts except the act of love. Hence, the only thing that can justify an act is if it is done following ends or purposes. This is not to say that any end justifies any means, but only that a *loving* end justifies any means. For example, it might be the loving thing to steal a murderer's gun or to lie to a schizophrenic patient to keep him calm for treatment. What, asks Fletcher, justifies slicing into a human body with a knife? Surely not hatred of him as one's enemy. But would not the act of mutilating his body be justified if the end in view is to save his life from a disease or a cancerous organ? Does not the end justify the means in this situation?

In fact, what other than the end could possibly justify the means, asks Fletcher? The means cannot justify themselves. Only ends justify means. Indeed, "no act apart from its foreseeable consequences has any ethical meaning whatsoever."[18] The meaning of the act comes from its purpose or end. And the only justifiable purpose for performing ethical acts is agapic love. Any means which is sought for its own sake is wrong. In fact, all ends are only means to higher ends, until one arrives at last at the ultimate end of love itself.

In response to those who challenge, on the basis of the "wedge" principle, that it is dangerous to have exceptions to moral norms like telling the truth and saving lives, Fletcher argues that "abuse does not bar use." The fact that some people will abuse the situationist position of responsible love by irresponsible actions does not disprove the value of the love norm itself. And the so-called generalization argument—"What if everyone did it?"—is no more than obscurantism, a delaying tactic of static morality.

"Love's decisions are made situationally, not prescriptively." The final expository postulate of situation ethics strongly marks the differ-

17. Ibid., p. 114.
18. Ibid., p. 120.

ence between the basic ethical principle of the love norm and the application of that principle in a given circumstance. The love principle is a universal but formal norm. It does not prescribe in advance what specific courses of action will be loving. For the precise prescription of love, one will have to wait until he is in the situation. Love is free from specific predefinition. One cannot know in advance the "existential particularity" that love will take in a given situation. Love operates apart from a system of pretailored, prefabricated moral rules. Love functions circumstantially and neocasuistically. Love does not make up its mind before it has seen the facts, and the facts come from the situation.

What the situationist does have in advance is a general (though not specific) knowledge of what he should do (love), why he should do it (for God's sake), and to whom it should be done (his neighbors). He knows, of course, that love is altruistic and not egoistic. And he knows that it should be exercised toward as many neighbors as possible. He knows in advance how this love will probably operate in a general way by means of *sophia,* or wisdom. But he cannot say for sure what the loving thing to do will be in a particular case until all the particulars are known. For example, if Fletcher is asked, "Is adultery wrong?" he answers, "I don't know. Maybe. Give me a case." (In fact, Fletcher himself provides a case where adultery can be right if it is done in love.)

In brief, the situationist holds that the general what and why are absolute, but the how is relative. There is an absolute prescription, but it is only worked out in the relative situation. Love is ultimate, but just how one is to love is dependent on the immediate circumstances. By a closer examination of some difficult moral situations, we will be able to understand even better just how Fletcher's one-norm absolutism functions in different contexts.

Applying the Love Norm

By the use of provocative illustrations throughout his book, Fletcher is able to explain more fully just why he holds to only one absolute norm and how it would probably be applied under differing conditions. Some of these marginal moral cases merit further examination.

Altruistic adultery—A German mother of two was captured by the Russians near the end of World War II. The rules of her Ukrainian prison camp allowed her release to Germany only in the event of pregnancy, in which case she would be returned as a liability. So the woman asked a friendly camp guard to impregnate her. She was sent back to Germany, was welcomed by her family, gave birth to the baby, and made him a part of their reunited family. Was her adultery justified?

Fletcher does not say explicitly that it was, but implies the same by calling it "sacrificial adultery." Elsewhere, however, Fletcher speaks approvingly of wife-swapping for consenting adults, of a woman seducing a man pathologically attracted to a little girl, and of a young couple forcing parental approval of their marriage by engaging in intercourse. The direct implication is that all of these things can be done lovingly and can, therefore, be morally right.

Patriotic prostitution—A young woman working for a United States intelligence agency was asked to lure an enemy spy into blackmail by using her sexuality. In the guise of a secretary, she was to become involved with a married man working for a rival power. When she protested that she could not put her personal integrity on the block by offering sex for hire, she was told, "It's like your brother risking his life or limb in Korea. We are sure this job can't be done any other way." She was patriotic and wanted to serve her country. What was the loving thing to do? Here again Fletcher does not give his answer, but in view of the fact that he elsewhere approves of spies lying and men dying for their country out of love, there seems to be for him no reason why one might not be able to justify committing fornication for the fatherland, too.

Sacrificial suicide—Is taking one's own life always morally wrong? According to situation ethics, it is not; suicide can be done in love. For example, if a man has only the two choices of taking an expensive medicine, a course of action which will deplete his family's finances and cause his insurance to lapse, in order to live three more years, or else refusing the medicine and dying in six months, thereby leaving ample financial provisions for his family, which is the loving thing to do? It is not difficult to see how a situationist could approve of this rather indirect kind of sacrificial suicide. In fact, Fletcher speaks with approval both of Mother Maria's substitutionary death in the Nazi gas chambers for a young Jewess, and of a captured soldier's taking his own life to avoid betraying his comrades to the enemy. Suicide can be done for love's sake, in which case it is morally right according to a situationist ethic.

Acceptable abortion—Even though Fletcher favors birth control over abortion as a means of controlling the population, nonetheless there are circumstances when he comes out clearly in favor of abortion. He gives the example of an unmarried schizophrenic patient who became pregnant after being raped. Her father requested abortion but was refused by the hospital staff on the grounds that it was not a therapeutic abortion and was, therefore, illegal. Fletcher castigates this refusal as legalistic. "The situationist . . . would almost certainly, in *this case,* favor abortion and support the girl's father's request."[19]

In another case, Fletcher gives tacit approval to a Rumanian Jewish doctor who aborted three thousand babies of Jewish mothers in concentration camps because, if pregnant, the mothers were to be incinerated. That means that the doctor saved three thousand lives. And from the standpoint that the embryos were human lives (which Fletcher rejects), the doctor, by "killing" three thousand, saved three thousand and prevented the murder of six thousand. Surely this was the loving thing to do, according to situationism.

Merciful murder—Should we actually turn our back on a man who is hopelessly caught in a burning airplane and begs to be shot? Would it not have been right to assassinate Hitler? Fletcher offers both illustrations and seems to indicate that either one could be a merciful, and therefore justifiable, murder. He seems to favor the act of a mother smothering her crying baby in order to save her group from being detected and killed by hostile Indians. The direct implication is that such an act might be performed in sacrificial love for the good of the whole group.

Fletcher clearly approves of throwing some men out of an overloaded rescue boat to save them all from sinking. In 1841, the first mate of the ship *William Broilin* of Liverpool was in charge of an overcrowded lifeboat and ordered most of the males thrown into the sea to save the rest. Later, the seaman who threw them into the sea was convicted of murder, with mercy recommended. "Situation ethics says it was bravely sinful, it was a good thing."[20] According to Fletcher, the first mate actually acted in love for the greater number of lives.

There are many other marginal cases which Fletcher offers, including refusing to respirate a monstrously deformed child and carrying the inventor of a cancer cure out of a burning building rather than one's own father. He also recommends sterilizing someone marrying a syphilitic and providing motherhood for single women by artificial insemination. Time will not be taken here to discuss any more cases. The point, however, which arises from all of these situations and which needs emphasis here is that in each situation there is a conflict of moral norms which the situationist feels can best be resolved by appeal to a single higher norm.

Often the norms which conflict are held by some men to be unbreakable and universal. But how can two or more norms be universal and

19. Ibid., p. 38.
20. Ibid., p. 136.

unbreakable if they conflict? One cannot follow two opposing paths; he must choose. Surely he cannot be held responsible for obeying two conflicting norms when he can obey only one, can he? It is at this point that the situationist's solution shines. There is really only one universal and unbreakable norm—love. All the other norms are at best general and can be broken for love's sake. The simplicity and logic of the solution has strong appeal, but there are also some grave difficulties. Let us turn our attention now to an evaluation of the one-norm absolutism of situation ethics.

Situationism Evaluated

The goal in what follows is not to evaluate the whole of situational ethics comprehensively, but only insofar as it bears on the question of moral laws. In this respect the evaluation will be both positive and negative. First, there are some clear merits to holding only one absolute norm such as love.

Some Advantages of the Situational Position

Critics from more traditional and absolutistic viewpoints tend to overreact to Fletcher's relativism, pragmatism, emotivism, and radical examples. But what is sometimes forgotten is that all of this is in the context of a clear claim that his ethic is an absolutism—a one-norm absolutism. It is in this latter regard that many of the merits of the situational position emerge.

It is a normative position. First to be commended is Fletcher's attempt to lay down a *normative* approach to ethics. His second proposition states, "The ruling norm of Christian decision is love; nothing else." In view of the fact that he spends a whole chapter elaborating this, as well as repeatedly referring to this one absolute throughout the book, it seems quite unfair to summarily dismiss Fletcher as totally normless and antinomian. Indeed, Fletcher spends much of his first chapter explaining that his view is not antinomian but rather a one-norm absolutism. (In "What Is a Rule?" Fletcher later denies that his approach has any universal norms.[21]

Fletcher distinguishes between *formal* principles, such as "act as lovingly as possible," *substantial* principles, such as "the good which should be sought or done is utility," and *normative* principles, such as "loving concern for our neighbors calls for telling them the truth."

---

21. "What Is a Rule? A Situationist's View," in *Norm and Context in Christian Ethics,* ed. Gene H. Outka and Paul Ramsey (New York: Scribner's, 1968), p. 325.

Only formal principles, he says, are universal.[22] Possibly Fletcher means that there are no universals with substantive content, and that the love principle which he calls "the ruling norm of Christian ethics" is only formally universal.[23]

The reasons for commending a normative approach to ethics have already been given and need not be repeated here. It is sufficient to note in passing that norms are both inescapable and essential to a meaningful ethic. Without them one has no objective basis or guide for ethical decisions.

It is an absolutism. Fletcher's view is not only normative, it is *absolute*. There is one unbreakable law, the law of love. And even though Fletcher deliberately avoids such words as "never" and "always" with regard to every other norm, he does not hesitate to emphasize that there are no exceptions to the love norm. Only love and nothing else justifies what one does, he argues. Furthermore, there is no such thing as total relativity. Relative norms must be relative to a norm which is not relative. What, why, and who are the Christian's three universals, Fletcher says. That is, he knows that his neighbor should be loved for God's sake. These three universals are absolute; only the circumstances are relative. He clearly holds that one ought *always* to love and should *never* hate or be indifferent to his neighbors. "*Christian* situation ethics has only one norm . . . that is binding and unexceptionable, always good and right regardless of the circumstances"[24]— agapic love.

It resolves the issue of conflicting norms. Whatever one may think of the situationist's solution to the marginal cases where conflicting norms are involved, at least it presents a logical possibility. All other ethical norms are subordinate to the one absolute norm, in view of which it is ethically right to break any of them for the sake of this love norm. This solution is both logical and simple. It is simple because it does not involve a complicated series of exceptions to norms, nor does it present a pyramid of moral values. It posits a single norm which takes precedence over all others. It is logical in the sense that it is not internally contradictory. It never leaves any ethical dilemmas in conflict or tension; they are always resolvable (at least in theory) by appeal to the single law of love. In other words, situationism is never faced with the dilemma of having two absolute or universal norms in conflict, since it does not have two absolute norms. There is *one* absolute norm, no more and no less.

22. Fletcher, *Situation Ethics,* pp. 337–38.
23. Ibid., p. 69.
24. Ibid., p. 38.

It gives due value to differing circumstances. Another merit of situationism not to be undervalued is its emphasis on the fact that the circumstances or context of an ethical decision have a bearing on the rightness or wrongness of the act. However morally wrong falsifying may or may not be, surely it differs from context to context. Falsifying in fun to a friend is probably amoral, whereas serious falsifying before a judge and jury is not. The circumstances do make a difference in the moral rightness or wrongness of the act. Likewise, taking another life accidentally, or in self-defense, or letting one die as an act of mercy are all markedly different situations from an intentional and malicious murder of another human being. The situation does condition the way one's norm (or norms) should be applied. Without due stress on the conditioning influence of the moral situation, one's ethics become legalistic and even inhuman.

Indeed, as will be seen later, it is very difficult (if not impossible) to contend for a many-norm absolutism of any kind, unless contextual qualifications become part of the definition of the norm. Truthfulness and the duty to avoid or prevent taking life (or at least letting someone die) invariably come into conflict unless one has the prerogative to say that lying and taking life *in certain contexts* are wrong. This will be discussed more fully later. For now it is sufficient to note that giving attention to the circumstances or context of ethical decisions is both unavoidable and desirable in elaborating a good ethical position.

It stresses love and the value of persons. From a Christian point of view (and even from many non-Christian perspectives), the stress on agapic love as the ruling norm is certainly commendable. Bertrand Russell wrote *Why I Am Not a Christian,* but he also said elsewhere, "What the world needs is Christian love or compassion."[25] Seldom do strong voices arise in defense of selfish love. And from the Christian point of view, love is the absolute moral character of God. "God is love" and "love is of God," the New Testament says. And when all else fades, love will abide forever. Jesus summarized the whole of the Old Testament in the one word *love.* Indeed, according to Jesus, love was to be the earmark of his disciples. "By this all men will know that you are my disciples, if you love one another" (John 13:35).

In view of this, it is very difficult to criticize from a Christian point of view the preeminence Fletcher gives to Christian agapic love. Implied in this stress on loving others is the fact that they are to be treated as persons in the image of God and not as mere things. The neighbor is a thou, not an it. The other is a person to be loved, not a

25. Bertrand Russell, *The Basic Writings of Bertrand Russell,* ed. Robert E. Egner and Lester E. Denonn (New York: Simon and Schuster, 1961), p. 579.

thing to be used. Others are ends in themselves and not merely means for our own ends. But Fletcher's emphasis that humans are persons (like God) who have God-given value is commendable from a Christian perspective.

Some Inadequacies of One-Norm Situationism

From both a moralistic viewpoint in general and a Christian perspective in particular, not everything in Fletcher's situationism is praiseworthy. We will not take time here to elaborate on his critical and inconsistent view of the Gospel records of the New Testament, nor the implications of holding that God can be loved *only* through one's neighbor. We will rather center our attention on the inadequacy of having only one norm for an ethic.

One norm is too general. A one-norm ethic, especially when the norm is as broad and general as Fletcher's love norm, is in most (though not all) cases little better than having no norm at all. A single universal norm must by its very nature be broad and adaptable, or else it could not apply to all circumstances. But its versatility is also a liability, for it necessitates an ambiguity about what the norm means as far as concrete relationships are concerned. And if the absolute love norm is without concrete content apart from the relative situation, then the specific meaning of love is relative and not absolute.

Indeed, Fletcher admits that the content of love varies from situation to situation. Therefore, the command, "Love in all cases," means little more than "Do X in all cases." For unless there is advanced cognitive content to the term *love,* then one does not really know what one is being commanded to do. Fletcher clearly confesses that the love principle is empty of factual content: "This is why I say it is a 'formal' principle, which rules us and yet does so without content."[26]

In actual practice, Fletcher does seem to imply that there is *some* understanding of what love means in advance of the situation. But the question is, How much? Is there enough content in the universal love norm to raise it above a mere platitude? "Do the *loving* thing" is scarcely more specific than, "Do the *good* thing." The question in both instances is, What kinds of acts are good or loving? So his one moral law is too general to be helpful.

Fletcher's one-norm ethic of love is no more helpful than a view that says, "Follow nature," or "Live according to reason." Instead of "What does 'love' mean?" the question becomes, "What does 'nature' mean?" The result is the same, and one is left without any specific ethical direction. An appeal to the situation to provide content or

---

26. Fletcher, "What Is a Rule," p. 337.

meaning for love will not suffice. Fletcher admits that situations are relative and even radically different. If the meaning of love is dependent on the circumstances, then the significance of love is really relative to the situation and therefore not absolute. This leads to a second criticism.

The situation does not determine the meaning of love. The meaning of the love norm is not completely determined by the particulars of the situation but is merely conditioned by them. Circumstances do not effect norms which judge them; they only *affect* them. The context in which a norm is applicable does not dictate how the norm will be applied but only influences its application. If the complete determination of meaning came from the situation, then the alleged ethical norm would not really be normative at all. The situation would be determining the norm rather than the norm being determinative for the situation. Actually, the situation does not determine what is right; God does. The situation simply helps us discover which of God's laws is the one applicable there.

Fletcher does not claim that the situation completely determines what the norm means. He says only that what love will mean in advance of the situation cannot be known with any "existential particularity"; it can be known only in general. However, what is known in advance, "in general," may turn out to be the wrong meaning of love in a particular circumstance. No general wisdom (*sophia*) or norms are universal and unbreakable. There is no rule apart from the general (and ambiguous) rule of love which ought never be broken. But this is precisely the problem. The meaningful norms are breakable, and the only unbreakable norm is not meaningful in any specific or practical sense of the word. Perhaps Fletcher should not have dismissed so summarily the possibility that there are many universal and unbreakable norms.

The possibility of many universal norms. There seem to be several reasons why situationism dismisses the possibility of having many universal norms, though none of these reasons is definitive. First, Fletcher argues that the many-norm position would be legalistic. This does not follow. A many-norm ethic *may* be legalistic, but there is no reason why it *must* be legalistic. It all depends on what the norms are, how they are related to each other, and how they are applied to life whether or not the view is legalistic. As a matter of fact, one could be legalistic with one absolute norm such as, "Keep the Sabbath."

Second, it is implied that there is no other way to resolve the conflict of norms unless there is one absolute norm to which all other norms are only relative. But this is not so. There are at least three other ways to relate many universal norms: show how they really do not conflict;

or show why it is wrong to break either when they do conflict; or show how one of the norms is of a higher order and takes priority over those of a lower order.

Third, Fletcher sees no way to derive universal norms from a universal norm. He thinks that the concept of "middle axioms" is a contradiction in terms; they are "derived underiveds." But there is no reason a deduction cannot be as universal as its premises. Apart from whether there really *are* many universal norms, Fletcher certainly does not eliminate the possibility that there are such. He does not disprove that they can be arrived at by deduction the way postulates are derived from axioms in geometry. He does not disprove that they could come from revelation such as many Christians find inscripturated in the Bible. Nor does Fletcher definitely dismiss the possibility that many universal norms could be known intuitively to have a separate status of their own.

In brief, the possibility of there being many universal norms should not be given up until either it is shown to be logically impossible, or no universal norm other than love is ever found. In view of the fact that candidates for universal norms will be introduced and evaluated in subsequent chapters, we will withhold judgment until then whether or not there really are many universal norms. It will be enough at this point to observe that Fletcher does not prove that "there is *only* one universal norm," since he does not prove that it is impossible that there may be many universal norms.

A different universal norm is possible. Not only is it possible that there are many universal norms in contrast to Fletcher's single norm, but it is also possible to opt for a different single norm than the love norm Fletcher uses. Why not a one-norm ethic built on hate instead of love? Why not Buddhistic compassion instead of Christian love? Why not a "negative Golden Rule" that mandates, "Do *not* do to others what you do not want them to do to you," rather than the positive one? Surely Fletcher has not demonstrated that all ethical principles mean exactly the same thing (at any rate, not those as different as love and hate). Then on what basis is one to choose the single norm on which to build a whole ethic? There must be some way to justify one's basic ethical presupposition if it is not to be entirely arbitrary.

In brief, the problem of a one-norm ethic is: *which* norm? Prima facie, there are many ethical norms which claim obedience. Which one should be given the special position of being absolute and unbreakable? Could not a case be made for using truthfulness at any cost as the single absolute? Could not such a position be worked out with internal consistency in the same way as Fletcher's love norm can be? And if one absolute norm can be just as internally consistent as another, then on what basis is one norm to be preferred over another? By evaluating the consequences of each? If the one absolute norm is chosen on the ground that it brings the best consequences for most people in the long run, then there are several problems.

First, we do not know the long run, and some things that are not really best in the long run work well for many people in the short run (e.g., dishonesty and dictatorships). In fact, many things which are distinctly wrong on almost any ethical basis obviously work too well for too many people for too long a time (e.g., cheating, hating, warring).

Second, to choose the norm on the basis of its consequences (if this were possible) would be to depart from a normative basis for ethics in favor of a utilitarian basis, with all the problems that view entails. As a matter of fact, utilitarianism depends on norms for its own operation, which brings the argument full circle. That is, this would be saying that ends are needed to justify norms and these ends in turn depend on norms to establish them. But this really demonstrates that norms are the basis of ethics in either event. Norms are necessary. The question remains, *Which* norms and *how many* are there? We turn next to an examination of the many-norm view to seek an answer to these questions.

A many-norm ethic is defensible. A number of contemporary writers have shown how one may defend the validity of many ethical norms. On a popular level this has been done by C. S. Lewis in *Mere Christianity* and in a philosophical way by William K. Frankena in *Ethics*. In this latter category one may also place the works of Paul Ramsey (see *Deeds and Rules in Christian Ethics*). Indeed, there do seem to be many universally binding moral laws. Rape, cruelty, hatred, and genocide are universally frowned upon. And even if all do not practice them toward others, nevertheless all do seem to believe that others should treat them in accordance with these norms. (For an answer to this problem from a Christian point of view, see chap. 7.) And in view of the fact that Fletcher frankly but reluctantly admits his view is utilitarian, perhaps this criticism should be stressed more.

Fletcher is really a utilitarian. Fletcher admits that his view is utilitarian. As such, then, it is not really a one-norm absolutism but a form of generalism. This being the case, it is subject to the criticisms of utilitarianism (see chap. 4). As he says, the end justifies the means. He believes in the greatest love (good) for the greatest number of people in the long run. Not only do we not know the long run, but what is good for many may rob the minority of rights. Furthermore, just because an end is good does not make an act good. There are evil acts, such as rape, cruelty, child abuse, and murder. No amount of good intentions can make an evil act good.

Summary and Conclusion

Situationism claims to be a one-norm absolutism. It believes that everything should be judged by one absolute moral law—love. However, it turns out that this one moral principle is really only formal and empty. It has no content that can be known in advance of or apart from the situation. Different situations really determine what it means. So in the final analysis the one moral law turns out to be no moral law. Situationism reduces to antinomianism, for one empty absolute moral law is in practice no better than no absolute moral law.

Select Readings

Brunner, Emil. *The Divine Imperative*. Philadelphia: Westminster, 1947.

Fletcher, Joseph. *Moral Responsibility*. Philadelphia: Westminster, 1974.

————. *Situation Ethics: The New Morality*. Philadelphia: Westminster, 1966.

Kurtz, Paul, ed. *Humanist Manifestos I and II*. Buffalo: Prometheus, 1973.

Robinson, John A. T. *Honest to God*. Philadelphia: Westminster, 1963.

4

Generalism

Ethical positions can be divided into two broad classes: those that believe in binding ethical rules and those (such as antinomianism) that do not. The first group can be subdivided into those who believe there are universally binding ethical laws and those who believe they are only generally binding. This latter position is called generalism, and traditional adherents of this view include utilitarians.

Generalism Explained

Utilitarians are not antinomians, since they believe in the value of ethical laws in helping individuals determine which action will probably bring the greatest good for the greatest number of people. On the other hand, utilitarians are not absolutists, since they usually deny that there are universally binding ethical norms that represent intrinsic values.

It is true that some utilitarians say that rules should not be broken, but this is only because of the extrinsic value of the good results of keeping rules. The rule is kept, not because it is really intrinsically wrong to perform the forbidden act, but only because making exceptions to any ethical law is a practice which leads to greater evil than good. In other words, the act is not judged by its intrinsic and universal value, but by its results. Even those utilitarians who value rules, then, have no universal norms in the deontological and normative senses discussed in chapter 1.

This does not mean, of course, that utilitarians have no absolutes. They may have absolute ends, but they claim to have no absolute norms. They may have an absolute or ultimate result by which they judge all actions, but they confess no absolute rules enabling one to realize this ultimate end of the greatest good for the greatest number of people.

Jeremy Bentham: Quantitative Utilitarianism

Modern generalism is heir to ancient hedonism, which believed that pleasure is the greatest good (summum bonum) for man. Although the popular "eat, drink, and be merry" is a perversion of what Epicurus himself taught, his ancient followers set forth the classic doctrine that seeking physical pleasure and avoiding physical pain is the chief aim in life.

The pleasure calculus—Jeremy Bentham developed this ancient hedonistic pleasure calculus into a utilitarian position in his *Introduction to the Principles of Morals and Legislation* (1759). According to Bentham, "Nature has placed mankind under the governance of two sovereign masters, pain and pleasure" and "it is for them alone to point out what we ought to do, as well as what we shall do."[1] These are summed up in the principle of utility, which affirms the position "which states the greatest happiness of all those whose interest is in question, as being the right and proper, and only right and proper and universally desirable, end of human action."[2]

In view of this, "an action then may be said to be conformable to the principle of utility . . . when the tendency it has to augment the happiness of the community is greater than any it has to diminish it."[3] Furthermore, "when thus interpreted, the words *ought,* and *right* and *wrong,* and others of that stamp, have a meaning: when otherwise, they have none."[4] That is, no acts or words have any ethical meaning apart from their consequences. Everything is to be justified by its end, by whether it brings more pleasure than pain. But how is the principle of utility itself to be justified? Bentham answers that it is not susceptible to any direct proof, "for that which is used to prove everything else, cannot itself be proved."[5] Men everywhere naturally tend to em-

1. Jeremy Bentham, *Introduction to the Principles of Morals and Legislation* (reprint ed.; New York: Hafner, 1965), p. 1.
2. Ibid., p. 5. Note added by Bentham, July 1822.
3. Ibid., p. 3.
4. Ibid., p. 4.
5. Ibid.

brace the principle of utility, although some have inconsistently rejected it. However, "when a man attempts to combat the principle of utility, it is with reasons drawn, without his being aware of it, from that very principle itself."[6]

Further, if a person rejects the utilitarian principle in favor of his own feeling, "in the first case, let him ask himself whether his principle is not despotical, and hostile to all the rest of the human race," and "in the second case, whether it is not anarchical, and whether at this rate there are not as many different standards of right and wrong as there are men?"[7]

Calculating pleasure—If pleasure and the avoidance of pain are the ends of ethically good acts, then it is reasonable to ask how one is to measure relative amounts of these two elements. Bentham divides his answer into two parts, one for individuals and one for groups.

To an individual person, the value of pleasure or pain in itself will be determined by six factors: intensity, duration, certainty or uncertainty, propinquity or remoteness, fecundity (the chances of producing others of its kind), and purity (the chances of not producing the opposite kind of sensation). When applying the pleasure calculus to a group of people, a seventh factor of extent (the number of persons to whom it extends) must be considered in determining the value of pleasure or pain. So, to make a final calculation of the good of an act for a group, one must first determine how much more pleasure than pain it will give to each individual and then add these all together. The total balance of pleasure over pain will give the general good tendency of the act. If there is more evil than good, then the general evil tendency will be revealed.

Bentham admits that "it is not to be expected that this process should be strictly pursued previously to every moral judgment, or to every legislative or judicial operation."[8] Presumably this is because it is too psychologically and mathematically complex to be practical. It is at this point that the need for some kind of general norms is most obvious in Bentham's position. For if one cannot always calculate the balance of pleasure, then how is he to determine his course of action? The answer becomes more explicit in the utilitarian position of Bentham's successor.

John Stuart Mill: Qualitative Utilitarianism

John Stuart Mill made at least one modification to Bentham's position concerning how pleasure (the end) is conceived and developed

6. Ibid., pp. 4, 5.
7. Ibid., p. 6.
8. Ibid., p. 31.

a fuller statement regarding how general moral laws could function in a utilitarian context.

Pleasure is defined qualitatively—Bentham's hedonistic calculus (or pleasure principle) lends itself easily to a materialistic interpretation. He seems to be speaking of physical pleasure and pain, since they are measured by intensity and duration. Although Bentham tried in later years to soften the hedonistic implications of this by noting that "happiness" or "felicity" may be better words for describing what he meant by "pleasure," he did not deny the materialistic way this "happiness" was to be measured nor the mathematical way it was to be calculated.

Mill, on the other hand, argued that pleasures differ in kind, and higher pleasures are to be preferred over lower ones (*Utilitarianism* [1863]). Pleasures do not differ merely in their amount or intensity. One is higher and more valuable than another simply because most people who experience both decidedly prefer one over the other.

The reason humans give marked preference to some pleasures is that they have higher faculties than animals. "No intelligent human being would consent to be a fool, even though they should be persuaded that the fool, the dunce, or the rascal is better satisfied with his lot than they are with theirs."[9] Indeed, says Mill, "It is better to be a human being dissatisfied than a pig satisfied, better to be Socrates dissatisfied than a fool satisfied."[10] And if the fool and the pig are of a different opinion, says Mill, it is because the pig knows only one side of the question; the fool knows both sides.

Cultured pleasures are higher than uncultured pleasures. Intellectual pleasures are higher than sensual pleasures, and so on. There is a qualitative difference between them, and one is obligated to seek the highest kind of pleasure for the greatest number of people. But again it may be asked: How can one know what will bring about the highest good for the greatest number unless there are some guides or norms for the decisions? Surely the individual is seldom if ever in a position of being able to foresee the long-range results of his actions. Mill's answer to this question leads to the need for norms.

Pleasure is determined normatively—The utilitarian position is not without norms. Mill refers to the great usefulness of the veracity norm. "Yet that even this rule, sacred as it is, admits of possible exceptions is acknowledged by all moralists."[11] Truthfulness is a general rule, with some exceptions (lying is right to save a life), that can guide

9. John Stuart Mill, *Utilitarianism,* in *The Utilitarians* (Garden City, N.Y.: Dolphin Books, Doubleday, 1961), p. 409.
10. Ibid., p. 410.
11. Ibid., p. 424.

one in doing what will bring the greatest good to the greatest number of people.

Mill admits that one cannot always calculate the consequences of one's actions. This is precisely why rules and norms are needed. Mankind has had ample time to formulate a fund of human experience on which one may draw to help calculate the consequences of actions. "During all that time, mankind have been learning by experience the tendency of actions," Mill writes.[12] And unless we assume men to be complete idiots, "mankind must by this time have acquired positive beliefs as to the effects of some actions on their happiness."[13] And "the beliefs which have thus come down are the rules of morality for the multitude, and for the philosopher until he has succeeded in finding better."[14]

In short, there are valid moral rules, beliefs, and codes to guide human decisions toward maximizing the good in society, but none of these are universal rules. None of these is exceptionless; all of them can and should be broken for the principle of utility when the greater good is in jeopardy. For "the received code of ethics is by no means of divine right."[15] It admits of indefinite improvement. "But to consider the rules of morality as improvable is one thing; to pass over the intermediate generalization [i.e., rules and codes] entirely and endeavor to test each individual action directly by the first principle [of utility] is another."[16] Just because there is only the one ultimate goal of happiness, toward which all morality is directed, does not mean there cannot be many moral norms directing us toward that one goal. It means only that these many norms are not absolute, and when they conflict, the conflict must be resolved by the utilitarian principle. There is only one fundamental principle of morality and all others are subordinate to it.

The problem with exceptions—Mill admits that his position is open to the criticism that exceptions to moral rules will present a temptation to break moral rules indiscriminately for the supposed utility of it. His reply is twofold. First, this same criticism may be made of all moral systems. "It is not the fault of any creed, but of the complicated nature of human affairs, that the rules of conduct cannot be so framed as to require no exceptions. . . ."[17] And "there is no ethical creed which does not temper the rigidity of its laws by giving a certain latitude

12. Ibid., p. 425.
13. Ibid., pp. 425–26.
14. Ibid., p. 425.
15. Ibid.
16. Ibid., p. 426.
17. Ibid., p. 427.

. . . for accommodation to peculiarities of circumstances; and under every creed, at the opening thus made, self-deception and dishonest casuistry get in."[18] The utilitarian no more than other moralists must overcome the misuse of exceptions by intellect and virtue. To be utilitarian has a standard of morality, and though the application of it may be difficult, it is better than none at all. "While in other systems the moral laws all claim independent authority, there is no common umpire entitled to interfere between them."[19]

Second, Mill acknowledges that exceptions ought to be both recognized as exceptions and have their limits defined. The reasons for this, he says, are so that exceptions will not be multiplied beyond their need and so that they may not weaken one's confidence in the general rule. Mill merely mentions but does not elaborate on these points. Other utilitarians have adopted an alternate approach to that of Mill, arguing for exceptionless moral rules, or at least rules, though not exceptionless in themselves, that should never be broken for utilitarian reasons.

G. E. Moore: General Rules
and Universal Obedience

Utilitarians handle the problem of exceptions in two basic ways. One school, sometimes called act-utilitarians, holds that each particular ethical act must be judged by its consequences. Hence, there may be exceptions to any ethical rule or norm which in a particular case would justify breaking it. Another group, known as rule-utilitarians, argues that rules should never be broken (unless there is a conflict between them), since the consequences of rule breaking are bad. G. E. Moore's position in some respects seems to combine a bit of each view.

Rules are only generally valid—According to Moore the assertion, "I am morally bound to perform this act," means that the action will produce the greatest possible amount of good in the universe. That is, the results of acts determine their morality. Furthermore, "with regard then to ethical judgments which assert that a certain kind of action is good as a means to a certain kind of effect, none will be *universally* true; and many, though *generally* true at one period, will be generally false at others. . . . Hence we can never be entitled to more than a *generalization*—to a proposition of the form. 'This result *generally* follows this kind of action.' And even this generalization will only be true, if the circumstances under which the action occurs are

18. Ibid.
19. Ibid.

generally the same."[20] Rules and norms are generally useful but are not really universal.

In fact, ethical rules are not really categorical but prove to be only hypothetical. They say that if we act this way under these circumstances, then the greatest good will probably result. But since other circumstances may interfere, it is not possible to know this with any more than probability. So then "an ethical law has the nature not of a scientific law but of a scientific prediction: and the latter is always merely probable, although the probability may be very great."[21]

Murder, for example, cannot be known to be universally wrong, since "we do, as a matter of fact, only observe its good effects under certain circumstances; and it may be easily seen that a sufficient change in these would render doubtful what seem the most universally certain of general rules."[22] Thus, the general disutility of murder could be proved only if the majority of the human race persists in believing that life is worthwhile. "In order to prove that murder . . . would not be good as a means, we should have to disprove the main contention of pessimism—namely that the existence of human life is on the whole an evil."[23] So "when . . . we say that murder is in general to be avoided, we only mean that it is so, so long as the majority of mankind will certainly not agree to it, but will persist in living."[24] However, as long as most men continue to value life, the ethical consideration that "it is generally wrong for any single person to commit murder seems capable of proof."[25] The same holds true for other rules such as temperance and keeping promises.

Chastity, likewise, is only a general rule whose universal utility depends upon certain conditions which are considered necessary for the conservation of society. For instance, it is usually presupposed that chastity is necessary to avoid conjugal jealousy and to preserve paternal affection, and that both of these are necessary conditions to preserve society. "But it is not difficult to imagine a civilized society existing without them."[26] Hence, the rule of chastity is only a general and conditional rule that could be relinquished if society could survive without it.

Some general rules should never be broken—Notwithstanding the

20. G. E. Moore, *Principia Ethica* (Cambridge: Cambridge University Press, 1962), p. 22.

21. Ibid., p. 155.
22. Ibid., p. 156.
23. Ibid.
24. Ibid.
25. Ibid.
26. Ibid., p. 158.

fact that moral norms are only general rules which have individual exceptions, Moore argues that the individual ought never disobey a rule which is held by most men to be true in general. He gives the following reasons. First, "if it is certain that in a large majority of cases the observance of a certain rule is useful, it follows that there is a large probability that it would be wrong to break the rule in any particular case."[27] Further, "the uncertainty of our knowledge both of effects and of their value, in particular cases, is so great, that it seems doubtful whether the individual's judgment that the effect will probably be good in his case can ever be set against the general probability that that kind of action is wrong."[28] Also, "added to this general ignorance is the fact that, if the question arises at all, our judgment will generally be biased by the fact that we strongly desire one of the results which we hope to obtain by breaking the rule."[29] In view of these factors, "it seems, then, that with regard to any rule which is generally useful, we may assert that it ought *always* to be observed," wrote Moore, "not on the ground that in every particular case it will be useful, but on the ground that in any particular case the probability of its being so is greater than that of our being likely to decide rightly that we have before us an instance of its disutility. . . . In short, though we may be sure that there are cases where the rule should be broken, we can never know which those cases are, and ought, therefore, never to break it."[30]

Even if one were to perceive clearly that in his case breaking the rule would be advantageous, yet insofar as such a rule-breaking action tends to encourage other unadvantageous breaches of the rule, it has a bad effect. For "in cases . . . where example has any influence at all, the effect of an exceptional right action will generally be to encourage wrong ones."[31] According to Moore, the logic of this should be carried even one step further. For "it is undoubtedly well to punish a man, who has done an action, right in his case but generally wrong, even if his example would not be likely to have a dangerous effect. For sanctions [punishments] have, in general, much more influence upon conduct than example; so that the effect of relaxing them in an exceptional case will almost certainly be an encouragement of similar action in cases which are not exceptional."[32]

It should be noted that the position that one ought always obey

27. Ibid., p. 162.
28. Ibid.
29. Ibid.
30. Ibid.
31. Ibid., p. 163.
32. Ibid., p. 164.

rules that are admittedly only generally applicable is limited only to those rules or norms which are known "certainly" to be of general usefulness. In cases where there is doubt of the general utility of a rule, Moore appears to agree with the approach of the act-utilitarians. He says, "It seems that, in cases of doubt, instead of following rules, of which he is unable to see the good effects in his particular case, the individual should rather guide his choice by a direct consideration of the intrinsic value of vileness of the effect which his action may produce."[33]

In either event, there are no actions or kinds of action which really are universally wrong; there are only some things generally wrong which one ought (for utilitarian reasons) to avoid universally. So there are at least two ways in which Moore's position does not provide any truly universal norms. First, the norms which one should always follow do not represent acts which are really universally right or wrong, but only acts which are generally wrong. In specific cases an exception may be justified. But since it brings more evil than good to claim that any given case qualifies as a legitimate exception, it follows that the rule should never be broken.

Second, Moore's general rules which should always be obeyed are not really normative universals in a categorical sense, since they are norms justified only by their results. They are not deontological. They do not represent kinds of actions with intrinsic value. Moore is very clear in holding that no acts have intrinsic value; all acts are to be judged by their results.[34]

John Austin: No General Rules Should Be Broken

In the rule-utilitarianism of John Austin, the question of unbreakable rules is carried one step further than in the thinking of G. E. Moore. Moore argued only that some rules ought never to be broken, because of their general utility and because one could not be sure his case was a legitimate exception, and even if it were, other offsetting bad consequences and influences would result from making an exception of it. Austin, on the other hand, argues that rules about a class of actions which if generally done would bring bad results should never be broken.

Rules are justified by general results—Austin's position is decidedly utilitarian because the only justification for keeping the rules is the good result keeping rules brings. In *The Province of Jurisprudence Determined* (1832), he says, "Our rules would be fashioned on utility;

33. Ibid., p. 166.
34. See ibid., pp. 92, 93, 104, 105.

our conduct on our rules. . . ."[35] According to Austin's view, "our conduct would conform to *rules* inferred from the tendency of actions, but
would not be determined by a direct resort to the principle of general
utility."[36] That is to say, "utility would be the test of our conduct,
ultimately, but not immediately."[37] Rules are justified if keeping them
brings greater good, or if breaking them brings greater evil, on society.
However, rules are not about specific or individual acts but about classes
or kinds of acts.

Universal rule-keeping is justified by general results—Each individual act is not to be justified by its specific results as in act-utilitarianism. But the whole class of acts of that kind is judged by the results
which those kinds of acts bring. As Austin states it, "If we would try
the tendency of a specific or individual act, we must not contemplate
the act as if it were single and insulated, but must look at the class
of acts to which it belongs."[38] Further, "we must suppose that acts of
the class were generally done or omitted, and consider the probable
effect upon the general happiness or good. . . ."[39] For "the particular
conclusion which we draw, with regard to the single act, implies a
general conclusion embracing all similar acts."[40]

The only exception to this is when rules conflict or when a particular
act falls under no rule. Furthermore, these general rules are always
to be obeyed only if they are generally observed and generally useful.
If either (or both) ceases to be a fact, then they lose their force and
need not always be obeyed. Austin gives a number of examples of his
position. A poor man should not steal from his rich neighbor on the
grounds of the utility of this particular act (as an act-utilitarian would
say), for if stealing were general, the effect on society would be disastrous. Nor should one evade the payment of a tax to devote the
money to some good purpose, for "regular payment of taxes is necessary to the existence of the government. And I, and the rest of the
community, enjoy the security which it gives, because the payment of
taxes is rarely evaded."[41]

In a similar way, the punishment of an individual as a solitary
event may do more harm than good. "But, considered as part of a
system, a punishment is useful or beneficent. By a dozen or score of

35. John Austin, *The Province of Jurisprudence Determined* (1832; reprint ed., London: Weidenfeld and Nicolson, 1954), p. 47.
   36. Ibid.
   37. Ibid.
   38. Ibid., pp. 47, 48.
   39. Ibid., p. 48.
   40. Ibid.
   41. Ibid., p. 39.

punishments, thousands of crimes are prevented."[42] The individual punishment is justified by the good results of the general practice. Exceptions should not be made because the general results of disobeying general rules is generally bad.

Traditionally, utilitarians argued that an action should be judged on whether it would bring the greatest good to the greatest number of people. Professor Joseph Barnhart offers a modification to this utilitarian calculus. He believes we should act so as to bring the greatest good (happiness) to *every* individual, *including* oneself.[43] From a libertarian perspective, he believes this will better safeguard each individual's rights.

Generalism Evaluated

There are some positive values as well as serious drawbacks to generalism. Let us first consider some of the positive features of the generalist approach to ethical norms.

Some Values of Generalism

The values of generalism vary with its representations. But, taken as a whole, there are at least three that relate to a normative approach to ethics such as that taken by Christians. First, generalism reflects a need for norms. Second, it offers a possible solution to conflicting norms. Finally, some generalists even argue for "unbreakable" norms.

The need for norms—Generalists are not antinomian. They recognize the need for norms, for even utilitarian ends need normative means for attaining them. There must be a road map to one's ultimate goal. Moral ends are not self-attaining, and there is an evident need for criteria to guide one's conduct. It is to the credit of the utilitarians that they have recognized that without norms or other normative bases taken from the fund of human experience, there is no way of determining the long-range results of one's actions. That is, they are aware of the fact that in the absence of predictive powers, men must draw upon principles which are known to produce good results when followed.

Moore argued that in view of the fact that one does not know the long-range future, he must gauge his actions on the basis of the known short-range future, assuming they will be the same. But he frankly acknowledges that this is an unproven assumption. He adds, "It will be apparent that it has never yet been justified—that no sufficient

42. Ibid., p. 40.
43. Joseph E. Barnhart, "Egoism and Altruism," *Southwestern Journal of Philosophy* 7, 1 (Winter 1976): 101–10.

reason has ever yet been found for considering one action more right or more wrong than another [via results]."[44] In view of this, it is understandable that the utilitarian resorts to norms to save his position from collapsing.

A solution to conflicting norms—Generalism offers a solution to the problem of what to do when there is a conflict of duty, such as that between truthfulness and saving lives. For apart from rule-utilitarians, generalists believe that there are no universal rules which are really exceptionless. At best they are only general norms that may be broken if the occasion calls for it. In this way, lying to save a life can be right, even though lying is generally wrong. There is only one absolute end ("the greatest good") and all the means (rules, norms) are relative to that end. In any given instance, when there is a conflict of means or norms, it may be resolved by a direct appeal to the utilitarian end. If lying in a situation would be more useful or helpful to most men, then one ought to lie.

As has been mentioned, the generalistic solution is neither antinomian nor situational. Antinomians admit of the value of no laws at all, not even general ones. Situationists such as Joseph Fletcher claim to have one absolute norm, whereas generalists claim no absolute norms at all. Of course, generalism has one absolute end which functions like a norm in helping to determine a given course of action when there is a conflict of general norms. But technically, the greatest good for the greatest number is not considered by generalists to be a norm by which the best end can be attained, but it is the end itself in view of which the best norm should be chosen. So generalism evades the no-norm position and offers a reconciliation when there is a conflict among accepted norms. Its answer is simple: when moral principles conflict, the conflict is not absolute; there is always a possible exception. Moral duties are only general, not universal. And general principles admit of exceptions.

Some generalists have an "unbreakable" norm— Some generalists offer a case for rules or norms which should never be broken. Even though they admit that there are exceptional cases which might in isolation justify breaking a general rule, they offer practical arguments for never breaking a rule such as saving lives or keeping promises (unless, of course, there is a conflict of norms). The very desire to have meaningful and unbreakable norms for conduct is a commendable aspect of their ethic. It is a recognition of the many difficulties of an exceptive approach on the practical level.

Furthermore, generalists are not complete relativists. They have an

44. Moore, *Principia Ethica,* p. 153.

absolute, even though it is not always considered an absolute norm. It is an absolute end, and it is used by them to discern among their relative means. In fact, without an absolute end it is difficult to see how generalists could either justify their choice among means or how they could argue that some rules should never be broken. For if there is no ultimate criterion for deciding on these issues, then how could one relative be chosen over another? Ranking separate actions by intrinsic value is not something generalists of the utilitarian stripe are prone to do, for it is contrary to their premise of judging things by their extrinsic value (namely, their usefulness).

Some Inadequacies of Generalism

Despite some positive things that may be said of generalism, there are some serious problems with the position. Several of these will be briefly considered here.

The end does not justify the means—Utilitarianism believes that the end justifies the means. But this is clearly wrong. Hitler's goal to have a more perfect race was good, but his means of attaining it were evil. President Nixon's goal of national security was a noble one, but the criminal and unethical activity of Watergate was not justified to reach it. The end never justifies the means; the means must justify themselves. That is to say, an act is not automatically good simply because it has a good goal. The means to achieve it must be judged good by some objective standard of good. The road to destruction is paved with good intentions (Prov. 14:12). Something is not good because the intentions underlying it are good; it is good only if the actions are also good. From a Christian perspective, we must agree with Paul when he writes, "Shall we go on sinning so that grace may increase? By no means!" (Rom. 6:1).

Generalism has no universal norms—There is a distinct difference between a general norm, which for practical reasons one ought always to obey, and a truly universal norm which is always intrinsically right to follow. The latter represents an intrinsically good act. But the generalist offers only norms that have less than universal extension. There are always unspecifiable exceptions or else cases which are not covered by the rules. And even though generalists sometimes opt not to break these rules because of general utility, nevertheless the rule itself is not essentially unbreakable.

If one is in search of meaningful norms for conduct which he ought always to follow because they will guide him in performing acts which are always the right thing to do, then he will be disappointed in generalism. The best a generalist can offer is a set of general norms which neither cover all cases nor are nonconflicting and for which, in order for them to be effective, one must have some other means of applying them in specific and often crucial cases.

Utilitarian acts have no intrinsic value—Another criticism which may be directed toward the utilitarian generalists is that the norms which they do have do not represent any acts with intrinsic value. For example, the attempt to save a life is not an intrinsically valuable act. It has value only if the person is actually saved or if some other good comes from the futile attempt. According to the utilitarian premise, a gift of charity which never reaches the poor or an act of kindness to which there is no favorable response is not a good act. Indeed, no act is good in and of itself unless good results from it. And no act is morally right unless it brings the greatest good to the greatest number of men. No benevolence, no sacrifice, no love has any value unless it happens to have good results. And conversely, if an act brings about good, it is a good act whether it was intended that way or not.

Thus the utilitarian position reduces the ethical value of acts to the fates and fortunes of life. All is well that ends well. And what ends well is good. This would mean that the intentions of one's actions have no essential connection with the good of those actions. Presumably, one could will and perform an evil act which by chance turned out for good and be credited with performing a good act. Surely fortuity and morality do not belong in such proximity.

The need for an absolute norm—It is not possible to consistently maintain a group of general norms which may and do conflict without having an absolute norm by which the conflict can be resolved. This point seems to be evidenced by the need among utilitarian generalists to appeal to the end to resolve the conflict between norms. But when the end is so used, it serves a normative function. The end (the greatest good) becomes the means of determining which means will be best for attaining the end. Not only is there a manifest circularity in appealing to the end, but there is also an obvious need for an ultimate principle to resolve the tension among the less-than-ultimate principles or norms. To state the point another way, relative norms do not stand alone. They must be relative to something which is not relative. So unless there is an assumed nonrelative standard, the relative ones cannot function properly. General rules presuppose a universal norm or norms.

Whether the number of absolute or universal norms is one or many will be discussed more fully in the next three chapters. It is sufficient for now to note that there must be *at least* one norm which is true under all conditions if the other norms are to be true under any conditions.

The "end" is an ambiguous term—The generalist's ethic is based on what will bring the best results in the long run. But how long is "long"?

A few years? A lifetime? Eternity? Anything beyond the immediate present is outside of the human purview. Only God knows the future. Hence, only God could be a utilitarian, and he is not.

Certainly God knows that his moral principles will bring the best results in the long run. But he does not will them for this reason. Rather, he wills what is right because it is right. And it is right because it is in accord with his own unchangeable moral character. So appealing to long-range consequence as the basis for determining what rules we follow is out of the range of humans and out of the question for a morally perfect God.

The debate about whether the "greatest good" should in the end be understood quantitatively or qualitatively brings an ambiguity in the phrase into focus. How do we determine what is meant by "good"? As we saw in chapter 1, unless good has a divinely determined meaning there is no real basis for holding that anything is objectively good. And if moral good is not objective, then we are left with antinomianism.

The further ambiguity in the word *end* is brought to light by the disagreement about whether it means "for the greatest number" or for "*all* individuals," as some have suggested. It would make a significant difference which view is taken, particularly with respect to minority rights. For in many cases, more good could be achieved for the most people if basic rights were denied to some people.

The need for ethical norms—Even generalism does not avoid the need for some absolute norm or norms. First of all, without some basic value standard there is no means by which to measure the consequences to determine whether they are really good or bad. How can we know whether the results are better or worse unless we have some standard for what is best?

Second, the fund of human experience cannot serve as the ultimate measure. We cannot know what to put in the fund unless we have some moral standard outside of the fund by which to measure it.

Third, in utilitarianism the end serves as a norm by which actions are measured. It is the ultimate by which all else is measured, and hence its role is normative.

Summary and Conclusion

Generalism, in contrast to antinomianism, argues that there are some binding moral principles. But in contrast to absolutism, generalism insists that none of these moral laws is really absolute. Since every moral principle admits of exceptions, the generalist has an easy solution to moral conflicts. However, since he has no absolute moral principles, his view tends to be reducible to antinomianism. Unless there are some objective moral prescriptions of substantive content which are binding on all persons at all times, then at any given time it is possible that any action could be justified.

Select Readings

Austin, John. *The Province of Jurisprudence Determined*. 1832. Reprint ed. London: Weidenfeld and Nicolson, 1954.

Bentham, Jeremy. *Introduction to the Principles of Morals and Legislation*. Reprint ed. New York: Hafner, 1965.

Kurtz, Paul. *Forbidden Fruit: The Ethics of Humanism*. Buffalo: Prometheus, 1988.

Mill, John Stuart. *Utilitarianism*. In *The Utilitarians*. Garden City, N.Y.: Dolphin Books, Doubleday, 1961.

Moore, G. E. *Principia Ethica*. Cambridge: Cambridge University Press, 1962.

Singer, Marcus G. *Generalization in Ethics*. New York: Knopf, 1961.

5

Unqualified Absolutism

There are two basic kinds of ethical views: absolutism and relativism. The preceding three chapters (2–4) have examined ethical relativism. The next three chapters (5–7) will look at three forms of ethical absolutism.

Perhaps the most influential and widely held view among Christians is unqualified absolutism. The position was given its classic presentation by Augustine and has been defended by such a notable philosopher as Immanuel Kant and such theologians as John Murray and Charles Hodge.

An Exposition of Unqualified Absolutism

The basic premise of unqualified absolutism is that all moral conflicts are only apparent; they are not real. Sin is always avoidable. There are moral absolutes that admit of no exceptions and these never actually come into conflict with one another. On the classic question as to whether or not one should ever lie to save a life, the unqualified absolutist answers with an emphatic, "No!" The importance of this issue to Augustine can be measured by the fact that he dedicated two works to it, *Against Lying* and *On Lying*, plus made numerous other references to it throughout his writings.

Saint Augustine's Unqualified Absolutism

The medieval bishop Augustine has sometimes been misunderstood to be a situationist because of his statement that one should "love God and do as he will." While it is true that Augustine cast his whole ethical system in terms of love, it is not true that he based that system only on the one command of love. Augustine believed that love consummates the virtues, but it does not consume them. Rather, charity implies the other virtues.

Augustine's arguments against lying—There are many arguments offered by Augustine against ever telling a lie. For him telling the truth is an absolute, and absolutes cannot be broken. Augustine is quick to point out that not all falsifications are lies. Only those falsifications with intention to deceive qualify as lies. A person is to be judged as lying or not lying according to his intention, not by the truth or falsity of his expressions. Thus something said in jest or even something false, spoken by one who intends the hearer to understand something true by it, is not a lie. For example, if a man wants to reach a certain city, and asks directions of a friend he knows is a perpetual liar, the liar should give him directions that take him along the bandit-infested route. That way the friend will take the opposite route and avoid the robbers and possible death. This is not a lie.

Lying to ward off rape, or even to save a life, is strictly forbidden by Augustine's unqualified absolutism, for one's choice is really between the permission of another's sin or the commission of his own sin. Of a certain heretical group, the Priscillianists, who were lying to keep themselves from being discovered, Augustine insisted that Christians ought to condemn the impiety of lying as well as the heresy. Further, Christians ought not to lie to expose liars. In short, committing one sin to avoid another sin is still a sin.

Some had suggested that lying would be permissible as a means of getting another to heaven. But Augustine insisted that no eternal good could be accomplished by a temporal evil. He insisted that no one for any reason whatsoever ought to be deceived into the kingdom of Truth. Christian teaching is truth, and no falsehood should be part of Christian teaching.

Augustine insists that lying breaks down regard for the truth because lying destroys all certainty. When regard for the truth has been broken down or even slightly weakened, all things will remain doubtful. In brief, without truthfulness there is no integrity, and without integrity there can be no certainty. Once falsity is ever admitted into communication, then one can never again be certain the speaker is telling the truth.

Lying is a web that entangles more and more because lying necessitates more lying to explain and cover up for itself. Eventually, argued Augustine, this will lead to perjury or even blasphemy. If one becomes a habitual liar, then he might lie even to God.

Lying would weaken the Christian faith, for if we are untruthful in one area, then how can people believe us when we teach them Christian doctrine? When we are teaching the faith to them, they will say, "How do I know whether you are not lying to me now?"

Augustine borrowed a Platonic premise as a basis for his argument that one should never lie, even to avoid rape. He contended that one should endeavor to preserve chastity in both soul and body, but when both cannot be protected, he insisted that the latter must give way to the former because everyone knows intuitively that the soul is to be preferred to the body, and sins of the soul are worse than sins of the body.

Augustine cites numerous passages from the Bible (and Apocrypha) to support his unqualified absolutism. Psalm 5:5–6 is rendered, "Thou dost hate, O Lord, all who work iniquity; thou shalt destroy all who speak a lie." Wisdom 1:11 is also quoted by Augustine, "The mouth that belieth, killeth the soul." Thus Augustine concludes that since eternal life is lost by lying, neither should a lie be told for the preservation of the temporal life of another. In short, why lose eternal life in order to save a temporal life?

Augustine admitted that some acts are not good or bad in themselves. For example, giving to the poor is good at some times and bad at other times, depending on the motive for giving. But when the works themselves are already sin, such as theft, impurity, blasphemy, and the like, who would say that these evil acts should be done for good reasons? Some moral acts are intrinsically good and, hence, their violation can never be for a good purpose.

In his *Retractions,* Augustine confessed that some of his arguments were "obscure," but he never revised or corrected them. He apparently went to his reward firmly believing in an unqualified moral absolutism.

Augustine's treatment of difficult passages—On the face of it, the Bible seems to record many cases of justified lying. Augustine was aware of these passages and attempted to explain them in terms of his unqualified absolutism. Let us examine his interpretations of the stories of Rahab, the Hebrew midwives, and Lot, of David's oath to kill Nabal, and of the alleged falsehoods and deceptions of Abraham, Jacob, and Jesus.

The Hebrew midwives lied to Pharaoh, and yet God apparently blessed them for it (Exod. 1). Rahab's lie saved the Jewish spies, and she is commended for her faith in the "Hall of Fame" of the Letter to the Hebrews (11:31). Augustine's answer was that God blessed these women for their mercy but did not condone their impiety. God did not praise them because they lied but because they were merciful to the men of God. So, it was not their deception that was rewarded, but their kindness. God blessed in spite of their lie, not because of it.

Lot faced a moral conflict when the Sodomites demanded his guests for immoral purposes. To some, Lot's action of giving his daughters to appease the Sodomites seemed like an avoidance of a greater sin (homosexuality) by allowing a lesser one (rape). But Augustine emphatically rejects this position. His answer to this dilemma is to note two things. First, one must never commit a great crime of his own in order to avoid someone else's greater crime. Second, and more directly to the point of the dilemma, Augustine insisted that Lot himself did not sin; he merely allowed the Sodomites to sin by raping his daughters.

The Bible seems to say that an oath before God is inviolable (see Eccles. 5:1–6), and yet the Bible (and common sense) would seem to suggest that one should not keep a foolish or sinful oath. Augustine's response is that not everything done by righteous men of the past should be taken as normative. In short, the Bible records but does not approve of David's making such a sinful oath.

The Scriptures say that Abraham claimed Sarah to be his "sister" (she was his half-sister) in order to protect himself from being killed if the king discovered she was his wife (Gen. 20). Augustine insisted that Abraham was not lying here since he only concealed something of the truth but did not really say anything that was false. As to Jacob's alleged deception of his father, Isaac, in order to obtain God's blessing, Augustine argues that what Jacob did at his mother's bidding in seemingly deceiving his father was not a lie but only a "mystery."

The Gospel account tells us that Jesus asked, "Who touched me?" as though he didn't know. Later he indicated to the two disciples on the Emmaus road that he would go farther when he had not mentioned doing so (Luke 24:28). Augustine's answer here is that this was not really deception but instruction. Jesus pretended not to know who touched his garment in order that he might teach his disciples something they did not know. Since this teaching was true, no lie was involved. This answer seems to imply that as long as one conveys what is true in the light of his intentions, even if some deception is necessarily involved in doing so, then he has not lied.

Kant's Unqualified Absolutism

Immanuel Kant was one of the most influential thinkers of modern times. He was agnostic about knowing reality in itself, but he was a devout believer in God and was a moral absolutist.

A universal moral duty—Kant called the universal moral obligation

a categorical imperative. By that he meant that the duty was unconditional, not conditional. He eschewed any hypothetical ethics such as
if one does this, then this or that will result. He favored a categorical
(deontological) ethic where "one ought to do thus and thus." Duties are
duties regardless of the consequences. Kant stated the categorical imperative several ways. First, we should always treat others as an end
and never as a means to an end. And second, one should act so that
he could will his action a rule for all men.

Kant gave both proclaiming truth and protecting life as examples
of the categorical imperative. That is, both lying and murder are
universally wrong. His justification for this position is as follows. If
one were to will lying as a universal rule, then there would be no more
truth to lie about. Hence, it would be self-destructive to lie. But whatever we cannot will as a universal rule we should never do, for this is
what the categorical imperative demands. Likewise, one should never
kill, for if he does so, then he must will that all can kill. But if all
kill, then there will be no one left to kill. Therefore, murder should
never be permitted in even one instance.

The defense of universal moral duties—There are at least three
reasons stated or implied by Kant for his unqualified absolutism. All
of them reveal his strong commitment to a deontological (duty-
centered) ethic.

Moral duties by their nature admit no exceptions, since any exception to a moral law would indicate that it was not truly a rule. Kant
believed that moral laws, like Newton's law of gravitation, have no
exceptions. God does not tolerate the breaking of any of his laws,
whether ethical or natural. The universe runs according to universal
law.

Moral duties are intrinsic, not extrinsic, and whatever is intrinsically good cannot be evil. It is as absurd to call an intrinsically good
act evil as it is to call light darkness. Only what is neither good nor
bad in itself but dependent on something else for its goodness or evil
can be called evil at one time and good at another. Intrinsically good
actions are not like this; they are always good in and of themselves.
Since telling the truth is an intrinsic good and a lie is an intrinsic evil,
it follows that there can never be a good lie.

Kant's defense of universal moral laws is a kind of transcendental
argument. He argues that it is absolutely necessary to posit moral
duties as categorical and universal in order to live moral lives. Society
cannot function without law, and law must be universal in order to be
law. If it does not apply to everyone, then it is not a law. Hence, universal moral law, not what is simply socially or personally desirable,
is rationally necessary to posit for life.

Lying to save a life is always wrong—The fact that one should neither lie nor murder leads to the dilemma that Kant addressed in his
tractate, "On a Supposed Right to Tell Lies from Benevolent Motives"
(1787). His response to that supposition, like Augustine's response,
was a categorical no. He wrote, "Whoever then tells a lie, however
good his intentions may be, must answer for the consequences of it
. . . however unforeseen they may have been."[1] For "to be truthful (honest) in all declarations is therefore a sacred unconditional command
of reason, and not to be limited by any expediency."[2] Kant makes
several points in elaborating his view.

All social duties are moral contracts, and truth is the basis of all
contracts. Unless there is mutual trust in each other's word, there can
be no contract. Therefore, truth is the very foundation of all social
duties. Without it, all law is rendered useless and uncertain.

Kant is strongly opposed to the view that it is a duty to tell the
truth only to those who have a right to it. First, he insists that truth
is not a possession the right of which can be granted to one person and
refused to another. Second, the duty to tell the truth makes no distinction between persons but is an unconditional duty that holds in all
circumstances. Therefore, it is a duty to be truthful to everyone.

By lying to one person, we do injury to all persons, for falsehoods
violate the principle of justice which protects all from harm. Veracity
constitutes the condition of justice in utterances, and by lying one
offends all persons through violating the principle necessary for justice
in general.

Kant argues that "it is possible that while you have honestly an-
swered Yes to the murderer's question, whether his intended victim is
in the house, the latter may have gone out unobserved, and so not
have come in the way of the murderer. . . ."[3] Or, "if you had spoken the
truth as well as you knew it, perhaps the murderer while seeking for
his enemy in the house might have been caught by neighbours coming
up and the deed [have] been prevented."[4] Consequently, lying may not
be necessary to protect the innocent.

John Murray's Unqualified Absolutism

One of the best modern examples of unqualified absolutism in the
evangelical tradition is that of John Murray of Westminster Seminary.

1. Immanuel Kant, "On a Supposed Right to Tell Lies from Benevolent Motives," in
The Critique of Practical Reason, trans. Thomas Kinsmill Abbot, 6th ed. (London: Longmans Green, 1963), p. 363.
2. Ibid.
3. Ibid., pp. 362, 363.
4. Ibid., p. 363.

In *Principles of Conduct* (1957), Murray elaborates how he would maintain "the sanctity of truth" even in situations which would seem to call for a justifiable lie. There are two basic reasons for this: God is absolute, and truth is of the essence of God.

God's law is absolute—Like Augustine, Murray believes that God's law is absolutely binding. The will of God is a sovereign reflection of his unchanging character. Since God is truth and cannot ever lie (Heb. 6:18), then neither should we. The moral standard in Scripture is: "Be ye therefore perfect, even as your Father which is in heaven is perfect" (Matt. 5:48 KJV).

Lying is always wrong—Because the command to tell the truth flows from the absolute law of God, no exceptions can be made to it. Murray writes, "The necessity of truthfulness in us rests upon God's truthfulness. As we are to be holy because God is holy, so we are to be truthful because God is truthful."[5]

The explanation of alleged biblical lies—Murray offers an explanation for some of the difficult biblical passages, along the same lines as Augustine. With regard to Rahab's lie he says, "Although our purpose be to assist our brethren, to consult for their safety and to relieve them, it never can be lawful to lie, because that cannot be right which is contrary to the nature of God."[6] After reviewing several biblical examples of lying, Murray concludes, "We see, therefore, that neither Scripture itself nor the theological inferences derived from Scripture provide us with any warrant for the vindication of Rahab's untruth and this instance, consequently, does not support the position that under certain circumstances we may justifiably utter an untruth."[7]

One significant qualification—Murray believes all lying is wrong, but he does not hold that every intentional deception is a lie. For example, a general's troop maneuver may lead his enemy to an erroneous conclusion without lying. For according to Murray it is a "false assumption [to hold that] to be truthful we must under all circumstances speak and act in terms of the data which comes within the purview of others who may be concerned with or affected by our speaking or acting."[8] In brief, we may without lying intentionally act or speak in a way that we know will be misunderstood by others.

The Providence of God

Implied in unqualified absolutism is another premise: the providence of God. Since they are deontologists who believe that the result

5. John Murray, *Principles of Conduct* (Grand Rapids: Eerdmans, 1971), p. 127.
6. Ibid., p. 139.
7. Ibid.
8. Ibid., p. 145.

does not determine the rule, unqualified absolutists stress that in God's providence he always makes "a third alternative" in every apparent moral dilemma.

Several examples supplied from Scripture and elsewhere are used to show that God delivers his faithful from these dilemmas. The implication (seldom, if ever, stated) is that there are no real, unavoidable moral dilemmas. Daniel is often used as a prime example. The pagan king commanded that Daniel violate the law of God by partaking of forbidden meat and wine. But Daniel proposed "a third alternative" of vegetables and water, which God blessed and which thus brought him into the king's favor (Dan. 1).

It is also said that Sarah followed God's law and obeyed her husband's command, trusting that God would intervene and save her from having to commit adultery. This God did (Gen. 20). Of the many biblical examples where God did not intervene, it is implied that he would have intervened if the believer would have asked in faith for the deliverance, since "God is faithful; he will not let you be tempted beyond what you can bear" (1 Cor. 10:13). Those who admit there are some cases in which God does not intervene claim this is because there was antecedent sin in the person's life. For example, someone driving too fast might have to choose between hitting a school bus or hitting a pedestrian when there is no way between or around them. But the dilemma arises from the driver's own evil choice of fast driving.

In short, sometimes we make our own moral bed and we have to lie in it. But many of God's people do (and all could) manifest the kind of faithfulness that says, "I will tell the truth and leave the consequences to God." A case in point can be found in the story of Corrie ten Boom's life (*The Hiding Place*). When the ten Boom family told the truth to the Nazis, they said the Jews were hiding "under the table," but the Nazis did not see the fugitives because they were under the floor under the table. This, say some unqualified absolutists, is the sort of protection God will give if we trust him and never lie. Hence, there is never a need to lie or break any moral law in order to save a life or do any other moral good.

Summary of Unqualified Absolutism

There are several major premises that make up the unqualified absolutist's position, at least as it is held by Christians. Briefly stated they include the following:

1. God's unchanging character is the basis of moral absolutes.
2. God has expressed his unchanging moral character in his law.
3. God cannot contradict himself.

4. Hence, no two absolute moral laws can really conflict.

5. All moral conflicts are only apparent, not real.

Positive Aspects of Unqualified Absolutism

Unqualified absolutism has much to commend it as a Christian ethic. It is based in God's unchanging character, its nature is deontological, it has trust in God's providence, and it holds the belief that there is always a way to avoid sinning. Let us examine these in a little more detail.

It Is Based in God's Unchanging Nature

Most unqualified absolutists realize the need to anchor their universal moral duties in the unchanging character of God. Indeed, it is difficult to see how there can be any absolute moral prescriptions unless there is an absolute moral Prescriber. Absolutely binding moral laws come only from an absolute moral Lawgiver. This most commendable emphasis of unqualified absolutism points up the inconsistency of any form of moral relativism, such as antinomianism (chap. 2), situationism (chap. 3), or generalism (chap. 4).

It Stresses Rule over Result

Unqualified absolutism is a deontological ethic (see chap. 1). As such it rightly holds that the rule determines the result, and not the reverse. Here again, this is a necessary ingredient in an adequate Christian ethic. Something is not good simply because it brings about desired results. An act is good because it is good, regardless of the results. Of course, God designed good acts so that they would bring about good results. Moses told Israel "to observe the Lord's commands and decrees that I am giving you today for your own good" (Deut. 10:13). However, even though doing good is intended to bring good, nonetheless good is good no matter what evil may come from it. And evil is evil no matter what good may result from it.

It Shows Trust in God's Providence

Another positive dimension of unqualified absolutism is its manifest confidence in the providence of God. This is revealed clearly in the attitude of believers who, in the face of death, can say with Esther, "if I perish, I perish" (Esther 4:16), or, with the three Hebrew young men, "the God we serve is able to save us from it [the fiery furnace]. . . . But even if he does not, we want you to know, O king, that we will not serve your gods or worship the image of gold you have set up" (Dan. 3:17–18). Since an absolute ethic is based in a God who is in absolute control, the believer can trust him absolutely. God's providence makes it unnecessary to take things in our own hands. The Christian can confidently believe that since God made the rules, it is simply our duty to keep them and leave the results in his hands.

There Is Always a Way to Avoid Sinning

Another commendable feature of unqualified absolutism is its belief that it is not necessary to sin. God has so designed our moral laws and our duty that it is never necessary to sin. Ultimately, there is no moral conflict in the self-consistent God, nor are there any unresolvable conflicts in this moral world. There is always "a way to escape" (1 Cor. 10:13 KJV). It is never necessary to literally do the lesser evil. There is always "a third alternative." That is to say, the believer is never duty-bound to sin in order to avoid sin. God has set it up that way.

Negative Aspects of Unqualified Absolutism

Critics have pointed out a number of difficulties with unqualified absolutism. Since not all unqualified absolutists hold identical views, not all of these criticisms are applicable to all proponents. However, many of them will apply to all forms of the position.

Some Disputable or False Premises

Let us begin by examining presuppositions that are either unnecessarily or unjustifiably held by some proponents of unqualified absolutism.

Are sins of the soul greater? This Platonic premise held by Augustine has by no means experienced a universal acceptance. To be sure, many Christians still adhere to a dualistic hierarchy of this variety. This has led, not without justification, to the charge that such Christians neglect social concern because they are more interested in saving souls than helping bodies. The biblical teaching on the unity of man is the best corrective to this false dichotomy.

If Augustine were correct in this ethical dualism, then a "white lie" or minor "evil thought" would be worse than rape or murder, for any spiritual offense would be worse than a physical one. Furthermore, Augustine was not consistent in applying this principle. Otherwise he would not have rejected the view that David should have killed Nabal (the body) in order to keep his oath (the soul).

Can the lie to save lives be separated from mercy? Augustine says that God blessed the mercy but not the lie. However, it was by means of the lie that Rahab's mercy was expressed and the spies were saved. The same is true of the Hebrew midwives' lie (Exod. 1:15–16). There was no actual separation between the lie and the act of mercy. And a mere formal distinction will not suffice as an explanation, since in actuality there was only one act (which included the lie) under consideration, and this act was praised by God.

Are acts intrinsically good? Augustine argued that some acts are intrinsically good, apart from one's intentions or motives. If this is so, then theft or lying would indeed always be wrong. However, there are several objections to this view. First, if some acts were intrinsically good or evil, then an act of killing committed by an animal or an imbecile would have to be considered morally wrong. It will not suffice to add that only human acts of killing could be morally wrong, or else we would have to deny imbeciles are human, since they are not morally culpable for their acts. Furthermore, this would mean that they were wrong only because they were intended by someone, which is tantamount to saying that the act as such is not evil, but only the act as intended is evil.

Can a lie be defined without intention? Augustine defined a lie as an intentional falsehood. But if intention needs to be added to the act of falsifying in order to make it a lie, then it follows that the act of falsifying as such is not a lie. Further, if acts are intrinsically evil apart from intentions or motives, then any falsification or action contrary to a moral prescription in Scripture would be an evil. This would include unintentional falsehoods as well as accidental injury or death inflicted on persons. But this is not so. Finally, Augustine admitted that not all acts are intrinsically good or evil, as, for example, giving to the poor. If so, then he has already qualified his absolutism; perhaps the other acts, such as lying, are not intrinsically evil, either.

Does lying destroy all certainty? Augustine argued that lying would destroy all certainty. At best, this argument only proves that lying undermines some certainty, namely, that information based on the testimony of one known to have lied. Furthermore, the same argument could be made against anyone known to have made unintentional mistakes, which we all do. So Augustine's argument would prove too much. It would prove that one cannot be certain of anything that depends on any person. But his own Christian beliefs depended on the testimony of the apostles, which Augustine did not consider uncertain.

Is the choice between permission and commission? Unqualified absolutists believe there is no real moral dilemma in the case of lying or permitting a murder. They believe there is really only one moral obligation in this situation—to tell the truth. The only other duty, they say, belongs to the person threatening to do the killing. He is responsible for what he does with the truth we give him. But is this overlooking the fact that there is also a duty to save innocent lives, to show mercy? In short, is there a real conflict between truthfulness and mercifulness? In other words, the choice is really between an act of commission and one of omission. And a sin of omission can be just as much a sin as a sin of commission (James 4:17).

Does lying condemn a person to hell? Few Christians really believe, as Augustine suggests, that a single lie (even a few lies scattered through one's life) will send a believer to hell. Indeed, anyone who believes in salvation by grace alone, as Scripture teaches (Eph. 2:8–9), will not trouble himself long with this point. It is only those lives characterized by untruthfulness that eventuate in the lake of fire (Rev. 21:8). And these unsaved find themselves right alongside those who are "fearful." Yet who would say that everyone who has ever (or even occasionally) been fearful will be in hell?

Will God always save us from moral dilemmas? There are several reasons to suppose that divine intervention is not the solution to all moral dilemmas. First, nowhere does Scripture promise this to every faithful believer all the time. First Corinthians 10:13 is only a promise for victory in temptation—not a guarantee of intervention to avoid moral conflicts. Second, neither Scripture nor the history of the martyrs supports the position that God always delivers the faithful from moral conflicts. God did deliver Daniel and Sarah, but he did not deliver Abraham (Gen. 22), the midwives (Exod. 1), Rahab (Josh. 2), the three Hebrew children (Dan. 3), or the apostles (Acts 4). And yet the conflicts were just as real and the believers were just as faithful in these cases.

Further, not all real moral conflicts are brought on by a person's prior sin(s). Jesus seemed to face real conflicts between obeying his heavenly Father and his earthly parents (Luke 2), between showing mercy and keeping the Sabbath (Mark 2:27), and even between justice and mercy on the cross; yet he was without sin (Heb. 4:15). In fact, moral conflicts are often brought on by one's faithfulness to God. This was so of the midwives, of Daniel, of Abraham, of the apostles, and even of Corrie ten Boom. If she had not cared so much about those innocent Jews, she would never have found herself in the dilemma of needing to lie to save their lives.

Was Abraham's concealment a lie? Augustine insisted that Abraham's concealment of Sarah's identity as his wife was not a lie, since she was really his half-sister. But what about Isaac, who also claimed Rebekah was his sister, though she was not (Gen. 26:7)? Surely this was not even half true. Augustine does not address this problem, nor would his explanation for Abraham suffice for Isaac.

While one can agree that there is not always an obligation to tell the whole truth, as we have in the divinely approved case of Samuel's half-truth (1 Sam. 15), nonetheless concealment sometimes is a lie. If one knows exactly what the questioner wants and yet conceals the information by intentionally misleading him (though without direct falsification), is this not an intentional deception? And an intentional deception is a lie.

Fatal Qualifications

Unqualified absolutism does not need a thousand qualifications to kill it; it can die "a death by one qualification." As Kant acknowledged, even one exception to a rule proves the rule is not genuinely universal. By their own definition, an absolute rule has no exceptions, and yet there are many ways the proponents of unqualified absolutism have qualified their view or made exceptions to it.

Augustine's exceptions—Augustine admitted many exceptions to divine commands. He excused Abraham from the charge of intending to murder Isaac because Abraham was going to sacrifice his son "in obedience to God." Likewise, Jephthah's sacrifice of his daughter and Samson's sacrifice of his own life are "justified only on this ground, that the Spirit, who wrought wonders by Him, had given him secret instructions to do this."[9] But even one exception kills a universal rule as unqualified absolutists understand it; it is shown not to be genuinely universally binding without exception. Likewise, Augustine argues that there were exceptions to the divine command to obey human government. It should be noted in this connection that the Bible not only enjoins submission to the consequences of a law (for example, going to prison for disobedience, as in Dan. 6), but also demands obedience to the rules of government (1 Pet. 2:13–14). Paul enjoins both submission and obedience, saying, "Remind the people to be subject to rulers and authorities, to be obedient" (Titus 3:1).

John Murray's qualification—Murray contended that an intentional deception is not a lie. He claimed that it is a "fallacious assumption [to hold it] to be truthful we must *under all circumstances* speak and act in terms of the data which come within the purview of others who may be concerned with or affected by our speaking or acting."[10] But once this qualification is made, there are two momentous problems. First, how do we keep from allowing a thousand similar qualifications? At least Augustine limited the allowable instances of intentional deceptions to special cases involving supernatural intervention; Murray leaves the door wide open to all kinds!

9. Saint Augustine, *City of God,* in *A Select Library of the Nicene and Post-Nicene Fathers of the Christian Church,* ed. Philip Schaff, vol. 2 (Grand Rapids: Eerdmans, 1956), p. 15.
10. Murray, *Principles of Conduct,* p. 145.

Second, if a lie by definition is an intentional falsification, as Augustine said, then Murray is playing ball in another park, since he no longer defines a lie in the same way. But if one allows Murray this new definition of a lie, then Murray is no longer an unqualified absolutist in the original Augustinian sense. What is more, Murray by virtue of his tactic of redefinition, is subject to the criticism that he salvages "unqualified absolutism" by stipulative redefinition. But is this move really justified? Would it not be more honest to admit that there are actually times when one believes that a lie (an intentional deception) is justified, rather than redefining a lie to avoid admitting that lies are sometimes justified?

Hodge's limitation—Charles Hodge makes a distinction that would rescue Augustinian unqualified absolutism from collapse. He suggests there are limitations on what counts as a lie. These limits are contextual. That is, an intentional deception counts as a lie if and only if it is told in a context in which the truth is expected.[11] Since one does not expect a spy to tell the truth, it would follow that "lying" in spying is not really lying.

However, this solution presents unqualified absolutism with several serious problems. First, once this qualification is made, the view is no longer an unqualified absolutism. It is an admission that there are exemptions from the moral rule, "Thou shalt not intentionally falsify," which is what Augustine originally meant by a lie. Second, the only way one can know which moral law should be qualified is if he has knowledge of which is higher and which is lower. But this is a form of graded absolutism (see chap. 7), not unqualified absolutism.

Unsuccessful Qualifications

"Unqualified" absolutism is not really unqualified. It always seems to find some way to qualify divine commands. They reduce certain divine commands to less than an absolute level either by insisting that they flow only from God's will, not from his nature, or by saying some are purely civil or ceremonial in nature, not moral, or by claiming that the command applies only ceterus paribus, "all things being equal."

There are, however, several problems with these solutions. First of all, not all moral commands fit into these categories. Some are between two moral principles reflective of God's nature, such as truth and mercy. Second, the whole division of commands into civil, ceremonial, and moral is postbiblical, questionable, and probably of late Christian origin (possibly the thirteenth century). Third, such a move to subordinate

11. Charles Hodge, *Systematic Theology* (reprint ed.; Grand Rapids: Eerdmans, 1952), vol. 3, pp. 439–44.

some commands to others is not an unqualified absolutism but is a form of graded absolutism (see chap. 7). Finally, any subordination or qualification of any kind is a capitulation of unqualified absolutism, since it admits there are occasions when moral commands must be qualified.

Punting to Providence

An appeal to the providence of God to avoid moral conflict is ill-advised for several reasons. First of all, God does not always intervene and spare all the faithful from moral dilemmas. There is no evidence for this premise of unqualified absolutism either inside or outside the Bible. Indeed, the premise of supernatural intervention is in conflict with other premises held by these absolutists. To begin with, what need is there for divine intervention if all conflicts are only apparent and not real? The need for divine intervention is a concession to the position, which is contrary to the tenets of unqualified absolutism, that there are real conflicts. For once one admits that there are real moral conflicts and that they can be resolved by divine intervention, then he is no longer an unqualified absolutist but is some kind of graded absolutist.

Further, why the need for intervention if all moral dilemmas are caused by antecedent sin? God may sometimes in his mercy desire to intervene, but there is no reason to believe he must (or will) always do so. We should not always expect miracles to help us out of real moral conflicts.

Many unqualified absolutists "solve" the ethical dilemma with recourse to the belief that God will always spare the faithful. This, however, meets with several serious objections.

1. God nowhere promises that he will always intervene to save us from moral conflicts.
2. The three Hebrew children did not expect God to bail them out of their moral dilemma (Dan. 3).
3. Jesus spoke against expecting a miracle to get one out of difficult situations (Matt. 4:7).
4. Expecting a miracle shifts the responsibility from us to God. It is a kind of "if in trouble, punt to God" ethic.
5. We should not base the reality of a present decision on the possibility that God may perform a miracle in the future.
6. Believing that God will intervene if we do right begs the question. It assumes that there is always a way to do right without real moral conflict.
7. Such a view would demand frequent miraculous intervention.

But frequent miraculous intervention would make both life and miracles impossible, since both depend on regular patterns of activity for their operation.

8. Finally, there are some pertinent questions to answer if one always expects God to intervene. In the case of the Christian called upon to reveal the whereabouts of an innocent victim to a would-be assassin, why not trust God to intervene before speaking the truth (by making us temporarily mute)? That way the hiding place of the innocent is not disclosed. Or why not trust God to intervene and cause deafness in the would-be assassin?

Third Alternatives Are Not Always Available

It is both unrealistic and unbiblical to assume that moral obligations never conflict. Real life reveals this kind of conflict daily in hospitals, courtrooms, and battlefields. Sometimes one must kill or be killed. Other times the baby must die, or both the mother and baby will die (as in tubal pregnancies). Likewise, the Bible tells of no third alternative for Abraham in killing Isaac (Gen. 22), or for the Hebrew midwives (Exod. 1), or the three Hebrew children (Dan. 3). It is naive to assume that these kinds of situations never happen. And, if the Christian ethic is adequate for all situations, it must have an answer for these real moral conflicts.

Not All Moral Conflicts Are Self-Made

Further, prior personal sin does not cause all moral dilemmas. Even if Adam's sin (Rom. 5:12) is the ultimate cause of original sin and imputed sin, it cannot be blamed for each personal sin since then. And it is certainly not the cause of every individual moral dilemma since then; otherwise there would be no need for confession of personal sins (1 John 1:9). To argue to the contrary would be to confuse total depravity and ethical responsibility. At best, prior personal sins cause only some of one's personal moral conflicts, not all of them. Some are caused by others who force the conflict on the innocent. Indeed, sometimes just the opposite is true, namely, personal moral dilemmas are precipitated by one's faithfulness or righteousness.

A Basic Inconsistency

Most unqualified absolutists are inconsistent. For while they condemn lying to save a person, they engage in intentional deception to save their property. Most people, for example, leave their lights on while away from home in order to deceive potential thieves. But if one will lie to save his property from a potential thief, then why not lie to save an actual life from a murderer? While condemning Corrie ten Boom for lying to protect Jews from being killed, they lie to save their jewels from being stolen. But persons have more value than things.

Falling into Sins of Omission

Another problem is that the unqualified absolutist often ends up committing unmerciful acts. He performs greater sins of omission in order to avoid what he believes to be sins of commission. Plato's example is instructive.[12] Who would return a weapon one had borrowed from a man if he requested it back in order to kill someone with it? The law of mercy is higher than the law of property. Likewise, the Scripture indicates that saving the lives of the innocent (mercy) is a greater duty than telling the truth to the guilty (Exod. 1:15–16). So, in failing to show mercy to the innocent by withholding truth from the guilty, the unqualified absolutist falls into a sin of omission while attempting to avoid a sin of commission.

The Tendency to Legalism

Another difficulty with unqualified absolutism is that it often tends toward legalism by neglecting the spirit of the law in order to avoid breaking the letter of the law. This attitude is precisely what Jesus condemned when he said, "The Sabbath was made for man, not man for the Sabbath" (Mark 2:27). After her torturous internment experience, is it not a cold indifference to demand that Corrie ten Boom not sign the prison release stating that she had been "treated humanely"? When lying and lives are weighed, are not lives more important?

Silence Is Not Always Possible

It is not always possible, as some unqualified absolutists suggest, to avoid falsification by partial truths or silence. Samuel was able to avoid Saul's wrath by the partial truth that he had come to offer a sacrifice, when he had really come to anoint David king. But what if Saul had asked him what other mission he had in mind? At that point he would have had to either lie, be silent (which would have implied he had another purpose for coming), or else risk the death of the innocent and be unmerciful. Even silence before an interrogator who says, "I will kill these people unless you speak," can be an unmerciful sin of omission.

Summary and Conclusion

Despite the positive aspects of unqualified absolutism, and its noble efforts to preserve unmodified absolutes, there are some serious defi-

12. Plato, *The Republic* (New York: Oxford University Press, 1967), 1.330.

ciencies in the position. It is unrealistic, unmerciful (even legalistic at times), and unsuccessful in avoiding the inevitable modification of its absolutes in order to give an adequate answer to numerous biblical and real-life conflicts of divine commands.

While it is no doubt true that moral conflicts are not God's ideal, it is also a fact that this is not an ideal world. It is a real and fallen world. And if the Christian ethic is adequate for this real world in which we live, then it must not retreat into unqualified absolutes. It must find a morally acceptable way to preserve absolutes while honestly and adequately providing an answer for every moral situation.

Select Readings

Augustine, Saint. *On Lying.* In *A Select Library of the Nicene and Post-Nicene Fathers of the Christian Church,* edited by Philip Schaff, vol. 2. Grand Rapids: Eerdmans, 1956.

————. *To Consentius: Against Lying.* In *A Select Library of the Nicene and Post-Nicene Fathers of the Christian Church,* edited by Philip Schaff, vol. 2. Grand Rapids: Eerdmans, 1956.

Hodge, Charles. *Systematic Theology.* Reprint ed. Grand Rapids: Eerdmans, 1952.

Kant, Immanuel. "On a Supposed Right to Tell Lies from Benevolent Motives." In *The Critique of Practical Reason.* 6th ed. Translated by Thomas Kinsmill Abbot. London: Longmans Green, 1963.

Lutzer, Erwin W. *The Necessity of Ethical Absolutes.* Grand Rapids: Zondervan, 1981.

Murray, John. *Principles of Conduct.* Grand Rapids: Eerdmans, 1971.

Plato. *The Republic.* New York: Oxford University Press, 1967.

6

Conflicting Absolutism

Evangelicals have generally held to some form of ethical absolutism. In contrast to situationism, they have claimed that there are many moral absolutes. Within the camp of those holding to two or more absolutes, a special problem arises: What about moral conflicts? What should one do when two or more of his absolute obligations come into unavoidable conflict?

Basically, there are three answers to this question. First, unqualified absolutism affirms that all such conflicts are only apparent; they are not real. In short, no two absolute obligations ever come into unavoidable conflict. Second, conflicting absolutism admits to real moral conflicts but claims that one is guilty no matter which way he goes. Third, graded absolutism (or the greater-good position) agrees with the view that real moral conflicts do sometimes occur, but maintains that one is personally guiltless if he does the greatest good and chooses the lesser evil in that situation. This chapter will consider the second view.

An Explanation of Conflicting Absolutism

The central assumption of the ethical position of conflicting absolutism is that we live in a fallen world, and in such a world real moral conflicts do occur. The accompanying premise, however, is that when two duties conflict, man is morally responsible to both duties. God's law can never be broken without guilt. In such cases, therefore, one must simply do the lesser evil, confess his sin, and ask for God's forgiveness.

The Historical Background
of Conflicting Absolutism

Conflicting absolutism has roots in the Greek world, was incorporated into Reformation thinking, and finds expression in both modern existential and popular thought. The colloquial "I did the lesser of two evils" is an expression of it. In fact, it can be called the lesser-evil view.

Although there are Christian roots for conflicting absolutism, they grow in Greek soil. The ancient Greek tragedies often portrayed lesser-evil situations. In the fifth century B.C., Sophocles and Euripides wrote dramas about heroes who contended against forces of fate they could not avoid. These dramatized dilemmas reflected the nature of the real world of moral conflicts with which conflicting absolutism struggles.

The concept of lesser evils was given a new dimension with the Reformation doctrine of depravity, particularly as that was developed by Martin Luther. There are two things imbedded in Lutheran thought which give rise to a form of conflicting absolutism, the first being Luther's theory of two kingdoms. He believed that Christians live simultaneously in two kingdoms, the kingdom of God and the kingdom of this world. Since they are opposed and since Christians have responsibility in both, it is inevitable that there will be conflicts.

Second, Luther's famous statement to Melanchthon that we must "sin boldly" is amenable to a lesser-evil interpretation. Luther wrote: "Be a sinner and sin boldly, but believe even more boldly and rejoice in Christ, who is victor over sin, death and the world."[1] Commenting on this quote, the Lutheran scholar Helmut Thielicke noted that "it is not a case of compromise being justified. . . . The truth is rather that Christ conquers and overcomes the *skama* [form] of the world, the structure within which such compromise is necessary."[2] In short, even though sin is sometimes unavoidable, it is conquerable through the cross. In a fallen world sin is inevitable, but in a redeemed world it is also forgivable.

Helmut Thielicke

Perhaps the most comprehensive contemporary exposition of the conflicting absolutist view is found in Thielicke's works. There are

1. Letter to Melanchthon, August 1, 1521, in *Letters I,* vol. 48 of *Luther's Works,* ed. and trans. Gottfried G. Krodel (Philadelphia: Fortress, 1963), p. 282.
2. Helmut Thielicke, *Theological Ethics,* ed. William H. Lazareth, vol. 1 (Philadelphia: Fortress, 1966), p. 504.

several elements in Thielicke's form of conflicting absolutism. Fundamental to his view is the belief in real, unavoidable moral conflicts, for "to deny the conflict situation is to deny decision."[3] In conflict situations, says Thielicke, "I may have to face the possibility that what is involved here is a borderline situation which does not allow of any easy solution." And "I can reach such a decision only by going through the conflict and enduring it, not by evading it in the name of some kind of perfectionism."[4]

In the conflict situation sin is unavoidable, for we "constantly fall into sin in the borderline situation."[5] In view of human depravity, these kinds of conflicts should be expected, since "the form of this world is no more able to produce absolute righteousness than our human heart." The consequence is that in this fallen world "conduct is *de facto* a compromise between the divine requirement and what is permitted by the form of this world, . . . by the manifold conflicts of duty."[6] Even the so-called just war unavoidably involves injustices. For "there is no such thing as a wholly just war, and my decision to endorse a given war and participate in it can be made only from the standpoint that I see, or think I see, greater wrong on the one side than the other. . . ."[7]

Moral depravity is the cause of moral dilemmas. A moral conflict is "not due to the character imparted to the world by creation, as though 'from the beginning' (Matt. 19:8). . . ." No, "it is due rather to the complex of wrong decisions which lie behind us, which have their ultimate root in that primal decision recorded in the story of the fall."[8] In brief, moral conflicts arise out of the fact this is a fallen world. In a sinless world there would be no moral dilemmas. There will be none in heaven. God did not design, nor does he desire, moral dilemmas. They are not his ideal. But, on the other hand, this is not an ideal world; it is a real and fallen world. In such a world, there will be times when we cannot avoid evil.

When decisions are made in conflict situations, we must choose the lesser evil, for "there are heavier sins and lighter sins." They are both sins, but "they do not have the same weight."[9] Thielicke makes it clear that there is no justification of doing the lesser evil.[10] Neither

3. Ibid., p. 610.
4. Ibid., p. 612.
5. Ibid., p. 653.
6. Ibid., p. 499.
7. Ibid., pp. 414–15.
8. Ibid., p. 596.
9. Ibid., p. 620.
10. Ibid., p. 602.

is there any pragmatic justification. For "the slogan 'to prevent something worse' is always ethically destructive because it subjugates our action to a non-Christian pragmatism."[11] In fact, "readiness to do wrong in order to 'prevent something worse' is a very dubious principle, because it implies that the end justifies the means. . . ."[12] We must simply recognize that in conflict situations both commands are our moral duty and that sin is inevitable.[13] Nonetheless, since there are lesser and greater sins, the Christian should do the lesser sin, knowing forgiveness is available. "He knows that here in this world there is no perfect righteousness, but he does not therefore draw the conclusion that everything is under the same condemnation and that everything is equally permissible. . . ." On the contrary, he realizes that there is a "quantitative distinction between reprehensible and less reprehensible, between good and less good possibilities."[14]

According to Thielicke, "we can undergo and endure borderline situations and . . . inescapable conflicts only under forgiveness."[15] The Christian knows "that even in a war which—given things as they are—is 'just,' [he] must always stand in need of forgiveness"[16] Thus our "certainty that acts done under the guidance of the Spirit are, despite their 'crooked' form, done in God's name as *his* affair, and that at the same time they nonetheless stand in need of forgiveness. . . ."[17] Thus in the conflict situation the Christian "acts in the knowledge that even those actions which conform to the ultimate norms perceptible in this aeon must stand under forgiveness. . . ."[18] In short, even our best effort in obeying God's commands is an evil that needs to be forgiven.

The Basic Tenets of Conflicting Absolutism

There are four basic premises in conflicting absolutism. First, God's law is absolute and unbreakable. Second, in a fallen world unavoidable conflicts between God's commands occur. Third, when moral conflicts happen, we should do the lesser evil. Fourth, forgiveness is available if we confess our sins.

11. Ibid., p. 625.
12. Ibid., p. 590.
13. Ibid., p. 488.
14. Ibid., p. 501.
15. Ibid., p. 654.
16. Ibid., p. 655.
17. Ibid., p. 659.
18. Ibid., p. 431.

God's Moral Law Is Absolute

"The law of the LORD is perfect" (Ps. 19:7). The psalmist confessed to God, "Every one of thy righteous ordinances endures for ever" (Ps. 119:160). God has not made his law to be broken. The psalmist exclaims, "Thou [God] hast commanded thy precepts to be kept diligently" (Ps. 119:4). "The ordinances of the LORD are true and righteous altogether"; and "in keeping of them there is great reward" (Ps. 19:9, 11). Further, "Jehovah will not hold him guiltless" who breaks his commands (Exod. 20:7 ASV).

In short, God is absolutely perfect and his law is a reflection of his character. "You, therefore, must be perfect, as your heavenly Father is perfect" (Matt. 5:48). Anything that does not measure up to the absolute perfection of the law of God is sin. Whenever God's law is broken, the lawbreaker sins, for "sin is lawlessness" (1 John 3:4). God does not change (Mal. 3:6), nor does the moral law that reflects his character. "It is impossible for God to lie" (Heb. 6:18). Therefore, it is inexcusable for us to lie, even if it is necessary to save a life.

Moral Conflicts Are Unavoidable

The second premise of conflicting absolutism springs from the depravity of man. Man has broken God's law and finds himself inextricably bound in a web of sinful relationships in which sin is unavoidable. Before the fall of man, Adam was able not to sin, but since the fall, man is unable to avoid sin. Not only can man not avoid sinning in general, but there are tragic moral dilemmas in this fallen world in which all alternatives are wrong. Sometimes no matter what one does, he cannot avoid breaking one of God's laws. That is the reality of a fallen world. Sometimes one must sin. He must, of course, choose the lesser evil, but he must sin, regardless.

Conflicting absolutism runs contrary to the Kantian dictum that "ought implies can." Man is always called upon to obey a standard of perfection he cannot reach ("You, therefore, must be perfect, as your heavenly Father is perfect" [Matt. 5:48]). Further, in moral dilemmas one is morally obligated to keep both laws, even though one of them must be broken. Such it is in this sinful world, says the conflicting absolutist. Ideally, God did not design it this way. But then again, this wicked world is far from ideal.

The Duty to Do the Lesser Evil

Not all sins are created equal. Jesus said to Pilate, "The one who handed me over to you is guilty of a greater sin" (John 19:11). One sin is so bad that it is unpardonable—the blasphemy against the Holy

Spirit (Matt. 12:32). This being the case, there is an obligation to do the lesser evil. Whenever our moral duties conflict, we should obey the greater one, realizing that breaking the other is a sin. Nonetheless, it is the lesser sin in the situation. It is always our responsibility to do our best, even when it is not good. We must maximize the good, even when it is minimal.

Forgiveness Is Available

The fourth premise associated with conflicting absolutism is that even though sin is sometimes unavoidable, God's forgiveness is always available through the cross of Christ. One of the happy by-products of this sad world is that the unavoidability of sin drives men to the cross for forgiveness. There is a way out of the dilemma. It is not a way to avoid sin; sin is unavoidable by the nature of the case. Rather, it is a way to avoid bearing long the guilt of the sin. In brief, the way out is, on our part, confession and, on God's part, the sacrifice of Christ on the cross. All one need do in lesser-evil situations is to do the lesser evil, confess that he has broken God's law, and receive forgiveness through Jesus Christ. Sin is unavoidable, but salvation is available.

Some Positive Contributions of Conflicting Absolutism

Conflicting absolutism has many merits as a form of moral absolutism, but it is subject to some serious objections as well. First, let us consider four of the positive contributions it makes to Christian ethics.

It Preserves Moral Absolutes

Whatever its weaknesses, conflicting absolutism preserves moral absolutes intact. God's law is absolute, and there are absolutely no occasions when it is morally justifiable to break it. God is absolutely good, and his law is a reflection of his nature. This being so, the breaking of a moral law is an attack upon his character. Hence, God can no more allow a moral law to be broken than he can allow his character to be violated. Conflicting absolutism is to be commended for this strong stand upon the unchangeable and unbreakable nature of moral absolutes.

It Has a Moral Realism

In spite of their tenacious grip on transcendent moral values, conflicting absolutists are in touch with the real world of moral conflicts and borderline cases. Not every decision is neat and clean. Everything is not black or white. There are real moral conflicts. This realistic recognition of moral dilemmas is commendable. There is no effort to explain away all conflicts as apparent, not real. The conflicting absolutist may have his head in a heavenly cloud of moral perfection, but his feet are planted solidly in the clay of earthly imperfection.

It Sees Moral Conflicts as Rooted in Man's Fallenness

Another important dimension of conflicting absolutism is its insight into the nature of moral conflicts. It sees moral dilemmas as rooted in moral depravity. In an unfallen world there would be no unavoidable moral conflicts. It is only because of sin that they occur. There are no moral conflicts in God, and there will be none in heaven. Moral dilemmas are of man's own making. This does not mean that each individual makes his own moral bed and has to lay in it. Some moral dilemmas result from Adam's sin (Rom. 5:12), some from the sins of others, and some from our own sins. However, sin lies at the root of moral conflicts. God did not design the world this way.

It Is a Solution Without Exception

There is an unadulterated simplicity about conflicting absolutism. It is a solution without exceptions. It cannot be accused of casuistry. It is simply *always* wrong to break an absolute moral law of God. There are no exceptions, exemptions, or divine immunity. Absolute moral laws are absolute, and that is that. In a complex world of confused circumstances there is an admirable simplicity about conflicting absolutism. In this respect it has an uncluttered and unadorned appeal.

Some Criticisms of Conflicting Absolutism

In spite of its many appealing features, a number of objections have been leveled against the lesser-evil view. We will consider four of them here. The first two may be called moral and the latter two christological.

A Moral Duty to Sin Is Morally Absurd

According to conflicting absolutism, in real moral conflicts we have a moral duty to do the lesser of the two evils. That is, one is morally obligated to do evil. But how can there ever be a moral obligation to do what is immoral? It seems a morally absurd claim.

There are three basic alternatives for the proponent of the lesser-evil position in view of this criticism. First, he might claim that there is no moral obligation or divine command to do the lesser evil. It is simply what one "ought" to do, on some kind of pragmatic or utilitarian grounds, for personal or social reasons. This alternative would

seem to be particularly embarrassing for the biblical Christian, since
he would be faced with some of life's most difficult situations without
any direction or command from God. Christianity would have an incomplete ethic. It would be able to handle the ordinary situations, but
for the really difficult ones—the ones involving tragic moral choices—
it would give absolutely no divine direction.

There is another way out of the dilemma for the lesser-evil proponent. He may admit that there is a moral obligation, not to do evil,
but simply to maximize good or minimize evil in an evil situation. But
if he takes this route, then his position really collapses into the greater-
good view. For if he is actually obligated to do a maximal good, then
why call it evil? For example, the doctor who amputates a patient's leg
to save his life is not guilty of the sin of mutilation, but is to be
commended for doing the maximal good. As tragic as amputation is,
surely there is no basis in Christian ethics to consider amputation
done to save a life as a culpable act. Likewise, why call the act evil,
as the lesser-evil view would seem to do, when it is the greatest good
under the circumstances?

Finally, of course, the proponent of the lesser-evil view could simply
admit the absurdity and unavoidability of sin and claim that one is
morally obligated to do what is morally wrong, absurd as this is.

The Unavoidable Is Not Morally Culpable

This leads to a second criticism, that conflicting absolutism holds
that one is personally responsible for what is personally unavoidable.
Those who espouse this view challenge the underlying premise of their
opponents that responsibility implies ability, that "ought implies can."
They may point to biblical instances where God commands the impossible, such as, "Be perfect, as your heavenly Father is perfect" (Matt.
5:48). They may point to the doctrine of depravity which declares it
impossible for a man not to sin though God commands a man not to
sin.

But in these cases one need simply note that "ought implies can"
only in the sense that one can, by the enabling grace of God, do what
is utterly impossible by human standards. In this sense, the "ought
implies can" thesis is not a violation of these biblical truths. Furthermore, to focus on the "ought implies can" principle misses the real
issue. The moral absurdity of the lesser-evil position is not based on
the truth or falsity of "ought implies can." From a Christian standpoint it is morally absurd to say "one ought to do an evil," since "ought"
means "God has commanded it"; and God does not (I would say, *cannot*)
command one to do what is morally evil. God is good, absolute good,
and as such he can neither perform nor promote that which is evil. For

God to command one to do evil would contradict his very will, his very nature.

Of course, one might respond here by claiming that whatever God commands is ipso facto good and not evil, since one could define good as that which God commands. However, this response would be fatal to the lesser-evil view, for if what God commands in so-called lesser-evil situations is really good simply because he commanded it, then it is not an evil. In fact, if the act is good in this conflict situation because God commanded it, then the lesser-evil view has really collapsed into the greater-good view. The good act one performs at the command of God is not sinful but commendable because it is done in obedience to God.

Before we leave this point, it should be noted that making a distinction between good and right does not help the lesser-evil position. One cannot simply claim that the lesser evil is the "right" thing to do in a given situation, for one can always ask the question: Was the "right" act morally good or evil? Was the act culpable or not? If it is morally evil or guilt-inducing, then we are back where we started and the preceding criticisms apply. If, on the other hand, the "right" act was good or guiltless, then the view has collapsed into the greater-good view.

The essential difference between these two positions is that according to conflicting absolutism the tragic moral act is guilt-inducing and calls for confession and forgiveness, whereas according to the greater-good view the tragic moral act is guiltless. One may regret having to make the decision, but he need not repent of it. Indeed, according to the greater-good view, doing the greatest good leads to reward—not to punishment. At any rate, the lesser-evil view is not redeemed from its difficulties by calling the lesser-evil the "right" act in contrast to a "good" act. The question still remains: Is one personally guilty or not for performing this act? If one is guilty, then God is commanding an act which is unavoidably sinful. If one is not guilty, then the act is morally acceptable and we are driven to the greater-good position.

There is another distinction sometimes made in an attempt to rescue the lesser-evil position. It is occasionally claimed that one is not blamed for doing his best in conflicting situations, but rather he is blamed *in* doing his best, for even the most faithful servant is unworthy (Luke 7:6–10). In this sense it might be claimed that it would be morally absurd to blame one for doing his best, but it is not necessarily absurd to blame one for doing evil in the process of doing his best. Might it not be that the act of lying is evil but the whole process of showing mercy to the innocent is the greater good? Hence, one should confess the lie in particular even though the act as a whole was the greater good. Perhaps God blames a man for whatever sinful acts are part of an overall good performance.

In response to this distinction, we might simply note that the ethical complex must be thought of as a whole. Certain things done in one context are morally good and in another are morally evil. For example, cutting off a man's leg is good if done by a doctor as a necessary means to save a life, but evil if done as an act of sadism. It is the moral context as a whole that gives meaning to the act. Hence, one cannot separate specific evil parts from an overall ethical performance and call the whole act good. As an intention-act complex, amputation is either good or evil. One cannot claim that the overall amputation process was good but the actual cutting off a human leg was evil.

This discussion brings up a more principal issue beneath the whole discussion, specifically, the relation of intention to action in judging the morality of an act. It appears that the difficulty with much of the discussion on these issues hinges on the question of whether an act is intrinsically good or evil or whether it is the intention-act complex that must be considered. An adequate discussion of this is beyond the scope of this volume. Suffice it to say here that it seems most reasonable to assume that the latter is the case. Good intentions alone are not sufficient to make an act morally right. Hitler may have intended to produce a better world by attempting genocide, but the murder of millions of Jews was not made morally good by admirable motives. Likewise, an act as such apart from its motive or intention is not necessarily good. For instance, those who give to the poor in order to receive the praise of men are not to be morally commended. If this is the case, then the lesser-evil position is wrong to separate an act from its total intention-act complex and pronounce it evil and declare the overall process good.

Jesus Must Have Sinned

According to conflicting absolutism, sin is unavoidable in real moral conflicts. However, according to the Bible, Jesus was tempted in all points such as we are (Heb. 4:15). So, if there are real moral dilemmas, then either Jesus faced them or else he did not. If he did, then according to the lesser-evil view, which states that evil is indeed unavoidable, Jesus must have sinned. But the Bible says Jesus did not sin (Heb. 4:15; 2 Cor. 5:21). Hence, the only alternative here is that he never faced real moral conflicts. Assuming there are real moral conflicts, several explanations for this dilemma can be offered. First, perhaps the lesser-evil view is incorrect, and Jesus never sinned when he faced real moral conflicts because one is not held sinful when he does the greatest good in a moral conflict. Perhaps "stealing" bread from the temple (that is, taking it without permission of the proper authority) is not morally wrong when starvation of God's servant is the other alternative. Is this not what Jesus implied in Matthew 12:3–8?

But let us not so readily assume that conflicting absolutism is defenseless in the face of this charge. It may be that Jesus never sinned in the area of moral conflicts simply because he never faced any. There are two explanations for this position. First, it may be that God providentially spared Jesus from facing moral conflicts in order to preserve his sinlessness. But if this is the case, then the Christian may ask why he, too, is not spared from them if he is faithful to God. In fact, this is precisely what many nonconflicting absolutists hold, specifically, that there is always a third alternative for the faithful. Daniel did not have to either eat the pagan meat and drink the pagan wine or suffer the consequence of his disobedience (Dan. 1). There was a prayerful third way out. Is this not what 1 Corinthians 10:13 seems to imply, that there is always "a way of escape"? If the conflicting absolutists wish to take this alternative of arguing that God will always provide a way out for those who are faithful to God's will, as Jesus was, then their view really collapses into nonconflicting absolutism. For, in the final analysis, the lesser-evil view is saying there is no unavoidable moral conflict for those who do God's will. It would be special pleading to declare that the providential way out applies only to Christ but not to other servants of God who are faithful to his will.

A more plausible suggestion is that Jesus never faced any moral dilemmas simply because he never committed any antecedent sin to get himself into these tight spots. Only those who make their moral beds have to lie in them. Jesus never sinned and, hence, he never found himself in unavoidable moral conflicts. On the face of it, this view has merit. It does seem to be often the case that our previous sins get us into a moral pickle. We do reap what we sow. However, in order for this obvious truth to rescue the lesser-evil position from collapse, it must be universally true. That is, it must always be the case that moral dilemmas we face are created by our own antecedent sins. However, this seems patently false by counterexample. Sometimes it is the innocent who are faced with moral difficulties. What sin did innocent German Christian families commit that placed them in the dilemma of either lying or watching Jews go to the gas chamber? Were these believers more sinful than others in the world? One is reminded here of Jesus' statement about those on whom the tower fell: "Do you think that they were worse offenders than all the others who dwelt in Jerusalem?" (Luke 13:4).

Indeed, not only is it not true that moral dilemmas are always

brought about by antecedent sin, but sometimes it is antecedent righteousness that precipitates the dilemma. Daniel and the three Hebrew
children were not confronted with their dilemma because they were
backslidden (Dan. 1, 3, 6). Nor were the apostles doing evil when they
were commanded not to preach, thus forcing a choice between the command to obey government and the command to preach the gospel
(Acts 4). The same is true of Abraham's dilemma over whether to kill
his son or to disobey God (Gen. 22). Indeed, many times in life it is
one's dedication to God that precipitates moral conflicts. That is, it is
his righteousness, not his antecedent sin, that occasions the moral
conflict. If this is the case, then the lesser-evil position has not redeemed itself against the criticisms. It has not explained away the
christological dilemma. It has not shown that Jesus never faced moral
dilemmas simply because he never committed any previous sins.

Before the opponents of the lesser-evil view rejoice too quickly, there
is another point to consider. Perhaps there is always antecedent sin in
our case, but never in Christ's case—because we are fallen but he is
not. Adam's sin is antecedent in the case of all men except Christ.
Hence, because we are part of a fallen world, previous sin (that is,
Adam's; see Rom. 5:12) is responsible for subsequent moral dilemmas
we will face but Christ did not.

There is a certain plausibility about this suggestion that cannot be
denied. It would seem to point to a clear difference in Christ's case, as
well as to recognize antecedent sin in our case. There are, however, at
least two problems here. First, moral conflicts due to the antecedent
sin of Adam are not unique to fallen man; Christ also lived in this
fallen world. And even though he never personally sinned, Christ was
nevertheless immersed in a world of moral conflicts due to Adam's and
others' sins. It must be remembered that not all moral conflicts are
due to one's own antecedent sin. The sins of others can force a dilemma
on those who did not personally create the tragic situation. The question would then be, Why did not Christ face any moral conflicts forced
on him by the sins of others?

Second, the attempt to explain why Christ did not face moral conflicts by way of Adam's fall confuses collective and personal guilt.
There is a corporate sense in which everything done by fallen man is
sinful. In this sense, sin is inevitable for all fallen men. This, however,
is quite different from saying that a man is personally guilty for creating the situation, or that any particular sin is unavoidable. The
immediate moral choice may not induce guilt because it is unavoidable. However, were it not for Adam's fall, that kind of situation would
never have occurred. For example, one would never have to kill in self-
defense were it not for Adam's fall. There would, presumably, be no

need to kill for any reason in a paradise. Nonetheless, killing in self-defense is not a personally culpable act according to the law of God (Exod. 22:2).

We may still ask: Did Jesus really face moral dilemmas in which two or more commands of God came into unavoidable conflict? An examination of the Gospels yields several illustrations. At age twelve Jesus faced a conflict between his earthly parents and his heavenly Father. Although he later submitted to his earthly parents, initially he left them in order to fulfill God's will (Luke 2). It is parenthetically noteworthy in this context that Jesus justified his disciples' action of taking grain by approving David's "stealing" of the consecrated bread in the tabernacle (Matt. 12:3–4). In this regard Jesus said to others, "He who loves father or mother more than me is not worthy of me" (Matt. 10:37). On many occasions, Jesus faced conflict between obeying the religious authorities, which he himself taught his disciples and others to do (Matt. 23:3), and following the law of mercy by helping those in need (Luke 14:1–6). For example, he chose to heal a man on the Sabbath. When challenged, he said the law of the Sabbath should be subordinated to man, not vice versa. On another occasion Jesus approved of the disciples plucking grain on the Sabbath (Luke 6:1–5).

The greatest moral conflict that Jesus faced, however, was his trial and cross, where mercy and justice came into direct and unavoidable conflict. Should he speak in defense of the innocent (himself) as the law demanded (Lev. 5:1), or should he show mercy to the many (mankind)? Further, should he take his own life in a self-sacrifice for others (cf. John 10:10), or should he refuse to die unjustly for others? In both cases Jesus chose mercy over justice. But did he sin in so doing? God forbid! The cross was not the lesser of two evils; it was the greater good ("greater love hath no man . . ."). It appears that the lesser-evil view, then, literally stands at the crossroads. If it is a sin to do the greatest good in a morally conflicting situation, then Jesus would have been perhaps the greatest sinner who ever lived. Perish the thought! Indeed, God himself faced a moral conflict in the cross: Should he sacrifice his Son or should he allow the world to perish? Thank God, mercy triumphed over justice. Surely the sacrifice of Christ was not a lesser evil; it was indeed the greatest good God could do (cf. John 15:13; Rom. 5:8–9).

Christ Must Have Faced Moral Conflicts

The fourth objection is another christological problem with the lesser-evil view. If Christ is our complete moral example, then he must have faced morally conflicting situations in which both alternatives were sinful. But if Christ never sinned, then Christ never faced them. Hence, we have no example from Christ to follow in some of life's most difficult moral decisions. But does not Hebrews say he was "tempted in every way, just as we are" (4:15)? Does not Paul exhort us to be followers of Christ (1 Cor. 11:1–2)? But how can we follow him in ethical dilemmas if he never faced them?

Some proponents of conflicting absolutism frankly admit Christ is not our complete moral example. But it is unacceptable to grant this point. It concedes that the ethic of following Christ is incomplete for the followers of Christ. Indeed, a proper understanding of the New Testament would dictate that we give up claims of the lesser-evil view rather than sacrifice the completeness of Christ's moral example.

The proof that one can face real moral dilemmas without sinning is that Jesus faced them but never sinned. If this is so, then it follows that moral dilemmas do not necessitate personal guilt. There is always "a way of escape" through doing the greater good. In conflicting situations, keeping the higher law (for example, obedience to God over government) is the guiltless way out.

Summary and Conclusion

Conflicting absolutism believes that there are many moral absolutes that sometimes conflict. This view is rooted in the premise that God's laws are absolute and hence can never be violated. On the other hand, it recognizes that this is a fallen world. And in such a world there are real moral dilemmas. When such a real, unavoidable conflict occurs, it is our obligation to do the lesser evil. However, we must recognize such an act for what it is, confess our sin of breaking God's law, and accept his forgiveness.

Conflicting absolutism has the merit of retaining absolutes and yet being realistic about the fallen world in which we live. However, it does not appear to have successfully defended itself against either the moral or the christological charges leveled against it. It seems morally absurd to say there is a moral duty to sin or to blame someone for what was unavoidable. Furthermore, if Christ was tempted in all points as we are, then he must have faced moral dilemmas. But if he did, then he must have sinned. If he did not, then he is not our perfect moral example. In short, when pushed to the wall, it seems to collapse into either nonconflicting absolutism by claiming special providential intervention for Christ to save him from moral dilemmas, or into graded absolutism by claiming that one is morally obligated to maximize good. In short, in spite of its helpful insights, it seems to have no firm ground of its own on which to stand.

Select Readings

Luther, Martin. "Letter to Melanchthon." In *Luther's Works,* edited and translated by Gottfried G. Krodel. Philadelphia: Fortress, 1963.

Lutzer, Erwin W. *The Morality Gap.* Chicago: Moody, 1972.

Montgomery, John. *Situation Ethics: True or False.* Minneapolis: Dimension Books, Bethany Fellowship, 1972.

Thielicke, Helmut. *Theological Ethics.* Edited by William H. Lazareth. Philadelphia: Fortress, 1966. Vol. 1.

7

Graded Absolutism

Total ethical relativism is not an option for an evangelical. God's character is unchanging, and his law reflects his character (see chap. 1). Of the options within ethical absolutism, evangelicals must choose between unqualified absolutism (see chap. 5), conflicting absolutism (see chap. 6), or graded absolutism (see chap. 7). Our previous analysis, however, has indicated serious problems with the first two of these views. There remains one alternative to discuss, namely, graded absolutism.

The Historical Roots of Graded Absolutism

Of the three forms of absolutism held by evangelicals, unqualified absolutism is associated with the Anabaptist tradition, conflicting absolutism with the Lutheran tradition, and graded absolutism with the Reformed tradition. Before we examine the basic premises of graded absolutism, a brief look at some of its roots is in order.

Saint Augustine

Like most other Reformed traditions, the roots of graded absolutism can be traced to Saint Augustine. Although he defends the unqualified absolutist position on the issue of lying (see chap. 5), at times Augustine's answers to conflicting situations are similar to those of graded absolutism. For example, both views hold that there is a hierarchy of

113

virtue, that moral duties sometimes conflict, and that we are not culpable for obeying the higher duty.

Like graded absolutists, Augustine believes there is a hierarchy of sins, some being worse than others.[1] Since Augustine's ethic is centered in love, he sees an ordered priority in the things we are to love. God, of course, is to be loved more than man, and man more than things.[2] Thus, there is a pyramid of value with God on the top and things on the bottom.

Augustine also believes that moral duties sometimes come into conflict. Even in his advocacy for never telling a lie (see chap. 5), Augustine recognizes the clash of different duties which is one of the central premises of graded absolutism. Likewise, he sees moral conflicts in other life-and-death situations. Even though he views suicide as morally wrong, Augustine nevertheless justifies Samson's suicide, saying, "However, there are some exceptions made by the Divine Authority to its own law, that men may not be put to death. These exceptions are of two kinds, being justified either by a general law, or by a special commission granted for a time to some individual."[3] In this latter category Augustine places Abraham, Jephthah, and Samson, all of whom he believes were given a divine command to kill that overrode the general moral law against intentionally killing another human being.

In harmony with graded absolutists, Augustine believes that it is the greater good, not the lesser evil, to follow the higher moral duty in conflicting situations. For example, Abraham and Samson are commended for their willingness to kill at God's command. When two moral duties clash, the believer is exempt from his duty to the lower by virtue of his obedience to the higher. In this sense, Augustine is a precursor to the graded absolutist.

Charles Hodge

In his *Systematic Theology*, Charles Hodge defends a form of graded absolutism, as is illustrated by his discussion of uttering intentional falsehoods. In spite of the fact that Hodge holds that truth is absolute, being based on God's very nature, he believes that it is sometimes

1. Saint Augustine, *Enchiridion*, in *A Select Library of the Nicene and Post-Nicene Fathers of the Christian Church*, ed. Philip Schaff, vol. 3 (Grand Rapids: Eerdmans, 1956), p. 245.
2. Saint Augustine, *On Christian Doctrine*, in *A Select Library of the Nicene and Post-Nicene Fathers of the Christian Church*, ed. Philip Schaff, vol. 2 (Grand Rapids: Eerdmans, 1956), p. 530.
3. Saint Augustine, *City of God*, in *A Select Library of the Nicene and Post-Nicene Fathers of the Christian Church*, ed. Philip Schaff, vol. 2 (Grand Rapids: Eerdmans, 1956), p. 15.

right to intentionally falsify. He believes "truth is at all times sacred, because it is one of the essential attributes of God, so that whatever militates against, or is hostile to truth is in opposition to the very nature of God."[4] However, there are occasions when one is justified in intentionally deceiving another. He says, an "intention to deceive, therefore, is an element in the idea of falsehood. But even this is not always culpable."[5] Hodge uses both the Hebrew midwives (Exod. 1) and Samuel (1 Sam. 16) as examples of justifiable deception. (The latter is a divinely appointed falsehood.)

Hodge also believes "it is lawful not only to conceal intended movements from an enemy, but also to mislead him as to your intentions."[6] The reason for this is that "there may be any combination of circumstances under which a man is not bound to speak the truth, those to whom the declaration or signification is made have no right to expect him to do so."[7] For example, "if a mother sees a murderer in pursuit of her child, she has a perfect right to mislead him by any means in her power, because the general obligation to speak the truth is merged or lost, for the time being, in the higher obligation."[8] According to Hodge, "the principle that a higher obligation absolves from a lower stands firm."[9]

Hodge believes this kind of graded absolutism is a "dictate even of the natural conscience." For example, "it is evidently right to inflict pain in order to save a life. It is right to subvert travellers to quarantine . . . to save a city from pestilence." Indeed, he believes that "the principle itself is clearly inculcated by our Lord when He said, 'I will have mercy and not sacrifice;' and when he taught that it was right to violate the Sabbath in order to save the life of an ox, or even to prevent its suffering."[10]

Furthermore, Hodge contends that when one subordinates a lower moral duty to the higher, he has not sinned. He rejects the position that "it is ever right to do a wrong."[11] However, he believes that it is right to intentionally deceive in order to save a life. And even though Hodge does not wish to call this a "lie," a term he reserves for an unjustified intentional deception, he does believe it is morally right to intentionally falsify in these circumstances. It is right because there

---

4. Charles Hodge, *Systematic Theology* (reprint ed., Grand Rapids: Eerdmans, 1952), p. 437.
5. Ibid., p. 440.
6. Ibid., p. 441.
7. Ibid.
8. Ibid., p. 442.
9. Ibid., p. 441.
10. Ibid., p. 442.
11. Ibid.

is "no right for expectation" and "no obligation to speak the truth" in those cases where there is a greater duty.[12]

The Essential Elements of Graded Absolutism

Hodge's analysis sets forth the essential elements of a graded absolutism or ethical hierarchicalism. There are three essential premises in the biblical argument for graded absolutism, and each is based on relevant Scripture.

There Are Higher and Lower Moral Laws

Not all moral laws are of equal weight. Jesus spoke of the "weightier" matters of the law (Matt. 23:23) and of the "least" (Matt. 5:19) and the "greatest" commandment (Matt. 22:36). He told Pilate that Judas had committed the "greater sin" (John 19:11). Despite a rather widespread evangelical distaste for a hierarchy of sins (and virtues), the Bible does speak of the "greatest" virtue (1 Cor. 13:13) and even of "greater" acts of a given virtue (John 15:13).

The common myth that all sins are equal is often based on erroneous interpretations of James 2:10, which does not speak of the equality of all sins but rather of the unity of the law: "Whoever . . . fails in one point has become guilty of all of it" (RSV). It does not say he is equally guilty of all, nor that all infractions bring equal guilt (compare James 3:1). However, it is true that any violation of the law brings some guilt.

Others have supposed wrongly that simply because Jesus said that one can lust and even murder "in his heart" (Matt. 5:28) that this means it is equally evil to imagine a sin as it is to do it. In the same sermon, Jesus rejected this view, indicating there are at least three levels of sins with corresponding judgments (5:22). Indeed, the whole concept of degrees of punishment in hell (Matt. 5:22; Rom. 2:6; Rev. 20:12) and graded levels of reward in heaven (1 Cor. 3:11–12) indicates that sins come in degrees. The fact that some Christian sins call for excommunication (1 Cor. 5) and others for death (1 Cor. 11:30) also supports the general biblical pattern that all sins are not equal in weight. In fact, there is one sin so great as to be unforgivable (Mark 3:29).

Perhaps the clearest indication of higher and lower moral laws comes in Jesus' answer to the lawyer's question about the "greatest commandment" (Matt. 22:34–35). Jesus clearly affirms that the "first" and "greatest" is over the "second," that loving God is of supreme importance, and then beneath that comes loving one's neighbor. This

12. Ibid., p. 447.

same point is reaffirmed when our Lord says, "He who loves father or mother more than me is not worthy of me" (Matt. 10:37). Numerous other scriptural passages may be cited to support this same point (see Prov. 6:16; 1 Tim. 1:15; 1 John 5:16; and Matt. 5:22). The popular belief is wrong; all sins are not created equal, for there are clearly higher and lower moral laws.

It is of more than passing significance to note that both other Christian options admit the truth of this same point. The conflicting absolutist speaks of the lesser evil, plainly implying that not all evils are equal. Likewise, the unqualified absolutist admits that moral laws are higher than civil or ceremonial laws commanded by God, and that many laws are binding only if all things are equal, which they sometimes are not. The real question, then, is this: Are the moral laws hierarchically graded?

The answer is affirmative for several reasons. First, all ethical obligations are moral laws, and Christians do have an ethical obligation to obey civil laws (see Rom. 13:1–6; 1 Pet. 2:13–14). It is not simply a civil duty to obey civil laws, since such obedience is enjoined by the moral Lawgiver (God) for "conscience['s] sake" (Rom. 13:5). Second, even the commands to obey government or perform ceremonial duties are divine commands and, as such, involve a moral duty. By its very nature, a divine command is one which one ought to obey; it is an ethical responsibility. Otherwise it would be a mere declarative or descriptive statement, not an imperative. Third, the distinctions between civil, ceremonial, and moral laws are not rigid (if maintainable at all). The law of God is unified and interpenetrating, so that there are moral implications to civil and ceremonial commands. Whatever God commands his children to do—whether to love their neighbors or offer sacrifices—demands moral obedience. Finally, some of the conflicts in commands are clearly between two commands which are both moral in nature, even by those who distinguish between moral and civil or ceremonial laws (Gen. 22; Matt. 22; Exod. 1). We conclude, then, that there are graded levels of moral commands in Scripture.

There Are Unavoidable Moral Conflicts

Some personally unavoidable moral conflicts exist in which an individual cannot obey both commands. The arguments in support of this observation come from many sources—both inside and outside of the Bible. Several of them will suffice to establish this point.

First, the story of Abraham and Isaac (Gen. 22) contains a real moral conflict. "Thou shalt not kill" is a divine moral command (Exod. 20:13), and yet God commanded Abraham to kill his son, Isaac. That Abraham intended to kill Isaac is clear from the context (and from Heb. 11:19, which informs us that Abraham believed God would raise

Isaac from the dead). Further, the fact that Abraham was not required to go through with the act does not eliminate the reality of the moral conflict, since the intention to perform an act with moral implications is itself a morally responsible act (cf. Matt. 5:25). Neither will it suffice to say that this is a specially approved divine exception, because the "exception" (or exemption) must be made in view of some higher moral law; this is precisely the point graded absolutism wishes to make. Furthermore, the very fact that an "exception" (or exemption) is called for indicates that the two laws are in genuine conflict.

Second, the story of Samson contains a conflict of two divine commands. Samson committed a divinely approved suicide (Judg. 16:30) despite the moral prohibition against killing a human being, including oneself. Both commands were divine and moral—"Do not kill" and "Take your life"—yet when there was a real conflict between them, God apparently approved of Samson disregarding one in order to obey the other.

Third, the passage detailing Jephthah's sacrifice of his daughter (Judg. 11) shows a real moral conflict between a vow to God (which is inviolate [Eccles. 5:1–4]) and the command not to kill an innocent life. The usual answer of unqualified absolutists, that one is not obligated to keep a vow that necessarily involves sin, will not work here. According to that explanation, Jephthah should not have kept his vow to kill his daughter. But the Scripture appears to approve of Jephthah keeping the oath to kill. Some have suggested that Jephthah did not sacrifice his daughter's physical life but her marital life, making her a perpetual virgin. However, this interpretation is difficult to justify in view of the vow (v. 31) in which Jephthah says "whatever comes out of the doors . . . I will offer it up as a burnt offering" (NASB). Burnt offerings customarily were killed, not consigned to singlehood.

Fourth, there are several biblical illustrations in which individuals had to choose between lying and not helping to save a life (that is, not showing mercy). The Hebrew midwives (Exod. 1) and Rahab (Josh. 2) will suffice as examples. Regardless of whether they were right or wrong in lying, the point here is that the conflict was genuine and both obligations were moral ones. It is not sufficient to claim silence as a "third alternative," because even silence can lead to murder when deception is necessary to ward off an assassin. This is often the case, and it is unmistakably the case if the assassin says, "Either speak up or I will kill them." Nor will it do to claim that there is no real conflict in these cases on the grounds that in telling the truth the midwives would not be murdering the babies (Pharaoh would). For in the very act of telling the truth, the midwives would be unmerciful. To avoid what they believed to be the lesser sin of commission (lying), they would be engaging in a greater sin of omission (not showing mercy).

Fifth, there is a real moral conflict in the cross, one so great that many liberal theologians have considered the doctrine of the substitutionary atonement to be essentially immoral. The two moral principles are that the innocent should not be punished for sins he never committed, but that Christ was punished for our sins (Isa. 53; 1 Pet. 2:24; 3:15; 2 Cor. 5:21). Some have tried to solve the problem by suggesting that Christ submitted to this punishment voluntarily, and hence the moral responsibility for the conflict disappears. But this is like saying it was not immoral for Jim Jones to order the Jonestown suicide because his followers did it willingly! Other attempted explanations make God's actions in the cross entirely arbitrary, with no necessary basis in his unchanging moral character. But this reduces God to an unworthy being and takes away the need for the cross. If God could save men apart from the cross, then Christ's death becomes unnecessary.

Sixth, there are numerous cases in Scripture in which there is a real conflict between obeying God's command to submit to civil government and keeping one's duty to some other higher moral law. For example, the Hebrew midwives disregarded Pharaoh's command to kill all male infants (Exod. 1); the Jewish captives disregarded Nebuchadnezzar's command to worship the golden image of himself (Dan. 3); Daniel disregarded Darius's command to pray only to the king (Dan. 6). In each case there was plainly no other alternative; those involved had to follow one or the other of the two commandments. Even the unqualified absolutist admits the unavoidability of the conflict, since he reduces one command (the civil one) to a lower level. This maneuver, however, does not take away from the fact that both are commands of God with moral implications, and that the situation was personally unavoidable. That is, there was no prior sin on the part of those in the dilemma that precipitated it. In all these cases, it was because they were moral, godly people that they found themselves in the dilemma.

There are many other biblical examples of genuine, unavoidable moral conflicts, but the foregoing examples suffice. Even one clear case of an unavoidable conflict is enough to prove the point. Let us move, then, to the next premise.

No Guilt Is Imputed for the Unavoidable

God does not hold the individual responsible for personally unavoidable moral conflicts, providing he keeps the higher law. There are a number of ways of seeing the truth of this point. First, logic dictates that a just God will not hold a person responsible for doing what is

actually impossible. And it is actually impossible to avoid the unavoidable. It is impossible to take two opposite courses of action at the
same time.

Second, one is not morally culpable if he fails to keep an obligation
he could not possibly keep without breaking a higher obligation. This
is evident to all, even to those who hold opposing ethical views. Clearly
a person is not blameworthy for breaking a promise to meet his wife
for dinner at six o'clock if he has been delayed by helping to save a
life. Likewise, who would blame a man for refusing to return a gun to
an angry neighbor who wants to kill his wife? In each case, the praiseworthy and exemplary conduct of keeping the higher obligation absolves one of any responsibility to the lower duty.

Third, the Bible includes many examples of persons who were praised
by God for following their highest duty in situations of conflict. Abraham was commended of God for his willingness to sacrifice (kill) his
son Isaac for God (Gen. 22; Heb. 11). Likewise, Daniel (Dan. 6) and the
three Hebrew children received divine approval for their disobedience
of human government. The Hebrew midwives were blessed of God for
their disobedience to the king's command (Exod. 1). David and his men
who broke into the temple and stole the consecrated bread were declared guiltless by Christ (Matt. 12:3–4). In each case there was not
only no divine condemnation for the moral law they did not keep.
There was, rather, evident divine approval. The same is true of other,
similar cases in which moral commands to obey parents (Luke 2:41–42)
or God-ordained authorities are concerned (e.g., Exod. 12; Acts 4–5;
Rev. 13).

Graded Absolutism Is True

Therefore, in real, unavoidable moral conflicts, God does not hold
a person guilty for not keeping a lower moral law so long as he keeps
the higher. God exempts one from his duty to keep the lower law since
he could not keep it without breaking a higher law. This exemption
functions something like an ethical "right of way" law. In many states
the law declares that when two cars simultaneously reach an intersection without signals or signs, the car on the right has the right of
way. Common sense dictates that they both cannot go through the
intersection at the same time; one car must yield. Similarly, when a
person enters an ethical intersection where two laws come into unavoidable conflict, it is evident that one law must yield to the other.

An Elaboration of Graded Absolutism

The most obvious and basic of all divisions or levels of duty is
between the command to love God and the command to love one's
neighbor. The former always takes precedence over the latter.

Love for God over Love for Man

Jesus explicitly declares the commandment to love God to be the "first" and "greatest." Further, he teaches (Matt. 22:36–38) that one's love for God should be so much more than his love for parents that the love for the latter would look like hate by contrast (Luke 14:26). One implication of this is that if parents teach a child to hate God, the child must disobey the parents in order to obey God. This is true despite the fact that the Bible enjoins children to be obedient to parents in all things (Col. 3:20). The fact that the parallel passage in Ephesians (6:1) adds, "in the Lord" indicates that a hierarchy is envisioned that places filial duty on a lower level, under the duty to love and obey God.

Obey God over Government

God ordained human government and commands the Christian to "submit" to and "obey" those in authority, even if they are evil men (Rom. 13:1–2; Titus 3:1). Peter goes so far as to say we should submit to "every ordinance of man for the Lord's sake" (1 Pet. 2:13). The attempt of some to differentiate between submission and obedience—and thus claim that Christians need only submit but not obey government—fails for several reasons. First, it is plainly opposed to the spirit of the passages which enjoin Christians to follow the laws of their land. Second, the passage in First Peter demands submission to "every ordinance," not merely to the consequences of disobeying an ordinance. And submission to a law is obedience. Third, the word *submission* as used in the New Testament implies obedience. It was, for example, what a slave was to do toward his master (Col. 3:22). Finally, the words *submission* and *obedience* are used in parallel in Titus (3:1); thus Christians are told "to obey" governmental authorities.

It is clear that Christians are commanded of God to obey government. Hence, when disobedience to government is approved of God, it is clearly in view of a higher moral law. Several biblical instances illustrate this point. First, worship of God is higher than any command of government (Dan. 3). Second, no governmental law against private prayer should be obeyed (Dan. 6). Further, if a government commands a believer not to preach the gospel (Acts 4–5), or if it decrees participation in idolatry (Dan. 3) or even the murder of innocent victims (Exod. 1), it should not be obeyed. In each case the moral obligation to pray, worship God, preach the gospel, and so forth, is a higher duty than the one to obey government.

Mercy over Veracity

There is no question that the Bible commands Christians to not "give false testimony" (Exod. 20:16). We are also told to "put off falsehood and speak truthfully with his neighbor" (Eph. 4:25). Indeed, deception and lying are repeatedly condemned in Scripture (see Prov. 12:22; 19:5). On the other hand, the Bible indicates that there are occasions when intentionally falsifying (lying) is justifiable. Rahab intentionally deceived to save the lives of Israel's spies and was immortalized in the spiritual "hall of fame" (Heb. 11). It should be noted that first, nowhere does the Bible condemn her for this deception; second, her falsehood was an integral part of the act of mercy she showed in saving the spies' lives; and third, the Bible says, "Rahab . . . shall be spared, because she hid the spies we sent" (Josh. 6:17). But the real concealment was accomplished by deceiving the authorities at her door. It seems that God blessed her because of it, not in spite of it. Hence, her "lie" was an integral part of her faith for which she was commended of God (Heb. 11:31; James 2:25).

In the story of the Hebrew midwives we have an even clearer case of divinely approved lying to save a life. For Scripture says, "God dealt well with the midwives; and . . . he gave them families" (Exod. 1:20–21 RSV). Nowhere in the text does God ever say they were blessed only for their mercy and in spite of their lie. Indeed, the lie was part of the mercy shown.

It should not be surprising that mercy is considered to be higher than truth. Common sense dictates that Corrie ten Boom's acts of mercy to the Jews, which involved lying to the Nazis, were not evil but good. Indeed, those who say that one should not lie to save a life are inconsistent, for they leave their lights on when they are away from home. This is an intentional deception to save their property. Why not do the same to save a life? Is not a life worth more than a lamp? Are not persons more valuable than property? Why lie to save jewels but refuse to lie to save Jews?

There are other biblical examples of graded absolutism, but these will suffice to illustrate that there are "weightier matters" of the law and greater and lesser commands of God. It is the Christian's obligation in every morally conflicting situation to search Scripture for an answer. If one does not know what to do in certain situations, he should heed Jesus' words, "You are mistaken, because you know neither the scriptures nor the power of God" (Matt. 22:29 NEB).

Objections to Graded Absolutism

Like all other views, graded absolutism is subject to criticisms, both positive and negative. A number of objections have been raised against this kind of graded absolutism, and a brief discussion of each is now in order.

How Does Graded Absolutism
Differ from Situationism?

First, Joseph Fletcher's situationism (see chap. 3) does not hold that there are any absolutes with substantive content; graded absolutism does. According to graded absolutism, the universal commands of Scripture such as the prohibitions against blasphemy, idolatry, adultery, murder, lying, and so forth are absolute, and these are binding on all men at all times and all places. Second, graded absolutism holds that there are more absolutes than one. Fletcher believes in one and only one absolute, and that absolute is formal and empty. Third, Fletcher believes that the situation determines what one should do in a given case; graded absolutism holds that situational factors only help one to discover what God has determined that we should do. That is, the situation does not fill an empty absolute with content and thereby determine what one should do. Rather, the situational factors merely help one discover which command of God is applicable to that particular case.

Do Graded Absolutism and Situationism
Agree in Practice?

This question suggests that the two views differ only in theory but not in practice. This criticism, however, is misdirected. First of all, even if the two views agreed on given courses of action, nevertheless the reasons for that accord would be quite different. Hence, the similarities are only accidental and not essential. Fletcher concludes something is right or wrong because the "existential particularities" of the situation determine it. Graded absolutism, on the other hand, concludes something is right or wrong because God has declared it so. Second, there are numerous and significant differences in conclusion between situationism and graded absolutism. For example, in contrast to Fletcher, graded absolutism does not approve of wife-swapping, adultery to get out of prison, blasphemy, abortion of unwanted babies, harlotry to teach maturity, premarital intercourse, or a host of other sins. In brief, whether in principle or practice, any relation to situationism is purely coincidental. Indeed, the same accidental similarities could be drawn between most other views and situationism.

Is Graded Absolutism a Form of Subjectivism?

Doesn't each person have to decide for himself what is the greatest good? And doesn't this amount to subjectivism? In response, two things should be noted. First, if someone makes up his own hierarchy of values based on his own subjective choices, then this is subjectivism.

But this is emphatically not what Christian graded absolutism holds. Second, in graded absolutism the Christian does not decide for himself what the ethical priorities are. It is God who establishes the pyramid of values in accordance with his own nature. These are recorded in Scripture and, hence, they are no more subjective than is anything else revealed in Scripture. The priority of values is objective and determined by God; the only subjective factor is our understanding and acceptance of God's values. But this is a limitation shared by the other Christian views as well.

In What Sense Is Graded Absolutism an Absolutism?

If obedience to lower commands is sometimes unnecessary, then in what sense is it proper to call this view an absolutism? In response to this question, two things should be noted. To begin with, there are three ways in which graded absolutism involves absolutes. It is first of all absolute in its source. All norms are based in the absoluteness of God. God does not change, and principles based on his nature are likewise unchanging. Furthermore, each particular command is absolute in its sphere. Each moral law is absolute as such. It is only when there is a conflict between two of them that appeal must be made to the higher in order to resolve the conflict. Finally, it is absolute in its order of priority. The very gradation of values by which the conflicts are resolved is absolute. It is, for example, absolutely established by God that in an unavoidable conflict between God and parent, one must put God first.

Second, there is of course a sense in which graded absolutism is not an unqualified absolutism (see chap. 5). Graded absolutism may be called qualified absolutism or contextual absolutism, as some do. However, it is not improper to designate it as a form of absolutism because it does maintain, in contrast to situationism, that moral laws are absolute in their source, in their sphere as such, and in their order of priority.

If God Is One, How Can There Be Many Moral Laws?

If God is one in essence, then how can there be many moral laws based on his nature? The response is quite simple: God is one in nature but he has many moral attributes. Each absolute moral law is traceable to one of God's unchangeable moral attributes. Each of these is absolute insofar as it reflects his nature, but there are many of them. Just as the many radii of a circle are based in and spring out of the one center, even so God's many moral characteristics are rooted in his one essence. For example, God is unchanging love and he is also immutably holy. Love and holiness are two different moral attributes, but they are both true of God's one essence.

Is There a Hierarchy within God?

If there is a gradation of moral principles that are based on God's moral nature, then is there a hierarchy within God? By way of response, two things can be observed. First, there is no hierarchy within God's essence. God is absolutely one in essence, and any form of hierarchy implies two or more things. So whatever ordering of values there may be within God would have to be within his attributes, not his essence. For example, mercy as an attribute of God could take priority over justice when two moral principles based on them come into an unavoidable conflict.

Second, it is not necessary to graded absolutism that there be a hierarchy in God's attributes. The hierarchy may only be in God's laws based on those attributes. That is, the priority may not be in the basis of the values but in their expression in moral laws. So the real hierarchy may not be in God's attributes but in the application of them to his creatures. For example, light is one, yet when it passes through a prism it is manifest in a whole array of colors from higher to lower wavelengths. In like manner, all the many moral attributes are one in God, but they diffuse into many laws, ranging from higher to lower, as they pass through the prism of the finite world. In any case, it is not necessary for graded absolutism that the hierarchy is in God but simply that it is revealed by God and reflects the absolute nature of God.

Did Jesus Face Real Moral Conflicts?

The Bible teaches that Jesus was tempted in all points as we are and that he is our complete moral example. Certainly there would be something lacking in the basis for Christian ethics if the model of our morality did not face the most difficult kinds of situations that we his followers face. Yes, Jesus faced real moral conflicts without ever sinning (Heb. 4:15). Specific examples in Jesus' life are the moral conflicts between obedience toward parents and God (Luke 2), Sabbath regulations and healing (Mark 2), and government and God (Matt. 22). But the greatest conflict Christ faced—the conflict of the cross—is often overlooked. Here he was squeezed between the demands of justice for the innocent (himself) and mercy for mankind (the guilty). It is noteworthy that he chose mercy for the many over justice for the one. This conflict was without question the greatest ever faced by man, and it dramatizes the supremacy of mercy over justice in unavoidable moral conflicts.

Do We Create Our Own Moral Conflicts?

Are not our moral dilemmas of our own making and therefore shouldn't we be held responsible for them rather than being exempted from them by some "greater good"? Two things should be pointed out in response. First of all, it is true that we do sometimes create our own conflicts, and in those cases we are guilty. If we make our moral bed, then we must lie in it. Many moral conflicts can be avoided, and when they are not, then we are responsible for the resulting dilemma.

Second, while some moral conflicts are avoidable, it is a mistake to suppose that all of them are a result of prior personal sins. As a matter of fact, sometimes it is one's virtue that precipitates a moral conflict. This was true of the Hebrew midwives (Exod. 1), the three Hebrew children (Dan. 3), and Daniel (Dan. 6). On other occasions, it is neither one's sin nor his righteousness that occasions the moral conflict. For example, an abortion to save a mother's life or a crisis caused by too many people in a lifeboat is not usually the result of the prior sins of the individuals involved. It is to these kinds of personally unavoidable conflicts that graded absolutism is addressed. And both Scripture and human experience provide significant and numerous examples of these real but unavoidable conflicts.

How Can a Lesser Evil Ever Be the Good Thing to Do?

Is not graded absolutism nothing more than pronouncing evil good, which the prophet forbade (Isa. 5:20)? This question confuses graded absolutism with conflicting absolutism. The latter believes that the right thing to do in unavoidable moral conflicts is a lesser evil, but the former believes it is the greater good. The graded absolutist does not proclaim that the evil is a good thing to do, but rather that the highest obligation in the conflict is the good thing to do. For example, in falsifying to save a life, it is not the falsehood that is good (a lie as such is always wrong), but it is the act of mercy to save a life that is good—despite the fact that intentional falsification was necessary to accomplish this good. In other words, it is unfortunately true that what is called "evil" sometimes accompanies the performance of good acts. In these cases God does not consider a man culpable for the concomitant evil in view of the performance of the greater good.

In this respect, graded absolutism is similar to the principle of double effect, which states that when two results—a good result and an evil result—emerge from one act, the individual is held responsible only for the good one he intended and not the evil one which necessarily resulted from the good intention. For example, when a doctor amputates to save a life, he is not morally culpable for maiming but is to be morally praised for saving life.

Is Graded Absolutism Really Utilitarianism?

Isn't doing the greatest good what utilitarianism holds? How does graded absolutism differ from it? There is a basic difference between graded absolutism and utilitarianism. First of all, utilitarianism is teleological (end-centered), but graded absolutism is a deontological (duty-centered) ethic (see chap. 1). When graded absolutists speak of "greater good," they do not mean greater results but the higher rule. They are not referring to a higher end but a higher norm. Furthermore, the basis for their action is not future consequences (the long run) but present commands (the short run). Of course, any ethic is obliged to consider the possible results of actions, but this does not make them utilitarian (see chap. 4). But graded absolutism, in contrast to utilitarianism, holds that following moral rules God has established will bring about the best results. It does not believe that man's calculation of the best results will determine what the best rules should be. We keep the rules and leave the long-range consequences to God.

How Do Exemptions Differ from Exceptions?

Graded absolutism does not believe there are any exceptions to absolute laws, only exemptions (see chap. 1). But is not this merely a semantical difference, not a real one? No, the difference is more than verbal. First of all, an exception would violate the universality and absoluteness of a moral law, whereas an exemption does not. If there is an exception, then the law is not absolute and, hence, does not reflect the nature of God, but at best describes only what is generally the right course of action. Absolute norms, on the contrary, are based on God's unchanging nature and have no exceptions. If they did, it would be much like saying that God is truthful or loving only at certain times but not at others.

Second, an exception means that the lying as such is sometimes right, under certain circumstances. Not so with an exemption. Lying as such is always wrong; it is only the life-saving activity of which the falsehood may be a necessary concomitant that is good—not the lie as such. Third, in an exception, the general rule is not binding on that particular case, and so there is no real conflict. However, where an exemption is made to following a universal law, the law is still binding; that is what makes the conflict real. For instance, the law of filial piety is still binding on the child when he refuses to obey his parents' command to worship an idol; that is precisely what makes the conflict so real.

Finally, an exemption only eliminates the individual's culpability in not performing the demands of that lower law; it in no way changes either the basis or the nature of the law as an absolute in its domain. An exception, on the other hand, would prove the law is not absolute. The difference between an exemption and an exception can be illustrated as follows. When one kills another human being in self-defense, he is exempt from guilt (Exod. 22:2). Yet there is no exception made to the law which requires us to always treat another man—even a would-be murderer—as a human with intrinsic value. There is never a moment when the murderer ceases to be human. If there were, then there would be a legitimate exception to the law of demanding respect for humans. However, despite the fact that he is always human, and that the law to treat him as such still stands, the potential victim is exempt from the moral consequences of disobeying this law in view of the overriding value of defending his own innocent life.

How Can Conflicts Be Real Yet Resolvable?

This question wrongly assumes that a conflict is not real if it is resolvable. But this overlooks several things. First, if this were so, then any conflict that is ultimately resolved would turn out to be only apparent or illusory. But surely no biblical theist would seriously hold that the conflict between good and evil is not real simply because it will be resolved in the eschaton (end). Nor does the fact that one triumphs over temptation make the sin's allure unreal, for this would make Christ's temptation unreal.

Second, to claim a conflict is not real because it is resolvable is justification by stipulation. It is simply a decree by definition. If we stipulate that whatever is resolved is not a real conflict, then this question seems pointless. Moral conflict can be real and unavoidable and yet be capable of a final resolution, with the lower yielding to the higher.

Third, the conflict is real because it is unavoidable, but it is not irresolvable because in such a case we are exempt from obedience to the lower command. The conflict is real because neither law "backed down"; both continued to be binding even though one was more binding than the other. That is, God's absolute nature does not change simply because finite and fallible man finds himself in unavoidable moral conflicts. But in moral conflicts God's justice provides a way out of the dilemma, since it was not of our making.

How Can a Moral Law Be Absolute Yet Not Obeyed?

It seems contradictory to claim that a moral principle is absolute when it can sometimes be broken. For what has exceptions is not universal, and what is broken is not absolute.

In response to this criticism several things can be said in defense of graded absolutism. First, the lower command is not really broken when the higher command is followed. Just as a magnet does not break the law of gravity in attracting a nail, killing in self-defense does not violate the law of respect and preservation of human beings. The overriding duty to keep the higher law simply renders it unnecessary for us to perform the demands of the lesser command.

Second, as was already noted, there are no exceptions to absolute moral laws, only exemptions from obeying them in view of higher ones. So its universalness is not contradicted by an exception.

Third, the command remains absolute even when it is not followed, for its absoluteness is based in the nature of God that does not change. The nature of truth does not change when men tell justifiable falsehoods in order to save innocent lives. If the real conflict is between truthfulness and mercifulness, both of which are grounded in God's nature, then there is no conflict between these in the nature of God. God is one, and all his attributes are harmonious. The real conflict is that on some occasions a man cannot perform both. In these cases God witholds culpability from the man who shows mercy to the innocent rather than telling the truth to the guilty. But this in no way means that both commands are not binding at all times; God never ceases to manifest absolutely what is absolutely right. However, in unavoidable clashes, God does not demand obedience to lower laws, nor does he exact personal culpability for failing to do so.

How Can Lying Flow from the Nature of God as Truth?

If all moral laws are rooted in God, then how can lying ever be right, since God is absolute truth? Very simply, the answer to this is that lying as such does not flow from God's nature. A lie can never be justified by an appeal to him who is truth. However, while lying as such is never justified, lying to save a life is. But "lying to save a life" is really an act of mercy, and mercy is an attribute of God. Cutting off a human leg as such is not right either. It is called mutilation. But cutting off a leg to save a life is right. It is called amputation. Second, God is both merciful and true. So even though lying to save a life cannot be based in God as true, nevertheless, it can be based in God as merciful. Life saving is an act of mercy, even if deception is necessary to accomplish it. Graded absolutism holds that when truth and mercy conflict, then the necessary act of mercy (in this case, lying) finds its basis in God's nature as merciful. Hence justifiable lies are not based in God's truthfulness but in his mercy.

Doesn't Graded Absolutism Deny Total Depravity?

This objection assumes that sin is unavoidable for fallen human beings. Hence, unavoidable moral dilemmas are merely an extension of our depraved condition. But this is a misunderstanding of depravity for several reasons.

First of all, total depravity does not mean that sin is unavoidable. This would contradict 1 Corinthians 10:13, which states that in every temptation there is always a way of escape. Depravity means it is inevitable that fallen man will sin, but not that it is necessary that he must sin.

Second, sin may be unavoidable by fallen man on his own, but all sin is avoidable by God's grace. That is, what we ought to do, we can do, by God's grace.

Third, to insist that sin is unavoidable is to negate human responsibility. God is rational and moral, but it is neither rational nor moral to blame someone for something he could not avoid.

Fourth, responsibility implies the ability to respond. And culpability implies avoidability. Depravity does not make sin unavoidable. If it did, then depravity would destroy man's ability to sin.

Does Graded Absolutism Involve a Contradiction?

It is charged that graded absolutism involves a contradiction because it holds that two opposing courses of action should both be done at the same time. But the law of noncontradiction says it is impossible to do opposites at the same time.

First, this is a misstatement of the law of noncontradiction. To be contradictory, the two opposing commands would have to be binding at the same time and in the same sense. But according to graded absolutism the commands are not binding in the same sense—one is binding in a higher sense.

Second, this criticism is a misunderstanding of graded absolutism. It does not hold that one do opposites at the same time and in the same sense, but only that one ought to do both. Of course God knows we cannot actually do opposites, so he exempts us from doing the lower duty, even though we ought to do it. That is, it is still binding on us even when we cannot do it because of our higher obligation. But since it is binding only in a lower sense, it is our obligation to follow the greater duty.

The Values of Graded Absolutism

There are a number of values of graded absolutism to be pointed out here. Each emerges from the foregoing discussion.

It Avoids Relativism

In contrast to antinomianism, situationism, and generalism (see chaps. 2–4), graded absolutism avoids the pitfalls of relativism. It stands firm on moral principles based in the absolute, unchanging character of God. These moral principles are absolute in their source, absolute in their sphere, and absolute in their order of priority. They are objective, propositional, and substantive in content. God's moral laws are specific and known in advance of the situation. Furthermore, there are no exceptions to them as such; they apply to all people in all places and all times.

It Successfully Answers Moral Conflicts

Another value of graded absolutism, in contrast to unqualified and conflicting absolutism, is that it gives a realistic and successful answer to the problem of moral conflicts. It neither closes its eyes to their reality nor blames an individual because of their unavoidability. It looks squarely at the total moral circumstance and acts responsibly without forsaking the absolute nature of moral principles. It avoids both legalism and antinomianism. It acts courageously but not recklessly.

It Makes Sense of the Cross

Apart from graded absolutism, it is difficult to make moral sense of the cross. From the standpoint of nonconflicting absolutism, the cross is a moral injustice, for on the cross the just was punished for the unjust (1 Pet. 3:18; 2 Cor. 5:21). There is no moral justification for this, unless there are higher and lower moral laws. In this way, mercy can take precedence over justice. The one (Christ) can suffer for the many that they may be saved (Rom. 5:6–18). But if mercy and love are not higher moral values than justice, then what God did to Christ, when it pleased him to "bruise" his son (Isa. 53:5), was a great injustice. But God cannot be unjust. Therefore, the cross makes sense only if the demands of justice are subordinated to the desires of mercy.

Summary and Conclusion

Graded absolutism is distinct from antinomianism, situationism, and generalism (chaps. 2–4) in that it believes in moral absolutes.

Moral laws are absolute in their source, in their own sphere where there is no conflict, and absolute in their order of priority when there is a conflict. In contrast to nonconflicting absolutism, graded absolutism believes there are real moral conflicts. But in distinction from conflicting absolutism, it holds that in these circumstances one is not culpable for subordinating the lower duty to the higher one.

The essential principles of graded absolutism are: There are many moral principles rooted in the absolute moral character of God; There are higher and lower moral duties—for example, love for God is a greater duty than love for people; These moral laws sometimes come into unavoidable moral conflict; In such conflicts we are obligated to follow the higher moral law; When we follow the higher moral law we are not held responsible for not keeping the lower one.

Select Readings

Augustine, Saint. *City of God.* In *A Select Library of the Nicene and Post-Nicene Fathers of the Christian Church,* edited by Philip Schaff, vol. 2. Grand Rapids: Eerdmans, 1956.

————. *Enchiridion.* In *A Select Library of the Nicene and Post-Nicene Fathers of the Christian Church,* edited by Philip Schaff, vol. 3. Grand Rapids: Eerdmans, 1956.

Davis, John Jefferson. *Evangelical Ethics: Issues Facing the Church Today.* Phillipsburg, N.J.: Presbyterian and Reformed, 1985.

Erickson, Millard J. *Relativism in Contemporary Christian Ethics.* Grand Rapids: Baker, 1974.

Hodge, Charles. *Systematic Theology.* Reprint ed. Grand Rapids: Eerdmans, 1952.

Kierkegaard, Søren. *Fear and Trembling.* Garden City, N.Y.: Anchor Books, Doubleday, 1954.

Ross, W. David. *Doing Evil to Achieve Good.* Chicago: Loyola University Press, 1978.

————. *Foundations of Ethics.* Oxford: Clarendon, 1951.

PART 2

Ethical Issues

8

Abortion

W e turn now from ethical options to ethical issues. Of all the moral issues, the most pressing are those involving life and death. And of the life-and-death issues, the one that bears on the most lives is that of abortion. So we will begin our discussion by examining when, if ever, it is right to terminate a life in the womb.

There are three basic positions on abortion, and they all center around the question of the human status of the unborn. Those who believe the unborn are subhuman favor abortion on demand. On the other hand, those who hold that the unborn are fully human are against abortion. And those who argue that the unborn is a potential human favor abortion in specified circumstances. The three views are outlined in table 8.1.

TABLE 8.1

Three Views of Abortion

Status of unborn	Fully human	Potentially human	Subhuman
Abortion	Never	Sometimes	Anytime
Basis	Sanctity of life	Emergence of life	Quality of life
Mother's rights	Life over privacy	Combination of rights	Privacy over life

The status of the unborn is crucial to the various views, for if the unborn are truly human, then the prohibition against taking human life applies to them as well. On the other hand, if the unborn are merely appendages or extensions of their mothers' bodies, then abortion is no more serious than an appendectomy.

Another important issue is the relationship between the right to life and the right of privacy. If human life takes precedence over personal privacy, then aborting a human fetus on the basis of the right to privacy is unjustified. If, on the other hand, the mother's right to privacy takes priority over the baby's right to life, then abortion is justified.

Abortion at Any Time:
The Belief that the Fetus Is Subhuman

Abortion on demand was recognized by the U.S. Supreme Court in its decisions on Doe v. Bolten and Roe v. Wade. In these decisions, the Court argued that the woman's right to privacy prevails over the states' interest in regulating abortions. As a result of these two decisions, abortion for any reason became legal in all fifty states. The Webster decision (1989) gave states more regulatory rights, but did not outlaw abortion.

The pro-abortionist's self-designation as "pro-choice" places emphasis on the right of the mother to decide whether she wants to have a baby. It reveals the belief that the right to privacy is dominant in the decision. Many proponents believe that no unwanted baby should ever be born. No woman should be forced to have a child against her will.

The Supreme Court clearly based its decision on this assumption, referring to the unborn as merely "a potential [human] life." At the same time, the Court also recognized explicitly that if the right of personhood is established, the "appellant's case, of course, collapses, for the fetus' right to life is then guaranteed specifically by the [Fourteenth] Amendment."[1] Hence, the pro-abortion position is dependent on the belief that the unborn is not fully human.

Biblical Arguments for Viewing the Fetus
as Subhuman

A number of Scripture texts are cited to support the view that an unborn child is not human. Brief comments can be made about and conclusions drawn from the most significant biblical passages used for this position.

Genesis 2:7 declares that man "became a living being" only after

1. Roe v. Wade 410 U.S. 113, 93 S.Ct. 705, 35 L.Ed. 2d 147 (1973).

God gave him life. Since breathing does not occur until birth, it is argued that the unborn are not human until they are born.

Job 34:14–15 says that if God "withdrew his spirit and breath, all mankind would perish." Here again, since life is connected with breath, it is reasoned that there is no human life before breath.

Isaiah 57:16 refers to "the breath of man that I [God] have created." This also seems to make the beginning of breath the point of the creation of a human being.

Ecclesiastes 6:3–5 declares that "a stillborn child" comes into the world "without meaning, it departs in darkness, . . . it never saw the sun or knew anything." This is taken to indicate that the unborn are no more than the dead, who also know nothing but lie in the darkness of the grave (9:10).

Matthew 26:24 records Jesus' statement about Judas that "it would have been better for him if he had not been born." The implication drawn from this is that human life begins at birth. Otherwise, Jesus should have said it would have been better for him never to have been conceived.

Other Arguments for Viewing the Fetus as Subhuman

There are several extrabiblical arguments presented by proponents of abortion. The most significant ones will be briefly considered here. Others will be considered later when objections to the pro-life view are discussed.

The argument from self-consciousness—It is argued by some that a baby is not a human until it possesses self-consciousness. Since no infant in the womb is self-conscious, this would argue in favor of a subhuman status for the unborn, and on this ground abortion would be permissible.

The argument from physical dependence—Another reason often given by proponents of abortion is that the baby is an extension of the mother's body, and the mother has the right to control her own body and reproductive system. Since the baby is intruding on the mother's physical domain, she has the right to abort it.

The argument from the safety of the mother—Here it is argued that illegal abortion is dangerous. Figures ranging between five thousand and ten thousand maternal deaths from illegal abortions are offered as evidence. By legalizing abortion, thousands of mothers can be saved from death by rusty coat hangers in back alleys.

The argument from abuse and neglect—Another argument given in favor of abortion is the need to prevent child abuse and neglect. Unwanted pregnancies lead to unwanted children, and unwanted children become abused children. Abortion will help prevent child abuse.

The argument from deformity—Why should any child be born deformed? Why should the family or society be forced to care for deformed children? Abortion based on prenatal tests can eliminate these unnecessary and undesirable births. Furthermore, abortionists argue that concern for the genetic purity of the human race should lead us to weed out bad genes from the human gene pool from which all future human beings will come.

The argument from privacy—The Supreme Court declared in Roe v. Wade that a woman's right of privacy over her own body is guaranteed by the Constitution. Others argue the same thing on ethical grounds. They reason that just as we have the right to evict an unwanted guest from our home, a woman likewise has the right to eject an unwanted baby from her womb.

The argument from rape—Pro-choice adovcates insist that no woman should be forced to have a child against her will. It is immoral to add the necessity of pregnancy to the indignity of a rape. No one should be forced to have a baby against her will.

An Evaluation of the View that the Fetus Is Subhuman

Now that the arguments have been outlined in favor of abortion, a brief evaluation is in order. First, a reply to the biblical arguments.

A Response to the Biblical Arguments for Viewing the Fetus as Subhuman

Breath is not the beginning of humanness—There are several reasons for not taking breath as the point of beginning of human life. If breath is equated with the presence of human life, then the loss of breath would mean the loss of humanness. But the Bible is clear that human beings continue to exist after they stop breathing (Phil. 1:23; 2 Cor. 5:6–8; Rev. 6:9). The Scriptures speak of human life in the womb long before breathing begins, namely, from the point of conception. David said, "In sin did my mother conceive me" (Ps. 51:5). And the angel said of Mary, "What is conceived in her is from the Holy Spirit" (Matt. 1:20). Also, medically many who stop breathing, later revive or live aided by a machine.

It should be noted that the verses on breath do not speak of the beginning of human life but simply the initial "coming out" event. Birth is the human debut into the world. These passages speak about the beginning of *observable* life, not the beginning of life. Even in

Bible times people knew the baby was alive in the womb. The mother could feel it move, at times even jump (Luke 1:44). Birth was not seen as the beginning of human life but simply as the beginning or emergence of life in the naturally visible world—as the human debut.

Adam was a unique case—Since Adam was directly created by God, he was a special case. Thus, the fact that he did not become human until he breathed is not decisive for determining when individual human life begins, and that for several reasons. First, Adam was never conceived and born like other humans; he was directly created. Second, the fact that Adam was not human until he began to breathe no more proves when individual human life begins today than does the fact that he was created as an adult prove that individual human life does not begin until we are adults. Third, "breath" in Genesis 2:7 means life (see Job 33:4). So this means that life began when God gave human life to Adam, not simply because he began breathing. Human life was later given to his posterity at fertilization or conception (Gen. 4:1). Fourth, other animals breathe but are not human (Gen. 7:21–22).

Knowledge is not necessary to humanness—When Ecclesiastes 6:3–5 speaks of "stillborn child[ren]" as not knowing anything, this does not mean they are not human. If this were the case then adults would not be human after they die either, for the same book also says there is no "knowledge" in "the grave where you are going" (9:10). In context, this passage is simply making the obvious point that people not in the world cannot enjoy its opportunities (see v. 9). If lack of knowledge rendered an individual subhuman, then the ignorant would not be human, and the educated would be more human than the uneducated.

A Response to the Nonbiblical Arguments for Viewing the Fetus as Subhuman

The extrabiblical arguments in favor of abortion all beg the question. They all assume what they were to prove, namely, that unborn children are not human.

Self-consciousness is not necessary to humanness—If self-consciousness is essential to humanness, then those who are in a state of dreamless sleep or in a coma are not human. This carries the additional absurd implication that if a wife were to awaken her sleeping husband, she would be calling him back into existence! Furthermore, little children do not gain self-consciousness until they are about a year and a half of age. This would mean, then, that infanticide would be justified on any child going on two years of age! Finally, well-educated people would be more human than less educated ones, since they are more conscious of the world.

An embryo is not an extension of the mother—It is a scientific fact that embryos are not physical extensions of their mothers. They have their own sex from the moment of conception, and half are male, while the mother is female. Beginning about forty days after conception, they have their own individual brain waves which they keep until death. Within a few weeks of conception, they have their own blood type, which may differ from the mother's, and their own unique fingerprints. Finally, the embryo is only "nesting" in his or her mother's womb. Birth simply changes the method of receiving food and oxygen.

Hence, embryos are no more a part of the mother's body than a nursing baby is part of her mother's breast or a test-tube baby is part of a Petri dish. So distinct is an embryo from a mother's womb that if a fertilized ovum from a black couple is transplanted into a white mother, she will have a black baby.

Legalized abortion does not save lives—Legalizing abortion has not saved thousands of mothers from dying, and it has killed millions of babies. Before the legalization of abortion in 1973, there were not thousands of women dying from illegal abortions. The U.S. Bureau of Vital Statistics reported that in 1973 there were only forty-five maternal deaths from abortion. One of the original leaders of the abortion movement, Dr. Bernard N. Nathanson, has subsequently admitted that proponents of abortion lied about the statistics.[2]

However, the maternal death rate for childbirth is only 1 in 10,000 births, or 1/100 of 1 percent. It is one of the safest medical procedures in the country. But the child mortality rate from successful abortions is 100 percent; it is the most fatal operation in America. If the embryo is human, then saving even hundreds of mothers would not justify killing millions of babies. Abortion takes the lives of 1.5 million babies a year in the United States. So the net effect of legalizing abortion has been to arrange that these deaths occur more sanitarily and professionally.

Abortion does not avoid child abuse—The argument for preventing child abuse as a rationale for abortion takes the focus off the issue of whether the unborn child is human. If the unborn is human, then abortion does not avoid child abuse. Rather, abortion is child abuse of the worst kind—abuse by a cruel death. According to U.S. Department of Health and Human Services figures, between 1973, when abortion was legalized, and 1982, child abuse increased more than 500 percent. Research reveals that the vast majority of battered children were

2. Bernard N. Nathanson, *Aborting America* (Garden City, N.Y.: Doubleday, 1979), p. 193.

wanted by their parents. One study showed that 91 percent of abused children were wanted children.[3]

Deformity is no justification for abortion—Once again, this argument for abortion makes sense only if the unborn are not human, which begs the question. If the unborn are human, then abortion of the deformed is no more justified than infanticide or euthanasia for genetic reasons. Abortion of the handicapped is not promoted by handicapped people. At last count, there was not a single organization for parents of handicapped children on record as favoring abortion of the handicapped. In short, it is not the handicapped or their parents who want abortions of babies who may be handicapped; it is those who are not handicapped. Let us allow the handicapped to speak for themselves.

Privacy rights are not absolute—The problem with the right-to-privacy argument for abortion is that it brings us face to face again with the basic issue: Are the unborn human? In other words, justifying abortion on the grounds of privacy makes good sense only if the embryo is not a human being. This is obvious for several reasons. First, we do not have the right to privately kill human beings. Abortionists would have to argue that we also have the right to engage in child abuse or rape as long as it is done privately. But certainly we have no right to kill privately. Second, abortion of human beings is significantly different from evicting someone from our home. Abortion is more like killing an indigent person in our home because he will not leave. After all, evicting a nonviable embryo is fatal. It is tantamount to killing it, since it cannot live on its own outside the womb. Third, with the exception of criminal rape, no pregnancy is unwilled. If one consents to intercourse, then one is responsible for the result of that free act. So, to carry the illustration through, in 99 percent of abortions the "guest" was invited to begin with. This being the case, abortion is more like inviting an indigent guest to our home and then killing him (or evicting him to a sure death) simply because he is not wanted.

Rape is not a justification for abortion—The rape of the mother does not justify the murder of the child. If the unborn is a human, then intentionally taking its innocent life is murder. So here again the real issue is the human status of the unborn. But appealing to sympathy for the rape victim does not avoid the question of justice for the abortion victim.

Abortion does not take away the evil of the rape; it adds another

3. E. Lenowski, *Heartbeat* 3, 4 (December 1980), quoted in J. C. Willke and Barbara Willke, *Abortion: Questions and Answers* (Cincinnati: Hayes, 1985), p. 138.

evil to it. The rape problem is not solved by killing the baby. We should punish the guilty rapist, not the innocent baby. Even if abortion were justified in a few extreme cases such as rape, this would in no way justify abortion on demand, such as the Roe court permitted.

If a rape victim gets immediate medical treatment, then conception can be avoided in all cases (since conception does not occur immediately). Due to understandable physical and psychological circumstances, few pregnancies ever occur from rape. The figure for criminal rape is well under one percent. But in those cases where pregnancy does occur, about half of rape victims want to have the baby. Should the mother not want the baby, there are lines of people waiting to adopt babies. Adoption, not abortion, is the better alternative.

Abortion Sometimes: The Belief that the Fetus Is Potentially Human

According to this opinion on abortion, the unborn child is merely a potential human being. Proponents argue that the humanness of the individual develops gradually between conception and birth. The fetus begins as a potentially human person and becomes fully human gradually. Of course, even as a potential human being, the fetus has more value than mere things or even animals. However, this emerging value must be weighed against such other considerations as the mother's rights and society's rights. Whether abortion is justified in a given case will depend on where the greater weight of these rights falls in the balance. Generally, those who hold this view favor abortion to save the mother's life, for rape, for incest, and (in many cases) for genetic deformities. The arguments offered in favor of this view can be categorized as biblical and nonbiblical.

Biblical Arguments for Viewing the Fetus as Potentially Human

There are several passages used to support the position that the unborn are only potentially human. The one most often appealed to is Exodus 21.

Exodus 21:22–23. This passage reads as follows:

If men strive, and hurt a woman with child, so that her fruit depart from her, and yet no mischief follow: he shall be surely punished, according as the woman's husband will lay upon him; and he shall pay as the judges determine. And if any mischief follow, then thou shalt give life for life . . . (KJV).

These verses are taken to mean that only a monetary fine was exacted for the death of the fetus, but capital punishment for the death of the mother. If so, then the mother's actual life was considered of more value than the fetus's potential life. Adherents argue that "her fruit depart from her" means a miscarriage in which the baby dies. Thus, that "no mischief follow" would refer to the mother, since the miscarriage has already brought death to the fetus. If this is so, then the mere fine, as opposed to capital punishment, for the death of the fetus would indicate that the fetus was not considered fully human.

Psalm 51:5. David confessed, "Surely I was sinful at birth, sinful from the time my mother conceived me." In what sense was David a sinner at the moment of conception? He obviously was not an actual sinner because he had not yet actually sinned. So, it is reasoned, David was a potential sinner. He was a potential sinner because he was only a potential person. Later, when he became an actual person, he became an actual sinner.

Psalm 139:13, 16. The Psalmist wrote of the process by which we are formed in our mother's womb, saying,

> For you created my inmost being;
> you knit me together in my mother's womb.
> When I was woven together in the depths of the earth,
> your eyes saw my unformed body.

From these verses it is argued that the fetus is not fully human because it is in the process of being "knit . . . together" and is called "unformed." Add to this the verses from Ecclesiastes (6:3–5) that the fetus does not have "breath" or "know" anything and the image develops of a potential but emerging human being in the womb. But it is argued from this that the fetus is not yet fully developed or fully human.

Romans 5:12. The Bible declares that "sin entered the world through one man [Adam], and death through sin, and in this way death came to all men, because all sinned [in Adam]." However, it is evident that all men were not in Adam actually. Hence, it is argued that all humans were in Adam only potentially. Thus it is concluded that we are only potentially human before we are born and only become actual human beings later.

Hebrews 7:9 says that "Levi . . . paid the tenth through Abraham, because . . . Levi was still in the body of [Abraham]." But since Levi lived hundreds of years after Abraham, it is clear that he was not actually in Abraham's body. He must have been there only potentially. Thus, it is argued by comparison that the unborn are only potentially human when they are in the body of the mother.

Other Arguments for Viewing the Fetus
as Potentially Human

In addition to the biblical evidence, there are several reasons offered to support the view that a fetus is only potentially human. Some of the most significant ones are summarized here.

Human personality develops only gradually—Observation reveals that human personality goes through a gradual process of development. One is not conceived with a sense of his or her personal identity. This develops gradually through relationships with other persons. Thus it is urged that one becomes a person only as his or her personality develops. Before that, one is only potentially and emergently human.

Human development is interconnected with physical development—It is evident that there is physical development between conception and birth. Not all bodily organs and functions are present at conception; they develop gradually throughout the prenatal period. But it is equally true that there is an interrelation between psychological and physical development. For example, a one-day-old baby's body does not have an eighteen-year-old's mind. This being the case, some argue that human personhood develops along with the human body.

The analogy with other living things—An acorn is not an oak tree, nor is an egg a chicken, and an embryo is to a human being what an acorn is to an oak tree, or an egg to a chicken. Just as an egg is not a chicken, so neither is a fetus a human. An acorn is a potential oak tree, and an embryo is a potential human being. Of course, a fetus has the potential to become human and the egg does not. This potential is of great value, in fact, more value than an actual chicken. However, a potential human is no more an actual human than an acorn is an oak tree.

The legal argument—The Supreme Court referred to a fetus as "a potential [human] life."[4] Some pro-abortionists claim that this idea is implied in the Fourteenth Amendment, which says:

> All persons born or naturalized in the United States, and subject to the jurisdiction thereof, are citizens of the United States and of the State wherein they reside. No state shall . . . deprive any person of life, liberty, or property, without due process of law. . . .

Since the amendment extends the rights of citizenship only to those who are born, pro-abortionists reason that the Constitution implies that the unborn are not fully human. Hence, the right to life of those already born would not apply to them.

4. Roe v. Wade.

An Evaluation of the View
that the Fetus Is Potentially Human

There are several serious problems with the position that the un-born are only potentially human. First, the interpretations of the bib-lical passages are questionable.

A Response to the Biblical Arguments Viewing the
Fetus as Potentially Human

Exodus 21 does not teach that a fetus is a potential human. Neither can this be legitimately inferred from the passage. The Hebrew word for "come forth" is *yahtzah,* which means "to give birth." It is the Hebrew word regularly used for live birth in the Old Testament. Hence, in this passage it refers to a live premature birth, not a miscarriage. The separate Hebrew word for miscarriage, *shakol,* is not used here. The word used for the mother's offspring here is *yeled,* which means "child." It is the same word used of babies and young children (Gen. 21:8; Exod. 2:3). If any harm came to either the mother or the child, the same punishment was given, "life for life" (v. 23). This reveals that the unborn was considered of equal value with the mother.

The famous Hebrew scholar, Umberto Cassuto, rendered this pas-sage as follows:

> When men strive together and they hurt unintentionally a woman with child, and her children come forth but no mischief happens—that is, the woman and the children do not die—the one who hurts her shall surely be punished by a fine. But if any mischief happens, that is, if the woman dies or the children die, then you shall give life for life.[5]

This makes the meaning clear; it is a strong passage affirming that the unborn are of equal value to adult human beings.

Psalm 51:5 does not support the potential-human view for several reasons. Even if it were teaching that humans are potential sinners from conception, it does not follow that they are potential humans. The very fact that humans are declared sinners from conception re-veals that they are human, that is, part of the fallen human race. It is only by virtue of being part of the Adamic human race that we are conceived in sin (see comments on Rom. 5:12).

Psalm 139 is a strong support of the view that the unborn are fully human, not potentially human. "Unformed" (v. 16) does not mean un-human any more than deformed does. The baby in the womb is referred

---

5. Umberto Cassuto, *A Commentary on the Book of Exodus,* trans. Israel Abrahams (Jerusalem: Magnes, 1974), p. 275.

to as "created" (*bara*), the word used of mankind in Genesis 1:27 to denote their being made in the "image of God." The unborn is referred to by personal pronouns (Jer. 1:5), and the unborn is "known" by God in the womb, a term implying personal relationship. Each unborn child in the womb is also written down in God's book in heaven.

Romans 5:12 implies that all humans were in Adam, but not that they were potential humans before they were born. The passage is not speaking about an embryo in the womb but about the fact that all humans were in Adam. The fact that we were all genetically or representatively in Adam, and therefore responsible in his sin, reveals that there is a corporateness about human nature. That is, there is a unity in humanity, so that we cannot totally cut off one member from another (Rom. 14:7) wherever we are located. The very fact that we are all declared sinners from conception (Ps. 51:5) by virtue of being in Adam reveals that, even at the point of conception, one is considered to be part of the human race.

Hebrews 7:9 is not speaking of an embryo, to say nothing of it being a potential human being. It does not say that Levi was potentially in Abraham. He was probably there representatively or figuratively. But even if Levi was potentially in Abraham, it certainly does not follow that he was an embryo in Abraham. If Levi, who was not even conceived when he was said to be "in Abraham," was a potential human being, then we are potential humans before we are even conceived. If this is so, then, even human sperm (before they fertilize an ovum) are potential human beings. But this is genetically incorrect. Sperm have only twenty-three chromosomes while embryos have forty-six. Embryos have human souls, but sperms do not.

A Response to the Nonbiblical Arguments for Viewing the Fetus as Potentially Human

The extrabiblical arguments for viewing the fetus as only potentially human suffer from many of the same weaknesses as the arguments for viewing the fetus as subhuman. Let us consider them in turn.

Personality differs from personhood—Arguing that the unborn are only potential persons because personality develops is a confusion of personality and personhood. Personality is a psychological concept; personhood is an ontological category. Personality is a property, but personhood is the substance of being human. Personalities are formed by their surroundings, but personhood is created by God. Thus, personality is developed gradually, but personhood comes instantly at conception. If personhood is identified with personality, then an improperly adjusted person is not properly human. Since personality involves consciousness, those who lack consciousness would cease to be human. On this ground, killing people who are unconscious would be justified.

The soul does not have to change with the body—Simply because the body develops does not mean the soul does. A jar can have the same form whether it is small or big. This sentence could be magnified (enlarged) without changing its meaning (form). Likewise, the small body of a fertilized ovum can have the same soul as the somewhat bigger one of a fetus, or even the much bigger one of an adult. So simply because the human body undergoes obvious development does not mean that the human person animating that body must also develop gradually. The soul can be present wholly and completely from the very beginning of the body's development.

Neither an acorn nor an embryo is a potential life—It is a misunderstanding of botany to say an acorn is a potential oak tree. An acorn is a tiny living oak tree inside a shell. Its dormant life does not grow until properly nourished by planting and watering, but it is a tiny living oak tree in a shell nonetheless. All the genetic information which comprises an oak tree is in the acorn. And all the genetic information which comprises an adult human being is in the fertilized ovum. All that is added to make an adult human from this tiny human is water, air, and food. An embryo is not a potential human life; it is a human life with great potential.

The unborn are constitutionally protected—There are a number of significant reasons why the Supreme Court was wrong when it declared that unborn children are not persons with a protected right to life. It is not simply those who are born in the United States who are protected under the Constitution. Otherwise, it would be legal to kill any alien within our borders. But the Fourteenth Amendment explicitly says that the state shall not "deprive any person of life, liberty, or property, without due process of law; nor deny any person within its jurisdiction the equal protection of the law."

Even corporations have been considered "persons" under the Fourteenth Amendment (Santa Clara County v. Southern Pacific R. R. Co. 118 U.S. 394 [1886]), and the Supreme Court also once mistakenly said that blacks were not citizens (Dred Scott v. Sanford 60 U.S. [19 How.] 393, 15 L.Ed. 691 [1857]) and was tragically wrong then too. The right to life is an inalienable God-given right according to the Declaration of Independence (1776), our national birth certificate. The fact that abortions were forbidden by law at that time and that an embryo was defined as a "child in the womb" shows that this right to life included unborn children as well. And only three years before Roe v. Wade a federal court referred to the unborn as persons (Steinberg v. Brown [1970]).

No Abortions:
The Belief that the Fetus Is Fully Human

The final view holds that the fetus is fully human. Therefore, any intentional taking of an unborn's life is homicide. This position is supported by both biblical and nonbiblical evidence.

Biblical Arguments for Viewing the Fetus as Fully Human

Since most of the biblical data has already been presented, the arguments pertinent to this position will simply be summarized here.

1. Unborn babies are called "children," the same word used of infants and young children (Luke 1:41, 44; 2:12, 16; Exod. 21:22), and sometimes even of adults (1 Kings 3:17).
2. The unborn are created by God (Ps. 139:13) just as God created Adam and Eve in his image (Gen. 1:27).
3. The life of the unborn is protected by the same punishment for injury or death (Exod. 21:22) as that of an adult (Gen. 9:6).
4. Christ was human (the God-man) from the point he was conceived in Mary's womb (Matt. 1:20–21; Luke 1:26–27).
5. The image of God includes "male and female" (Gen. 1:27), but it is a scientific fact that maleness or femaleness (sex) is determined at the moment of conception.
6. Unborn children possess personal characteristics such as sin (Ps. 51:5) and joy that are distinctive of humans.
7. Personal pronouns are used to describe unborn children (Jer. 1:5 LXX; Matt. 1:20–21) just as any other human being.
8. The unborn are said to be known intimately and personally by God as he would know any other person (Ps. 139:15–16; Jer. 1:5).
9. The unborn are even called by God before birth (Gen. 25:22–23; Judg. 13:2–7; Isa. 49:1, 5; Gal. 1:15).

Taken as a whole, these Scripture texts leave no doubt that an unborn child is just as much a person in God's image as a little child or an adult is. They are created in God's image from the very moment of conception, and their prenatal life is precious in God's eyes and protected by his prohibition against murder.

Nonbiblical Arguments for Viewing the Fetus as Fully Human

The extrabiblical evidence that prenatal life is fully human falls into the categories of scientific and social.

Scientific evidence for the humanity of the unborn—Modern science has placed a window in the womb. As a result, the evidence is now clearer than ever that individual human life begins at the very moment of conception or fertilization.

It is a genetic fact that a fertilized human ovum is 100 percent human. From the very moment of fertilization, all genetic information is present. All the physical characteristics of an individual being are contained in the genetic code present at conception. The sex of the individual child is determined at the moment of conception as well. A female ovum has only twenty-three chromosomes, and male sperm has twenty-three chromosomes, but a normal adult human being has forty-six chromosomes. At the very moment of conception, when the male sperm and female ovum unite, a new, tiny forty-six-chromosome human being emerges. From the moment of conception until death, no new genetic information is added. All that is added between conception and death is food, water, and oxygen.

At a U.S. congressional hearing in 1981, scientific experts from around the world testified about the beginning of an individual life:

In biology and in medicine, it is an accepted fact that the life of any individual organism reproducing by sexual reproduction begins at conception, or fertilization. (Dr. Micheline M. Matthews-Roth)[6]

To accept the fact that after fertilization has taken place a new human has come into being is no longer a matter of taste or opinion. The human nature of the human being from conception to old age is not a metaphysical contention, it is plain experimental evidence. (Jerome LeJeune)[7]

But now we can say, unequivocally, that the question of when life begins is no longer a question for theological or philosophical dispute. It is an established scientific fact. Theologians and philosophers may go on to debate the meaning of life or the purpose of life, but it is an established fact that all life, including human life, begins at the moment of conception. (Dr. Hymie Gordon)[8]

Modern fetology has brought to light some amazing things about the growth of this tiny person in his or her mother's womb. The following summary is vivid testimony to the full humanness of the prenatal child (a girl in this instance).

6. Subcommittee on Separation of Powers, report to Senate Judiciary Committee S-158, 97th Congress, 1st session, 1981.
7. Ibid.
8. Ibid.

FIRST MONTH—ACTUALIZATION
Conception—All her human characteristics are present
She implants or "nests" in her mother's uterus (one week)
Her heart muscle pulsates (three weeks)
Her head, arms, and legs begin to appear

SECOND MONTH—DEVELOPMENT
Her brain waves can be detected (forty to forty-two days)
Her nose, eyes, ears, and toes appear
Her heart beats and blood (her own type) flows
Her skeleton develops
She has her own unique fingerprints
She is sensitive to touch on her lips and has reflexes
All her bodily systems are present and functioning

THIRD MONTH—MOVEMENT
She swallows, squints, and swims
She grasps with her hands, moves her tongue
She can even suck her thumb
She can feel organic pain (eight to thirteen weeks)

FOURTH MONTH—GROWTH
Her weight increases six times (to one-half birth weight)
She grows up to eight to ten inches long
She can hear her mother's voice

FIFTH MONTH—VIABILITY
Her skin, hair, and nails develop
She dreams (REM sleep)
She can cry (if air is present)
She can live outside the womb
She is only halfway to her scheduled birth date

These characteristics make the identity of human embryos unmistakable. Human embryos are not mineral, vegetable, or animal. They are fully human.

Social evidence for the humanity of the unborn—In addition to the biblical and scientific evidence, there are many social arguments for protecting the human rights of unborn children. These are the most significant ones among them.

No one disputes that human embryos have human parents. Why then should anyone argue that a human embryo is not human? No biologist has any difficulty identifying an unborn pig as a pig or an unborn horse as a horse. Why then should an unborn human be considered anything but human?

Human life never stops and then starts up again. There is a continuous flow of human life from generation to generation, from parent to child. This flow of human life is uninterrupted. The way new individual human life appears is through conception. Hence, the new life that appears at that point is every bit as human as its parents. Otherwise, human life would have a discontinuity between conception and birth (or whenever it would begin again).

The father of modern fetology, Dr. A. Liley, noted that "this is the same baby we are caring for before and after birth, who before birth can be ill and need diagnosis and treatment just like any other patient."[9] But if it is the same baby and the same patient both before and after birth, then it is just as human before it is born as after.

Modern medical care has made it possible for premature babies to live outside the womb much earlier—some twenty-week-old fetuses have survived. But if they are human when they come out of the womb at five months, then they must be human if they stay in the womb. Then there are no grounds for killing them up to nine months, which is what U.S. law permits. This contradiction is often dramatized in a modern hospital where staff members in one room rush to save a five-month-old preemie, while in another room others may be killing (by abortion) a baby.

All the arguments for abortion apply equally as well to infanticide and euthanasia. If unborn children can be killed because of deformity, poverty, or undesirability, then both infants and the aged can be disposed of for the same reasons. There is no real difference between abortion and infanticide or euthanasia—they all involve the same patient, the same procedure, and end in the same result.

Abortion has been declared wrong by many societies and moralists, whether Christian or pagan, since the dawn of civilization. The Code of Hammurabi (eighteenth century B.C.) had a penalty for even unintentionally causing a miscarriage. Mosaic law (sixteenth century B.C.) exacted the same penalty for injury to baby or mother. Tiglath-pileser of Persia (twelfth century B.C.) punished women who caused themselves to abort. The Greek physician Hippocrates opposed abortion by oath, swearing, "I will neither give a deadly drug to anyone if asked for, nor will I make a suggestion to this effect. Similarly I will not give to a woman an abortive remedy." Even Seneca (second century), whose stoic compatriots allowed abortion, praised his mother for not aborting him. Saint Augustine (fourth century), Thomas Aquinas (thirteenth century), and John Calvin (sixteenth century) all considered abortion immoral. English common law exacted a punishment for taking life

9. Quoted in Willke and Willke, *Abortion,* p. 52.

by abortion, as did early American law. In fact, before 1973 laws in nearly all fifty states opposed abortion.

Discrimination against anyone's life based on circumstantial matters such as size, age, location, or functional ability is morally wrong. Yet these are the same grounds on which abortionists consider the unborn child to be nonhuman. On these same grounds we could discriminate against the lives of pygmies or preemies because they are too small, or against minorities because of where they live. Why then discriminate against babies who still live in the womb? Or we could discriminate against the handicapped or elderly because they lack certain functional abilities. And if we can eliminate babies from the human community because they are unwanted, then why not discard other undesired segments of society, such as AIDS victims, drug addicts, or derelicts?

A Response to Criticisms of the View that the Fetus Is Fully Human

Granting that a fertilized ovum is fully human leads to some difficulties. The most important ones are briefly noted here.

What if the Mother's Life Is Threatened?

Thanks to the advances of modern medicine, it is seldom necessary to abort the baby to save the mother's life. However, when it is necessary (such as in tubal pregnancies), it is morally justified to take every medical precaution to save the mother's life. This is not abortion as such, and for several reasons. First, the intention is not to kill the baby; it is to save the life of the mother. Second, it is a life-for-a-life issue, not an abortion-on-demand situation. Third, when one's life is threatened, as the mother's is, one has a right to preserve it on the basis of killing in self-defense (see Exod. 22:2).

Half of all Conceptions Spontaneously Abort

It is objected that if a fertilized ovum is a human being, then about one-half of all human beings are killed spontaneously anyway, for they never make it to the uterus to develop. However, this is not a legitimate ground for abortion. It fails to make the crucial distinction between spontaneous death and homicide. We are not morally culpable for the former, but we are for the latter. There is also a high infant mortality rate in some underdeveloped countries, but this does not justify intentionally killing these babies. There is a 100 percent mortality rate among people who are terminally ill, but this does not justify killing them. From a biblical standpoint, God is sovereign over life, not humans. The believer's attitude should be "the LORD gave and the LORD hath taken away; blessed be the name of the LORD" (Job 1:21 KJV; see also Deut. 32:39).

If All Fertilized Ova Are Human, We Should Try to Save Them

It is argued that if every fertilized ovum is human, then we are obligated to try to save all spontaneous abortions as well. But if we did, it would lead to overpopulation, death by medical neglect, and starvation. In response, several points should be made. There is no unqualified moral duty to interfere with natural death. Protecting life is a moral obligation, but resisting natural death is not necessarily a moral duty (see chap. 9). This also rejects God's sovereignty over life and death. God has appointed death for all persons (Rom. 5:12; Heb. 9:27), and we have no moral right to interfere with him when he does this. There is no inconsistency between preserving natural life by opposing artificial abortion and allowing natural death by spontaneous abortion. Both respect God's right over human life (Deut. 32:39; Job 1:21).

Twins Prove that Life Begins at Conception

Identical twins come from one fertilized ovum that does not divide until after conception. On this basis it is argued that human life could not begin at conception, since each twin's life did not begin until after conception. But this does not follow for several reasons. The original ovum was 100 percent human with forty-six chromosomes. From the instant the ovum split in two, each twin has 100 percent human characteristics and forty-six chromosomes. Twin splitting may simply be a nonsexual way of parenting. And we do not consider the parents of humans to be subhuman. The "parent" of a twin is just as human as would be the "parent" of a human clone. Both have human genetic characteristics.

Some Fertilized Ova Do Not Have Forty-six Chromosomes

Some babies have only forty-five chromosomes (Turner's Syndrome) and some have forty-seven (Down's Syndrome). This is used by some pro-abortionists to justify abortion of genetically imperfect babies, but this does not follow for many reasons. On this same ground we could also kill little children and adults with these same genetic imperfections. Many people with other than forty-six chromosomes live relatively normal lives. We do not treat the physically impaired as subhuman, and neither should we treat the genetically impaired that way.

A Human Being Is Not Necessarily a Person

This distinction admits the humanness of the embryo but denies that he or she is a person. But this will not help the pro-abortion cause. The distinction is arbitrary. There are no real essential differences between being human and being a human person, only functional ones. On the same grounds the personhood of the severely retarded, the unconscious, and the senile could be denied. Even if an embryo were not yet a person, it still would be wrong to kill innocent human beings. And they are unmistakably human in both parentage and genetic characteristics.

Summary and Conclusion

The abortion debate focuses the whole issue of the sanctity of human life. Both Scripture and science support the view that an individual human life begins at conception, and both special and general revelation declare it is wrong to kill an innocent human life. Furthermore, the same arguments used to justify abortion may also be used to justify infanticide and euthanasia. These reasons all violate the sanctity of human life.

Abortion is not just a threat to the unborn. As the English poet John Donne noted, "Any man's death diminishes me, because I am involved in mankind; and therefore never send to know for whom the bell tolls; it tolls for thee." In America it tolls more than four thousand times a day, once every twenty seconds!

Select Readings

Brennan, William. *The Abortion Holocaust: Today's Final Solution*. St. Louis: Landmark, 1983.

Burtchaell, James Tunstead. *Rachel Weeping: The Case Against Abortion*. San Francisco: Harper and Row, 1984.

Gardner, R. F. R. *Abortion: The Personal Dilemma*. Grand Rapids: Eerdmans, 1972.

Krason, Stephen M. *Abortion: Politics, Morality and the Constitution*. New York: University Press of America, 1984.

Nathanson, Bernard N. *Aborting America*. Garden City, N.Y.: Doubleday, 1979.

———. *The Abortion Papers: Inside the Abortion Mentality*. Hollywood, Fla.: Fell, 1983.

Roe v. Wade 410 U.S. 113, 93 S.Ct. 705, 35 L.Ed. 2d 147 (1973).

Webster v. Reproductive Health Services (1989).

Wennberg, Robert N. *Life in the Balance: Exploring the Abortion Controversy.* Grand Rapids: Eerdmans, 1985.

Willke, J. C., and Barbara Willke. *Abortion: Questions and Answers.* Cincinnati: Hayes, 1985.

9

Euthanasia

What should we do to a person hopelessly caught in a burning airplane who begs to be shot? Most humane persons would shoot a horse trapped in a burning barn. Why should a human not be treated as humanely as an animal? Or when a monstrously deformed baby is born and suddenly stops breathing, is the doctor morally obligated to resuscitate it? Would it not be more merciful to let it die? Again, perhaps a person with an incurable disease is being kept alive only by a machine. If the plug is pulled he will die; if he lives it will only be artificially in a kind of "vegetative" existence. These and many similar situations focus the ethical problem inherent in euthanasia and infanticide. When, if ever, is a "mercy killing" morally justifiable?

Active Euthanasia:
Taking Lives to Avoid Suffering

Euthanasia means "good (or happy) death." There are two kinds of euthanasia: active and passive. The former is taking a life to avoid suffering, and the latter is simply allowing death to occur in order to avoid suffering. Euthanasia can be either voluntary or not voluntary. In the former the patient consents to his death, and in the latter he does not. The death can be self-caused or caused by another. In the former case it is a form of suicide, and in the latter case it is a homicide.

Those subjected to humanely initiated death can be young or old.

157

The former is infanticide and the latter is generally just called euthanasia. In this section the discussion is concerned with active euthanasia, or the intentional taking of another life, whether by one's self or another, whether one is young or old. None of these are natural deaths; all are unnatural. They are not the result of natural processes, but are humanly initiated deaths.

The very word *euthanasia* gives a positive connotation to the act. It is an attempt to have a happy or painless death. The most basic reason for this is to avoid suffering, usually of a physical nature. The proponents of active euthanasia offer the following reasons in favor of it.

There Is a Moral Right to Die with Dignity

It is argued that everyone has a right to die with dignity, and that this is part of what it means to have a human kind of life. Death is a part of that life, albeit the last part. But a slow, painful, and merciless death is not a dignified death. Rather, it is a dehumanizing death like that of an animal (or even a vegetable in some cases). Thus, proponents of active euthanasia insist that it is a necessary means to guarantee a dignified death. Without it we humans have no choice in our own destiny or demise. We have no control over catastrophe. We are mere pawns on the chessboard of pain.

The Constitutional Right of Privacy Includes Death with Dignity

The argument for euthanasia is an extension of the one used by the Supreme Court to justify abortion. The Court contends that there is a constitutional right to privacy implied in the Fourteenth Amendment. This guarantees a woman's right to have her unborn baby put to death by abortion. But if the right to privacy includes taking the life of the unborn, then why not of the newly born by infanticide, or the almost-dead by euthanasia? If we have the constitutional right to decide who lives, then why not the right to decide who dies?

It Is an Act of Mercy to the Sufferer

We shoot horses trapped in burning barns to prevent their suffering. Why not be at least as humane with humans? Not allowing euthanasia merely prolongs suffering. Why must we perpetuate human misery? The most compassionate thing to do is to put the sufferer out of his misery. It is not kind or considerate to insist that one must go through endless pain for nothing. Mercy dictates that we alleviate the pain in the most effective and permanent way possible, that we give a suffering person a good death. Nobel prizewinner Dr. James Watson writes,

If a child were not declared alive until three days after birth, then all parents could be allowed the choice only few are given under the present system. The doctor could allow the child to die if the parents so chose and save a lot of misery and suffering.[1]

It Is an Act of Mercy to the Suffering Family

The patient is not the only one suffering. The family suffers also. Hastening an inevitable death not only will relieve untold suffering for the patient, but also will take an incalculable burden from the family. Their social sacrifice and psychological suffering can be every bit as great as the physical suffering of the one dying. Thus, it is also an act of mercy to the family to "pull the plug." In 1983 the Supreme Court of Indiana agreed with this reasoning and upheld the parents' right to allow "Baby Doe" to starve to death. Defenders of the decision considered it the compassionate thing to do.

It Relieves the Family of Heavy Financial Strain

Besides the social and psychological burden, the family also may be carrying a heavy financial load. Severe illness can wipe out a lifetime of savings in a short period. Often these are funds badly needed by the survivors for their own sustenance. At other times sickness can eliminate funds for future education or health care for the whole family. Hence, euthanasia is not only an act of mercy to the dying, but also to the living who are responsible for them.

It Relieves Society of a Great Social Burden

As medical costs soar and the number of elderly increases in society, the burden of caring for the suffering increases. In April of 1984, Governor Richard Lamm of Colorado declared that the elderly "have a duty to die and get out of the way." Indeed, there are now groups to help them. A voluntary euthanasia group in England is called Exit. In the United States one is called the Society for the Right to Die and another is called the Hemlock Society. The founder of the latter group, Derek Humphry, helped his wife to commit suicide in England in 1975. The society's book, *Let Me Die before I Wake,* includes case studies of suicides as well as the amount of drugs necessary to end one's life. Humphry boasts, "We have made it respectable to debate and discuss euthanasia. We've also helped a lot of people die well."[2]

1. J. C. Willke and Barbara Willke, *Abortion: Questions and Answers* (Cincinnati: Hayes, 1985), p. 204.
2. *Reader,* June 29, 1983.

It Is the Humane Thing to Do

Before a presidential commission appointed to study biomedical ethical issues (1982), philosopher Mary Anne Warren compared a severely disabled newborn child to a horse with a broken leg that should be killed to spare it from the agony of a slow and painful death.[3] Professor Peter Singer insists that "the life of a fetus is of no greater value than the life of a nonhuman animal at a similar level of rationality. . . . Now it must be admitted that these arguments apply to the newborn baby as much as to the fetus." Thus he concludes that "the life of a newborn baby is of less value than the life of a pig, a dog, or a chimpanzee."[4] A 1982 *Newsweek* article proclaimed in large print, "Biologists say infanticide is as normal as the sex drive—and that most animals, including man, practice it."[5]

An Evaluation of Active Euthanasia

The response to these arguments from a Christian perspective has been strong, for they are based on utilitarian presuppositions that deny deeply held Christian convictions about the sovereignty of God and the sanctity of human life made in his image.

There Is No Moral Right to Kill

The euthanasia proponents assume that there is a moral right to intentionally kill an innocent human. But the Bible says, "Thou shalt not kill" (Exod. 20:13 KJV). They believe that man is sovereign over human life, but Scripture declares that God is. "I put to death and I bring to life . . . and no one can deliver out of my hands" (Deut. 32:39). As Job declared, "The LORD gave and the LORD has taken away" (Job 1:21). God created human life (Gen. 1:27) and he alone has the right to take it (Heb. 9:27). So the basic fallacy of active euthanasia is to presume upon the sovereign right of God over human life. The proponents presume to play God rather than simply to be man.

The Constitution Gives No Right to Kill

First of all, there is no explicitly stated right to privacy in the U.S. Constitution; it is at best only implied. Second, even if there is a right of privacy, it does not take precedence over the emphatically stated

3. William Brennan, *The Abortion Holocaust: Today's Final Solution* (St. Louis: Landmark, 1983), p. 83.
4. Peter Singer, *Practical Ethics* (Cambridge: Cambridge University Press, 1979), pp. 122–23.
5. Sharon Begley, "Nature's Baby Killers," *Newsweek,* September 6, 1982, p. 78.

right to life in the Fifth and Fourteenth amendments. The Declaration of Independence calls the right to life an "unalienable" right with which we are "endowed by our Creator." So the right to life is absolute, but the right of privacy is limited. For example, the Constitution grants no right to abuse children or commit rape as long as it is done privately. And certainly there is no right to kill privately. But active euthanasia is killing. It is taking innocent human lives, and this is both unconstitutional and un-Christian.

It Is Not Merciful to Kill a Sufferer

First of all, the argument for euthanasia, like the argument for abortion, is misdirected. Killing an unborn human does not avoid child abuse; it *is* child abuse! Likewise, killing deformed infants and suffering adults does not avoid human misery; it inflicts the misery of death. Second, even if euthanasia avoids more suffering, this does not justify it. The end does not justify any means; it only justifies *good* ones. And killing innocent people is not a good act; it is an evil one (Exod. 20:13). Third, if any good end (avoiding suffering) justifies the means (killing), then killing, abortion, and euthanasia proponents could save millions of lives that are taken by these means. Yet no euthanasia proponent would allow this.

There Is Much to Be Learned Through Suffering

Much of the pro-euthanasia rhetoric emphasizes the avoidance of suffering. Suffering is a great evil to be avoided at all cost, even the cost of one's life. This is not a Christian view of suffering. James wrote, "Consider it pure joy, my brothers, whenever you face trials of many kinds, because you know that the testing of your faith develops perseverance. Perseverance must finish its work so that you may be mature and complete, not lacking anything" (James 1:2–4). The apostle Paul told the Christians at Rome that "we know that suffering produces perseverance; perseverance, character; and character, hope" (Rom. 5:3–4).

Far from being an evil to avoid at all cost, suffering can be a time of refining and character building (Job 23:10). James said of Job's suffering that "the Lord is full of compassion and mercy" (James 5:11). Of course, "no discipline seems pleasant at the time, but painful. Later on, however, it produces a harvest of righteousness and peace for those who have been trained by it" (Heb. 12:11).

There Is No Price Tag on Human Life

The pro-euthanasia argument concerning the relief of financial strain is based on the fallacious premise that a price tag can be placed on human life. It wrongly assumes that we should protect and preserve life only if we can afford it. But this is materialistic, not moral. It is a confusion of categories. No material value can be placed on a spiritual value such as life made in God's image. Jesus said, "What good is it for a man to gain the whole world, yet forfeit his soul?" (Mark 8:36). One human life is more valuable than any thing in this world (Matt. 6:26). Hence, to argue that we should take life in order to save money is a distorted and materialistic view of human life.

The End Does Not Justify the Means

The same basic utilitarian errors (see chap. 4 also) lie behind the argument that euthanasia will relieve society of a great burden. First, this overlooks the intrinsic value of an individual human life. Second, it wrongly assumes that the end justifies the means (killing). Third, it calculates results only in material but not in spiritual terms. Fourth, euthanasia can be a tyrannical tool (consider Hitler) with which to rob millions of their human rights.

Humans Are Not Animals

Another fatal assumption behind the pro-euthanasia arguments is that humans have evolved from animals and basically are animals. Thus, just as we weed out and breed out undesired traits in animals, even so we should eliminate undesired strains in the human race. As a matter of fact, the reason a Christian could shoot a horse hopelessly trapped in a burning barn, but not kill a suffering human being, is precisely because a human is not a horse! Once we reduce human beings to animals, then a host of horrendous evils follow logically, including human experimentation, killing AIDS victims, and even genocide. But even most ardent proponents of euthanasia oppose these practices.

Different Kinds of Passive Euthanasia

Now that we have explained and evaluated active euthanasia from a Christian perspective, it is time to look at what is often called passive euthanasia. Two distinct views go by this name and must be differentiated.

Active euthanasia means to *produce* death. Passive euthanasia, on the other hand, means to *allow* death. The former is morally wrong but the latter may be morally right, depending on whether it results from withholding natural means of sustaining life or from withdrawing unnatural means of resisting irreversible sickness. Passive euthanasia that withdraws natural means of life support in order to "allow" the death is called unnatural passive euthanasia. Passive euthanasia that withdraws unnatural life support is called natural passive euthanasia.

Unnatural Passive Euthanasia

Unnatural passive euthanasia is allowing someone to die by deliberately withholding natural means of sustaining life. Natural means are such normal methods of life sustenance as food, water, and air. Unnatural means include mechanical devices such as respirators and artificial organs. In view of this distinction, an important point must be made: not all so-called passive euthanasia is morally justified from a Christian point of view. For example, starving an infant is passive euthanasia, but by "allowing" the baby to die, one is really responsible for taking its life. This is morally wrong.

Natural Passive Euthanasia

Since the withholding of food, air, and water leads directly to the baby's death, it is negligent homicide. On the other hand, withholding unnatural means leads only indirectly to the individual's death. So withholding natural means is tantamount to active euthanasia, since the act leads directly to the death of the individual. Hence, when we speak about morally justified cases of passive euthanasia, we are referring only to those that fall into the category of *natural passive euthanasia*. Only in cases of irreversible disease should a person be allowed to die naturally by withholding unnatural life-sustaining equipment.

Discussion of Passive Euthanasia

The debate over euthanasia is basically a clash of world views. From a secular humanist perspective euthanasia makes sense, but within a Judeo-Christian context it is morally unacceptable. In order to understand the differences, it will be helpful to contrast them in table 9.1.

It Is Contrary to God's Sovereignty over Life

By "euthanasia," we mean active euthanasia and unnatural passive euthanasia (such as starving someone to death). Both are a direct human cause of death. This is morally unacceptable from a Christian perspective because it rejects God's sovereignty over human life. According to the Bible, God is the Creator and owner of all things (Gen. 1:1; Ps. 24:1). He made humans in his own image (Gen. 1:27) and holds them responsible to him for human life.

When Cain killed Abel, the blood of Abel cried directly to God for vengeance (Gen. 4:10). Moses was told by God, "I put to death and I

TABLE 9.1

The Secular Humanist and
Judeo-Christian World Views

Secular Humanist View	Judeo-Christian View
No Creator	A Creator
Humans not created	Humans are created
No God-given values	God-given values
Man determines right	Man discovers right

bring to life . . . and no one can deliver out of my hand" (Deut. 32:39). When Pharaoh challenged God's sovereignty saying, "Who is the LORD, that I should obey him?" he soon found out when God took the life of all Egypt's firstborn sons, including Pharaoh's (Exod. 11:4–7). When God (through Moses) produced life out of the dust, the magicians of Pharaoh cried out, "This is the finger of God" (Exod. 8:19). God alone is sovereign over life. And since human life is in his image, he has placed a social sanction upon it. God alone created human life, and God alone has the right to take an innocent life. Euthanasia is an attempt to preempt God of his sovereign right over human life.

It Is Against the Sanctity of Human Life

Not only is God sovereign over human life, but human life is sacred. It is made in the image and likeness of God (Gen. 1:27). Because of this, it is wrong to kill an innocent human being. When bloodshed and violence filled the earth, God destroyed it with a flood (Gen. 6:11) and then instituted human government with the authority of capital punishment. The reason for this was stated explicitly by God: "Whoever sheds the blood of man, by man shall his blood be shed; for in the image of God has God made man" (Gen. 9:6). Human life is sacred and God-like. For this reason it is even wrong to curse another human being (James 3:9).

Unlike animals, human beings are rational (Col. 3:10; Jude 10), moral beings. They resemble God and are morally responsible to him (Gen. 2:16–17). They can be holy as he is holy (Lev. 11:44) and are exhorted to moral perfection, just as their "heavenly Father is perfect" (Matt. 5:48). Because of the sacredness of human life, God has forbidden that anyone kill another, for he has thereby indirectly attacked God.

It Is a Form of Suicide or Murder

Scripture is emphatic in proclaiming that murder is wrong. It is one of the Ten Commandments: "You shall not murder" (Exod. 20:13). The penalty for violating this command is death (Exod. 21:12–13). Since suicide is also a form of homicide, it too comes under the prohibition against murder. Killing one's self is both a rejection of God's sovereignty over life and an attack upon the sanctity of life. It matters not whether the human life is our own or another's; it is still in God's image, and he is sovereign over it. Euthanasia is either voluntary or not voluntary. But whether it is self-inflicted or inflicted by another, it is still a form of homicide. In either case, the Bible prohibits it.

It Is Specifically Condemned in Scripture

Even the most desperate believer in the Bible who wished to die never contemplated taking his own life but prayed, like Jonah, "O LORD, please take my life from me, for death is better to me than life" (Jon. 4:3 NASB; see also Job 3). And the few cases of suicide recorded in the Bible are condemned by God. King Saul's suicide is a case in point (1 Sam. 31; 2 Sam. 1). So horrible was the crime that Saul's armor-bearer refused to obey the command of his mortally wounded master. As a result, "Saul took his own sword and fell on it" (1 Sam. 31:4). The same is true of Abimelech's assisted suicide (Judg. 9:54) of which the Bible says, "thus God repaid the wickedness that Abimelech had done" (v. 56).

Suicide is a particularly abhorrent crime, because it not only violates God's sovereignty and life's sanctity, but it also fails to take responsibility for the life God has entrusted to us. It fails to show the basic self-respect of which Paul spoke when he declared that "no one ever hated his own body, but he feeds and cares for it" (Eph. 5:29). Scripture commends giving one's life for another (John 5:13; Rom. 5:7).

It Is Based on a Humanistic Ethic

Humanist Manifesto II specifically recommends abortion, suicide, and euthanasia. This flows naturally from humanists' rejection of God-given values and acceptance of a situational ethic. They claim that "the nature of the universe depicted by modern science makes unacceptable any supernatural or cosmic guarantee of human values." This follows from their belief that "the universe is self-existing and not created."[6] If there is no Creator, then he cannot be the source or guarantor of any values. Thus, it would follow, as they claim, that "moral

---

6. Paul Kurtz, ed., *Humanist Manifestos I and II* (Buffalo: Prometheus, 1973), p. 8.

values derive their source from human experience. Ethics is *autonomous* and *situational,* needing no theological or ideological sanction."[7]

Of course, once God and God-given values are denied, then Dostoevsky was right when he said in *The Brothers Karamazov* if God is dead then "everything is lawful." Indeed, the *Humanist Manifesto* goes on to demand "an individual's right to die with dignity, euthanasia, and the right to suicide."[8] This actually confirms what is logically inherent in their position, namely, that euthanasia follows from a denial of divine sanctions on human life. Conversely, if God has created life in his image, then the reality of God is the basis for the sanctity of life and dignity of man. Since a secular humanistic ethic rejects this, it destroys the barriers that protect human life.

It Cheapens the Value of Human Life

Euthanasia, like abortion that leads to it (see chap. 8), cheapens the value of human life. A classic example is that of Dr. Bernard N. Nathanson, who operated one of the largest abortion clinics in the western world, responsible for killing some sixty thousand unborn babies. According to his own testimony, what guided him was "a humanistic philosophy drawn from modern biological data, not from religious creeds."[9] Using his own "humanistic" ethic, Nathanson was dehumanized by the process of performing abortions. Euthanasia is even more dehumanizing since, unlike abortion, the actual death is not usually seen by the doctor or nurses.

A society cannot engage in the wholesale slaughter of innocent life without paying a sobering price. The value of life is significantly cheapened by such callous disregard for human beings. When we do not respect life before birth, it affects our attitude toward life after birth. When we do not respect the dying, it affects our attitude toward the living. Human life is a continuous and communal web. "For none of us lives to himself alone and none of us dies to himself alone" (Rom. 14:7). Hence, what affects one member of the race affects all.

It Produces Guilt in the Family and Society

The decision to remove artificial life support from a loved one is a heavy load to bear, even when, as in some cases of indirect passive euthanasia, it may be morally justified. But when it is a humanly initiated act deliberately aimed at extinguishing a life that God in his

7. Ibid., p. 17.
8. Ibid., p. 19.
9. Bernard N. Nathanson, *Aborting America* (Garden City, N.Y.: Doubleday, 1979), p. 259.

sovereignty has not chosen to take, then the load of guilt is heavy. A society that permits the slaughter of innocents, whether young or old, will bear this heavy load of guilt.

Discussion of Natural Passive Euthanasia

Taking a human life by euthanasia is morally wrong no matter how well-intended the motives are for doing so. It is always wrong to intentionally take another human life as such. However, it is not always wrong to allow someone to die, especially if it is a natural death. Of course, withholding food and water to starve a person to death is murder, even though it is by definition a form of passive euthanasia. This is because withholding these natural life-sustaining elements leads directly to death. However, this leaves open the discussion of when, if ever, it is morally right to withhold unnatural life-sustaining means and allow someone to die naturally.

Some Important Differences

As we have already seen, taking a human life by infanticide or euthanasia is never right, but allowing someone to die is not always wrong. If we "allow" a person to die by deliberately withholding food and water, then it is murder, even though it is called "passive" euthanasia. This is because the action leads directly to death. But withholding unnatural means of sustaining life is not always wrong. It now remains to discuss precisely where the line is drawn between cases of passive euthanasia that are justified and those that are not. Table 9.2 summarizes the situation.

It is never right either to take a life or to withhold ordinary life-sustaining means such as food, water, and air. The only time allowing a death can be justified is when we are withdrawing unnatural life-saving mechanisms or for cases of irreversible disease.

Guidelines for the Decision

There are times when the heroic use of unnatural means are a hindrance, not a help, to the process of natural death, which is under

TABLE 9.2

Active and Passive Euthanasia

Active Euthanasia	Passive Euthanasia	
Taking life	Allowing death by withholding	
	natural means	unnatural means

God's sovereign hand (Eccles. 3:2; Heb. 9:27). This is when extraordi-nary human efforts are really prolonging death rather than prolonging life. When artificial life supports are interfering with the natural pro-cess of death, rather than enriching the person's natural life, then their use is wrong. It is resisting the hand of God involved in the very process of death.

Keeping a comatose person who has an incurable disease alive on a machine when he is irreversibly dying is unnecessary. In fact, it could be viewed as unethical because it is opposing the very processes of natural mortality that God has ordained. God has appointed that all must die (Gen. 2:16–17; Rom. 5:12). He has declared that there are natural limits to life (Ps. 90:10). Extraordinary efforts to fight the divinely appointed limits of our mortality are really working in op-position to God.

Usually the most important decision is the one made to put a person on a life-sustaining machine. Sometimes this is unnecessary, and it creates a later ethical dilemma concerning when the machine should be disconnected. Life has become so mechanized that technology has created its own new morality. The scientific advances that have made the extension of life possible have also made the process of dying longer; technology is a mixed blessing. Hence, an important moral decision should be made at a very early stage concerning whether it is necessary to put someone on a life-support machine or not.

Who makes these crucial decisions to connect an individual to or disconnect him from a life-sustaining machine? Some guidelines are in order.

The disease must be irreversible—No one should be allowed to die if we have the means at hand to save his life. If possible, correctable situations should be corrected. Unless the process of the disease is irreversible, even natural passive euthanasia is not justifiable.

The patient has veto power—First and foremost, if the patient is conscious and rational, then he has veto power over any decision not to extend his life by artificial means. If the patient is not conscious, then all other things being equal, his living will on the matter should be respected. If the patient is not conscious and has expressed no will on the matter previously, then others responsible for him must make the decision. In short, representative decisions, but not substitute de-cisions, can be made regarding procedures.

A collective decision—But who should make the decision when others cannot make it for themselves? The Bible says there is wisdom in joint decisions (Num. 35:30; Prov. 24:6). Since there are spiritual, legal, moral, and family implications to the decision, it seems wise to con-sider all aspects. So the decision should not be made until there is consent from pastor, doctor, lawyer, and family members. But even before this—pray. God should be consulted first before any decision is contemplated. After all, he is sovereign and supernatural. It may be his will to heal, and he is waiting for us to ask (James 4:2; 5:14–15). God is able to perform miracles, and he should be sought first on behalf of the sufferer. But if after fervent and repeated prayer, medical science is not able, nor is God willing, to perform a miracle, then we must rest assured that God's grace is sufficient (2 Cor. 12:9).

An Evaluation of Natural Passive Euthanasia in Irreversible Sickness

Even in this carefully circumscribed sense of limited passive euthanasia, there are some significant problems. The two most prominent ones deal with the meaning of "irreversible" and "unnatural means."

What Does Dying Mean?

The definition of "irreversible" is important to the decision because it circumscribes the legitimate occasions when withholding extraordinary means is called for. In practical terms a condition is "irreversible" when there are no known available medical means to correct the injury or disease process leading to death. In other words, there is no medical hope for recovery, and it is only a matter of time before a person dies. Medically, this means that even the best unnatural (mechanical) means will not stop death.

What Are Unnatural Means?

Natural means include food, water, and oxygen. Unnatural means would definitely include a respirator, an artificial heart, or a kidney machine. However, things which do not fall clearly into these categories, such as intravenous feeding, oxygen masks, and antibiotics, pose a problem. Although intravenous feeding is not natural in the sense of being produced by nature, neither is it purely artificial, since it is food and food is a natural means of sustaining life. Hence, to withdraw someone's intravenous feeding can be tantamount to starving him to death. The same would apply to artificially supplied oxygen. In these cases the morality of the decision will be conditioned by the availability of the technology. Obviously, if the special equipment is not available, there is no moral obligation to use it. The same is true of all technology and drugs. Heroic efforts with unnatural means are not a moral duty when one is irreversibly ill.

Is It Unmerciful Not to Relieve Pain by Death?

Are not some people suffering so intensely that only death will relieve their pain? Isn't it unmerciful to refuse to relieve their extreme pain? In response, several things should be noted. First, the Bible provides an answer to this question. Solomon wrote:

> Give strong drink to him who is perishing,
> and wine to those in bitter distress;
> let them drink and forget their poverty,
> and remember their misery no more.
> [Prov. 31:6–7 RSV]

Although strong drink is condemned as a beverage that causes drunkenness (Prov. 20:1; Isa. 5:11), it is recommended for those who are dying so that it can relieve them of their suffering. In brief, the Bible recommends that the dying be given a shot but not that they be shot. The dying should be shot with a sedative but not a bullet.

What if Pain Relievers Hasten Death?

Sometimes the treatment used to reduce pain also hastens death. Is this then an unjustified use of passive euthanasia? Not necessarily. In such cases the principle of double effect may be invoked. Where two effects, one good and one evil, follow from the same action, it is our moral responsibility to will the good one. The evil effect is simply a necessary concomitant of the good action that is taken; there is no moral culpability for it. For example, when it is necessary to amputate a leg with gangrene there are two effects. First, the life of the individual can be saved. Second, the body will be mutilated and handicapped. But this evil consequence of amputation is to save a life. Likewise, sometimes the pain is so great that the medicine necessary to counter it will also hasten death. Patients sometimes die from surgery, but the potential benefits outweigh the risks.

Is There a Right to Refuse Treatment?

Many moral dilemmas are created by the decision to place persons on life-saving mechanical devices. Is it morally wrong to refuse this kind of treatment? In responding to this, an important distinction should be made—the difference between repairing life to function naturally and sustaining life artificially. Certainly under most circumstances, it is morally wrong to refuse treatment that would save one's life. Life saving is an essential part of the medical service. Refusing to allow cuts and wounds that could cause one's death to be treated is tantamount to suicide. These are all ordinary medical treatments. It is the extraordinary treatment, involving life-sustaining or life-prolonging mechanisms, that is the question.

While there is clearly a moral obligation to accept treatment to repair life, there is no absolute obligation to accept treatment that would sustain life artificially. We should accept treatment that would preserve life, but need not accept treatment that really will only prolong death. There would be, for example, no moral duty for a Christian to take a pill (were it available) to double his life span. Likewise, there is no absolute moral duty to take kidney dialysis treatment or even chemotherapy. It may be desirable or even wise to accept such treatment, but it is not morally necessary as such. One can accept the natural consequences of disease and mortality that God has appointed (Gen. 3; Rom. 5). Indeed, eventually we must all do so.

Summary and Conclusion

Euthanasia means good or painless death. Active euthanasia is taking a human life, and passive euthanasia is simply allowing death. The former is morally wrong from a Christian perspective, but the latter may be morally acceptable, as long as it is a natural and irreversible death, not an unnatural or reversible one.

Natural passive euthanasia is allowing death to occur naturally by withholding unnatural means of sustaining life, such as heart-and-lung machines. Natural means of sustaining life include food, water, and air. Deliberately withholding these is unnatural passive euthanasia, and it is morally unacceptable from a Christian perspective.

Even in morally acceptable natural passive euthanasia, there are difficult decisions. It should be exercised only when someone is irreversibly dying and then not against his expressed will. Also, the decision should be by consensus of pastor, doctor, lawyer, and family. God should be sought first and repeatedly in prayer for healing. And when the course of death is medically irreversible and no divine intervention is forthcoming, it is morally justified to stop unnatural efforts to prolong the process of dying.

Select Readings

Grisez, Germain, and Joseph M. Boyle, Jr. *Life and Death with Liberty and Justice: A Contribution to the Euthanasia Debate.* Notre Dame, Ind.: University of Notre Dame Press, 1980.

Hauerwas, Stanley. *Suffering Presence: Theological Reflections on Medicine, the Mentally Handicapped, and the Church.* Notre Dame, Ind.: University of Notre Dame Press, 1986.

Hitler, Adolf. *Mein Kampf.* London: Hurst and Blackett, 1939.

Humphry, Derek. *Let Me Die before I Wake.* Los Angeles: Hemlock Society, 1985.

Koop, C. Everett. *The Right to Live; the Right to Die.* Wheaton: Tyndale House, 1976.

Moreland, J. P. "James Rachels and the Active Euthanasia Debate." *Journal of the Evangelical Theological Society* 31, 1 (March 1988): 81–90.

Rachels, James. "Active and Passive Euthanasia." *New England Journal of Medicine* 292 (January 9, 1975): 78–80.

10

Biomedical Issues

Technology has created new ethical issues. Artificial insemination, test-tube babies, surrogate mothers, organ transplantation, organ harvesting, gene splicing, and cloning are all medical realities. There is no longer a question of whether they *can* be done; it is only a question of whether they *ought* to be done. Here again the viewpoints can be broadly divided between two categories: a secular humanist approach and a Judeo-Christian perspective. There are intramural debates in each camp that will emerge as the discussion unfolds.

A Secular Humanist Perspective: Playing God

Nowhere are the lines of demarcation between the secular humanist and Christian perspectives clearer than in biomedical issues. This is because ethical decisions are not made in a vacuum. They are made from within a world view. And it is in the human role of deciding what is right and wrong that the two positions are most evidently in conflict. The differences are summarized in table 10.1. Given these differences, conflicts are inevitable. Such conflicts manifest themselves in many areas of biomedical concern. These will become evident as the two positions unfold in our discussion.

Secular humanists have stated their beliefs repeatedly and clearly. Their *Humanist Manifestos* (1933, 1973) support abortion, euthanasia,

TABLE 10.1

The Judeo-Christian and
Secular Humanist World Views

Judeo-Christian	Secular Humanist
There is a Creator	There is no Creator
Man was specially created	Man evolved from animals
God is sovereign over life	Man is sovereign over life
Sanctity-of-life principle	Quality-of-life principle
End does not justify means	End justifies the means

and suicide. They speak glowingly about technology and emphatically deny that there is any God in control. They affirm that "we need to extend the uses of scientific method. . . . Confronted by many possible futures, we must decide which to pursue."[1] They disavow any Creator or divine aid, boasting, "No deity will save us; we must save ourselves."[2] Hence, they "affirm that moral values derive their source from human experience. Ethics is *autonomous* and *situational,* needing no theological or ideological sanctions."[3] From this context several crucial elements of their position emerge in relation to biomedical issues.

Humans Are Responsible for the Quality of Life

Paul Kurtz, the author of *Humanist Manifesto II,* set forth the humanist position well in *Forbidden Fruit,* when he wrote:

> We, not God, are responsible for our destiny. Accordingly we must create our own ethical universes. We should seek to transform a blind and conscious morality into a rationally based one, retaining the best wisdom of the past but devising new ethical principles and judging them by their consequences and testing them in the context of lived experience.[4]

One consequence to be kept in mind is the "quality of life" which, according to Kurtz, can justify in vitro fertilization, and even active

1. Paul Kurtz, ed., *Humanist Manifestos I and II* (Buffalo: Prometheus, 1973), p. 14.
2. Ibid., p. 16.
3. Ibid., p. 17.
4. Paul Kurtz, *Forbidden Fruit: The Ethics of Humanism* (Buffalo: Prometheus, 1988), p. 18.

euthanasia.[5] Indeed, the same principle is behind the right to abortion and the right to suicide.[6]

Genetic improvement of the race is also based on the so-called quality-of-life principle. Nobel prizewinner Dr. James Watson argued that no newborn infant should be declared human until it has passed certain tests regarding its genetic endowment. "If a child were not declared alive until three days after birth, then all parents could be allowed the choice . . . [to] allow the child to die . . . and save a lot of misery and suffering."[7]

Individuals Have Sovereignty over Their Own Lives

For secular humanists God is not sovereign over life—man is. Each individual has the right to live and the right to die. Although most humanists encourage life, they insist that they have the right to end it as well. Thus suicide and voluntary euthanasia are defended as moral rights. Ironically enough, abortion is also considered a right, and this generally is based on the grounds of the freedom of choice of the mother. Although some admit that the unborn are human, others confess difficulty in knowing when human life begins. Some claim that human life does not begin until birth and others say it begins when one becomes a self-conscious individual, which is nearly two years of age.

Euthanasia is another manifestation of the humanist's belief that the individual is sovereign over his own life. This belief has given rise to voluntary euthanasia groups like the Society for the Right to Die and the Hemlock Society, whose book *Let Me Die before I Wake* provides information for those who wish to commit suicide. Its founder, Derek Humphry, boasts that he has helped make euthanasia respectable and "also helped a lot of people die well."[8]

The Duty to Create a Superior Race

All secular humanists believe in biological evolution. Many believe that because humans have advanced to such a technological level, they have a duty to guide the future evolution of the race. For some the hope goes beyond a bionic man to genetically engineered humans. Gene splicing holds the promise of creating and patenting new ani-

5. Ibid., pp. 217, 222.
6. Ibid., pp. 217, 220.
7. J. C. Willke and Barbara Willke, *Abortion: Questions and Answers* (Cincinnati: Hayes, 1985), p. 204.
8. Derek Humphry, *Reader,* June 29, 1983.

mals. Sperm banks, artificial insemination, and surrogate mothers now make it possible to breed superior human beings. The ultimate goal is a human being totally engineered to specifications, the creation of a superior breed. Prenatal tests can already warn parents of genetically impure offspring and abortion can eliminate them. The final goal is for a completely fabricated human being.

One signer of *Humanist Manifesto II,* Joseph Fletcher, believes that coercive or compulsory genetic control is justified in cases where carriers of genetic disease do not abstain voluntarily from having children. Here the end justifies the means. That is, the goal of a genetically purified race justifies the compulsory sterilization necessary to achieve it.

The End Justifies the Means

In *Situation Ethics,* Fletcher states flatly, "Only the end justifies the means; nothing else."[9] Although few humanists are this frank, most operate on the same principle, particularly when it comes to advances in medical science. For example, when it was discovered that brain tissue from aborted babies could aid in treating Parkinson's disease, this good end was considered by many to be justification for the means necessary to obtain the tissue (namely, an aborted baby). The brisk business in organ transplants has likewise created a need for more organs. Since fresh tissues are better, tissues are taken from live babies aborted by hysterotomy.

Because the advancement of medical science depends on experimentation, many have taken advantage of the abortion business to use the live babies for experimentation. Some scientists speak openly of growing fetuses for spare parts.

An Evaluation of the Humanist Biomedical Ethic

The humanists' approval of certain biomedical procedures for the supposed benefit of the individual or the race flows from their presuppositions. If there is no God and man is simply a higher animal, then there seems to be no logical reason to deny many of their conclusions. There are, however, some good rational grounds for challenging their presuppositions.

The "Quality-of-Life" Principle Is Utilitarian

The so-called quality-of-life principle is a thinly veiled form of utilitarianism. In addition to the arguments already given against ethical

9. Joseph Fletcher, *Situation Ethics: The New Morality* (Philadelphia: Westminster, 1966), p. 120.

utilitarianism (see chap. 4), there are good reasons for rejecting this medical form of it. First of all, what does "quality of life" mean? Is it a physical, social, or spiritual quality? If a combination, then in what proportion? Often, it is an ill-defined and ambiguous catch-all term used to justify actions that lack any proper ethical quality whatsoever. Second, who decides what "quality" means? The patient? The doctor? Society? Third, which people get this "quality" treatment? On what basis do we discriminate? Age? Race? Social rank? Fourth, how do we know for sure what procedures will bring about this elusive "quality of life." One would have to be God in order to know all the factors necessary to predict that our genetic tinkering would really improve the race. It might cure some problems and cause greater ones.

We Are Not Sovereign over Life

The Bible makes it unmistakably clear that we are not sovereign over our own life. "The LORD gave and the LORD has taken away" (Job 1:21). God said to Moses, "I put to death and I bring to life" (Deut. 32:39). God created life (Gen. 1:21, 27) and he alone sustains it (Acts 17:28). Hence, we have no right to take innocent life (Gen. 9:6; Exod. 20:13).

But in addition to these scriptural truths, there are many other obvious reasons for concluding that we do not possess sovereignty over life. First of all, it is evident to all that we did not create life. Life was here before man arrived on earth, and human life clearly did not begin as a result of human activity. Second, in spite of all our medical advances, we cannot avoid death. This too is out of human hands. Third, humans have not been able to create life, certainly not human life. Thus far human brilliance has produced only some biologically interesting chemicals (e.g., amino acids) and crossed and spliced existing forms of life. But humans have not created from scratch their own new living things, to say nothing of a full-fledged human being.

Even if we could produce some simple forms (and therefore had some kind of claim on them) there is no realistic prospect of creating anything like a human life. But if we did not bring human life into this world, then we have no right to claim sovereignty over when it leaves. The secular humanist pretension to sovereignty over life collapses in the face of the facts of life.

There Is No Duty to Produce a Superior Race

Evolutionists often boast of their desires to forward the evolutionary process and produce a superior race. Indeed, the subtitle of Darwin's famous book, *On the Origin of Species* (1859), has racist overtones: "The Preservation of Favored Races in the Struggle for Life." Carrying

Darwin's idea forward, Adolf Hitler used natural selection as his model for producing the superior race. He wrote, "If nature does not wish that weaker individuals should mate with stronger, she wishes even less that a superior race should intermingle with an inferior one." Why? "Because in such a case all her efforts, throughout hundreds of thousands of years, to establish an evolutionary higher stage of being, may thus be rendered futile."[10] The famous evolutionist Julian S. Huxley contended, "In the light of evolutionary biology man can now see himself as the sole agent of further evolutionary advance on this planet, and one of the few possible instruments of progress in the universe at large." Huxley sees man as "the business manager for the cosmic process of evolution."[11]

The exaggerated expectations of producing a superior race are unfounded for several reasons. First of all, there is no real evidence that the present race was produced by any naturalistic evolutionary process. Both Scripture and the scientific evidence point to God as the cause of the human species.[12] Second, science, with all its technology and touted brilliance, has not been able to permanently improve even a fruit fly. We have a long way to go to "improve" man. Third, even if we could make permanent changes in the human species there is no ethical reason why we should. "Can" does not imply "ought" any more than "is" implies "ought." Just because we can do something does not mean that we should do it. Ability does not imply morality. Fourth, even if we were able to actually produce changes in the human species, how would we know they were better, not merely different? By what standard would we judge them better? It would beg the question to answer, "by the desired human standard." And, as we will see for the secular humanist there is no revealed standard that sanctions such a procedure.

The End Does Not Justify the Means

Since the "end justifies the means" ethic has already been critiqued (see chaps. 3 and 4), we will only summarize the problems here. First, ends do not justify means. Means must have their own justification. Second, even ends need justification. Not every goal is good, even if it is highly desired by many people. Many Germans desired the obliteration of the Jews. This does not justify it. Third, if good ends justified any means, then killing political dissenters for national harmony would

10. Adolf Hitler, *Mein Kampf* (London: Hurst and Blackett, 1939), pp. 239–40.
11. Julian S. Huxley, *Essays of a Biologist* (Harmondsworth: Penguin, 1939), p. 132.
12. Norman L. Geisler and J. Kerby Anderson, *Origin Science* (Grand Rapids: Baker, 1987), pp. 127–57.

be justifiable, or killing AIDS patients in order to curb the spread of this deadly disease would be morally justified. Simple reflection reveals numerous similar illustrations of morally unacceptable consequences that would follow from applying such an ethic.

A Christian Perspective on Biomedical Ethics: Serving God

While the humanist approach to biomedical ethics is to play God, the Christian approach is to use medical advances to serve God. Humanists believe that man is sovereign over life; Christians hold that God is sovereign over it. This does not mean, of course, that there is no role for technology and medicine to improve human life. It means, rather, that we do not use it to create human life. It should be used to cultivate but not control what God has given.

A comparison of the two approaches to biomedical issues will help focus the differences and serve as a springboard for articulating the basic principles of a Christian approach to biomedical issues. Table 10.2 notes the major differences.

There is a marked difference between Christian and humanist approaches to biomedical ethics. Christians believe God is sovereign over life; humanists think man is sovereign. Hence, Christians believe that we should serve God, not play God. Treatment should always be voluntary, not compulsory. The medical task is to improve life, not to create it. God has only made us the maintenance crew, not the engineers of life. Our goal is the more modest one of genetic fitness, not the grandiose one of genetic fabrication. We work in cooperation with nature, not to have control over it. In fact we conform to nature as

TABLE 10.2

Christian and Humanist Approaches to Biomedical Issues

Christian View: Serving God	Humanistic View: Playing God
Voluntary treatment	Compulsory treatment
Improving human life	Creating human life
Repairing human life	Recreating human life
Maintenance of life	Engineering of life
Genetic fitness	Genetic fabrication
Cooperation with nature	Control over nature
Conformity to nature	Power over nature

God's creation; we do not seek power over it as our creation. In short, the legitimate role of the Christian in biomedical areas is therapeutic, not eugenic.

Some Basic Fallacies Exposed

There are some basic assumptions in the modern humanistic approach to biomedical ethics that need exposing from a Christian perspective. Often they are implied, not stated. But they are operative nonetheless.

What is being done ought to be done—As any student of logic knows, this is the famous is-ought fallacy. Just because we are aborting babies does not mean we should be (see chap. 8), any more than the fact that rape and child abuse are occurring means that they ought to be. Likewise, the fact that scientists are cloning, gene splicing, and harvesting organs does not automatically mean that they should be doing so. These activities need some moral justification of their own. "Is" does not imply "ought."

If it can be done, it should be done—Another similar and common ethical fallacy is that what can be done, ought to be done. There seems to be an implied ethic in the progress of science which dictates that whatever humans can invent, they should invent and use. Scientific progress has been absolutized. Just because something is technologically possible does not make it morally permissible. It is technologically possible to destroy the human race by nuclear war, but no one in his right mind believes the race should be destroyed! Technological progress is not necessarily ethical progress. It may be ethical regress instead.

The end justifies the means—This fallacy, already examined, becomes emotionally appealing when the factor of suffering is added. Why, we are asked, should not brain tissue from aborted babies be used to help cure those with Parkinson's disease? Why should people be allowed to suffer when we have the means of alleviating it? The answer, of course, is that the means are evil. Killing an innocent human being to alleviate the suffering of another is not a morally justifiable means of attaining this end.

Two wrongs make a right—Scarcely anyone admits to believing this, but many people act upon it. It is never right to correct a wrong by doing a wrong. Adding a wrong to a wrong does not take away the first wrong—it simply adds another wrong to it. Hence, the fact that the wrong of abortion is occurring does not justify adding to it the additional wrong of experimentation with the live aborted babies— regardless of the information that may be gained from it. There is no ethical obligation to know everything no matter how we get the information. If this were so, then government invasion of privacy would be justified by the wealth of helpful information it could provide to curb crime and help society.

Some Basic Principles Stated

Now that we have examined the difference between a Christian and a humanistic approach to biomedical issues and exposed some fallacious humanistic principles, let us state some of the basic principles involved in a Christian approach to these problems.

The sovereignty of God—First and foremost is the principle of God's sovereignty over life. God created every living thing (Gen. 1:21) and human beings in his image and likeness (1:27). God controls both life and death. He gives life and he takes it away (Job 1:21). From dust we come, and to dust we return (Gen. 3:19). The Lord kills and makes alive (Deut. 32:39). We are not our own but his. He has made us, and we belong to him. This being the case, humans have no right to seek control of human life, to try to "advance" its evolution or to tinker with it genetically.

The dignity of man—Another principle at the heart of a Christian biomedical ethic is the dignity of man. Humans are made in God's image and likeness (Gen. 1:27). They are the crown of his creation. Human beings both represent and resemble God. It is for this reason that murder is such a heinous crime, for it is killing God in effigy. This is why God instituted capital punishment for capital crimes (see chap. 11), saying, "Whoever sheds the blood of man, by man shall his blood be shed; for in the image of God has God made man" (Gen. 9:6). Human beings have such dignity that it is even wrong to curse them, because they "have been made in God's likeness" (James 3:9). This dignity of human life includes the body, which should be cared for (Eph. 5:29) and even buried with respect, anticipating its final resurrection (1 Cor. 15).

The sanctity of life—Human life has both dignity and sanctity. The former calls for respect; the latter for reverence. This is not to say that human life should be worshiped, but only that it should be considered holy. Human life should not be adored as the Creator is, but it should be revered as one of his creations. Humans are not God, but we are God-like. We were made "a little lower than the heavenly beings [angels]" (Ps. 8:5), but were also "crowned with glory and honor." Since God is holy (Lev. 11:44) and we are made in his likeness (Gen. 1:27), it follows that in some sense we share in this moral likeness. This sacredness of life, as it uniquely reflects the very character of God, is the basis for a pro-life stance from conception to death. No matter how badly human life may be scarred or disfigured, it is still God-like and deserves to be treated as the sacred thing it is.

The mortality of life—Another principle endemic to a Christian approach to biomedical issues is the fact of human mortality. This is a fallen world, and the consequence of the fall is death. Adam was told of the tree of knowledge that "when you eat of it you will surely die" (Gen. 2:17). The apostle Paul added, "Sin entered the world through one man, and death through sin, and in this way death came to all men, because all sinned" (Rom. 5:12). Thus "man is destined to die once, and after that to face judgment" (Heb. 9:27). Moses spoke of the limits of human life when he said, "The length of our days is seventy years—or eighty, if we have the strength . . . for they quickly pass, and we fly away" (Ps. 90:10). In short, there are limits to human life in this world. Man is mortal, and human attempts to avoid it or overcome this fact are futile and misdirected.

Charity toward human life—Love is the essence of Christian ethics, for Jesus said this is the greatest commandment: first, to love God and then to love other human beings as ourselves (Matt. 22:37–39). Therefore, it is necessary to apply this love toward human beings in every area of ethical responsibility, including biomedical issues. Christian love (*agape*) is not selfish love. It comes from God, who is love (1 John 4:16), and is to be directed toward others (John 15:13). It is a responsibility we have to God (Matt. 25:45) and to all who are less fortunate than we. Love is not an empty, vacuous feeling or attitude. It is fleshed out in specific commandments. Jesus said, "If ye love me, keep my commandments" (John 14:15 KJV). Hence, the Christian looks to Scripture for guidance in bioethical issues, as well as in other moral matters.

Some Basic Guidelines for Crucial Issues

The preceding discussion has presented a number of biblical guidelines which can be applied to a range of biomedical issues. We will first state the principle and its biblical support and then apply it to specific issues.

Voluntary versus compulsory procedures—Flowing from the fact of freedom and dignity is the principle of autonomy, which entails informed consent. Even otherwise legitimate medical procedures are morally wrong unless there is informed consent to them. The patient should be informed about the nature and possible consequences of the medication or operation, and must give free and uncoerced consent to it. Where the patient is not able to do this because of irrationality or unconsciousness, no organs should be taken, no medical procedure taken except that necessary to preserve his or her life. This is called a best-interest judgment, as opposed to a substituted judgment. The latter takes away the autonomy of the patient.

A forced cure, no matter how beneficial it may be for society, is immoral. For example, compulsory abortions to control population are wrong. Likewise, forced sterilization for eugenic reasons is morally wrong. Abstinence, birth control, or voluntary sterilization are better alternatives. A forced cure is immoral, whether it is imposed on citizens or prisoners. It is in the very nature of morally responsible human acts that they be free and uncoerced.

Informed consent is a necessary foundation for all bioethical decisions, including abortion. It is a tragic moral irony to require informed consent before a teenager in a public school can put an aspirin in her mouth, but not require informed consent before she can kill a baby in her womb.

Mercy-killing versus mercifully allowing death—As previously noted, there is an important difference between taking an innocent life and allowing a death. The former is always wrong; the latter is sometimes right. Intentionally taking an innocent human life is murder, but allowing a natural death may be an act of mercy. Thus mercy-killing is always wrong, but mercifully allowing death is sometimes right.

Preserving life versus prolonging death—The command "You shall not murder" (Exod. 20:13) implies that we should help prevent the unnatural death of innocent people as well. The Bible declares that sins of omission are wrong, as well as sins of commission (James 4:17). Failing to prevent such a death is as culpable as actually causing it. In this sense, there is a duty to prolong human life, and if medical or technical aids are available, they should be rightly utilized. However, the duty to preserve life should be distinguished from a supposed obligation to prolong death. Nowhere does the Bible declare a duty to prolong the agony of death. In fact, attempting to avoid the inevitability of death is contrary to the principle of human mortality (Rom. 5:12; Heb. 9:27).

Artificial means versus natural means—Every attempt should be made to preserve a human life, by whatever means are available. Certainly, food, water, and air should never be withheld from human beings, no matter how small, old, or sick they are. Taking away these natural means of sustaining life is tantamount to causing death. And knowingly causing the death of innocent human beings is murder. Furthermore, when heroic means (technology) are available, they should be used to preserve human life. However, there is no divine duty to use heroic or unnatural means to prolong human death. This is contrary to the principles of human mortality and Christian charity. There is no duty to prolong misery or to fight mortality. Hence, when sustenance of life is artificial and the process of death is irreversible, there is no moral obligation to prolong life by artificial means.

Birth control versus abortion—Some Christians oppose both abortion and birth control. Historically, Roman Catholics have opposed birth control and Protestants favored it. Today, the lines are crossed. However, both sides agree that there is a qualitative difference between taking a human life by abortion and preventing more human lives by birth control. Whatever one can say for or against birth control, it is not murder. It is simply a method of limiting how many children are born, not a method of killing unborn children. Of course, some methods of what is called birth control are really methods of abortion, since they lead directly to the death of a fertilized ovum (which is a human being). But methods of birth control, natural or artificial, that simply prevent fertilization from taking place are not murder. Both Catholics and Protestants agree that it is right to use birth control; the debate is over the legitimacy of *artificial* forms of it.

Correcting versus creating life—This is an imperfect world. God did not plan it that way; man has made a mess of it. The effects of the fall of mankind are evident in the physical world (Gen. 3; Rom. 5, 8) and have taken their toll on human health. There is no biblical imperative that says that we cannot work to correct these imperfections. In fact, the Bible recommends medicine (1 Tim. 5:23) and prayer for healing (James 5:14–15).

Jesus manifested his approval of a medically corrective ministry by spending much of his time healing those who were sick. Likewise, he gave his apostles the ability to "heal the sick" (Matt. 10:8). However, there is a significant difference between correcting imperfect humans and creating perfect ones of our own. Alleviating human suffering due to the fall is a moral duty, but fabricating human beings is not.

Some Basic Issues

Now that the basic principles and guidelines of Christian bioethics have been outlined, it remains to apply them to some of the pressing issues made possible by modern technological advances. Since we have already discussed abortion (chap. 8) and euthanasia (chap. 9), we will not include them here.

Organ transplants—Organ transplantation has become a reality. Heart, lung, and kidney transplants are now common. Hundreds of people have had their lives prolonged because of this corrective technology. Transplantation is in accordance with many biblical principles. First, the principle of charity (love): "Greater love has no one than this, that he lay down his life for his friends" (John 15:13). I find it hard to imagine giving an eye, lung, or kidney to someone who has none, yet some living human beings have done this. How little sacrifice is required to do so when we are dead and no longer in need of these organs! Organ transplantation need not be, as some suggest, a violation of the mortality principle. It can and should be used as a means of prolonging life, not as a means of avoiding the eventuality of death. In this regard it can be questionable when used on the very elderly. For here the chances for surviving the operation are lessened, as is the need for the operation.

There are serious moral questions involved in the transplantation procedure. First of all, it should involve informed consent. No one should be forced to donate his organs, and no organ should be taken without permission of the donor, especially from those who are unable to make this decision (such as the handicapped). No one else has the right to give away a person's organs for him. In this sense my body belongs to me, and death does not erase this right. It is still my body put in my grave. Respect for human dignity demands that the body, which is the remaining symbol of the person, not be pilfered. Just as a national flag is the symbol of the nation and should be treated with respect, even so the body is a symbol of the person and should be treated with the respect due the person who occupied it.

Second, there is a moral question about the life and death status of the donor. The fresher the organ, the greater chances of success in the transplant, and organs from living donors are the best. However, if taking the organ causes death, then it is wrong. With the exception of cases of taking "spare" organs, such as one kidney or one eye, the donor must be brain dead before the organ is taken. Death is difficult to define, but in general terms it means vital signs are lacking, such as breathing, pulse, nerve reaction, or brain wave (EEG). This does not mean that after the person dies that the body cannot be kept "alive" by machine to prevent organ decay. It simply means that we should not hasten death in order to get a fresh organ.

Genetic surgery—Genetic surgery is now a possibility. Is this permissible? Here again the answer depends on whether it is an attempt to correct and restore life as God created it or an attempt to reconstruct it in the way we want it. Is the surgery correcting or creating? Is the procedure maintaining the life God created or is it engineering life the way man wants it? If the surgery is for repairing, not for creating, then it is morally permissible. After all, God created perfect human beings, and he wants us to be as perfect as we can be, even in this fallen world.

There is another type of genetic surgery that is morally wrong from a Christian perspective. God created "male and female" (Gen. 1:27). The fact that they were told to reproduce their kind (v. 28) reveals that this was understood as biological maleness and femaleness. For this reason genetic surgery to change one's sex is morally wrong. Whatever our psychological or sociological tendencies, we should bring them into conformity to the way God made us.

Sex detection and selection—It is now possible to know the sex of the unborn well before birth. Hence, selection of the desired sex is possible. Is this morally right? In the light of the Christian principles stated above, the appropriate response seems to be: sex detection, yes; sex selection, no. There is nothing inherently wrong with knowing in advance whether the baby is a boy or a girl. Sooner or later we will know anyway. Science has now made it possible to know sooner. Science has made it possible to know a lot of things sooner—storms, earthquakes, tornadoes, hurricanes. Few of us would reject this knowledge, but neither should we use it to do evil.

There is an inherent danger in sex-detection methods: they often become means of sex selection. Unfortunately, the only way to select the desired sex *after* it has been detected is by abortion, and that is morally wrong (see chap. 8). So if one chooses to know the sex of one's child before birth (and there is no obligation to do so), one is just as morally obligated to accept it from God's sovereign hand as one is the day it is born. Sex selection *before* conception is not necessarily morally wrong, but it can be both socially and psychologically harmful.

Artificial insemination—There are two forms of artificial insemination: artificial insemination by the husband (AIH), and artificial insemination by a donor (AID). There seem to be no valid moral objections from a Christian perspective to the former. Once one accepts the premise that it is morally permissible to correct impediments to fulfilling God's command to propagate life, then AIH would seem to fit in this category. If not, then one would have to argue against other corrective operations, including those to restore sight.

Sometimes Exodus 4:11 is cited in defense of accepting all our imperfections, even if they are correctable. God said to Moses, "Who makes him deaf or mute? Who gives him sight or makes him blind? Is it not I the LORD?" However, to so use this verse is to wrench it out of context and to ignore much other clear Scripture. First of all, the verse is descriptive, not prescriptive. It is describing the situation the way it is, not necessarily the way it ought to be. Second, in context, it is a statement about God's ability to overcome these difficulties, not about the undesirability of doing so. God said this to Moses because Moses complained to God that he was not eloquent enough to fulfill God's command to speak to Pharaoh (v. 10). Third, if correcting blindness and deafness was wrong, then Jesus often sinned by healing these very imperfections (John 9; Mark 7).

AID raises some moral questions not involved in AIH. Some object that it is "adultery by proxy," since the sperm is not from the woman's husband. However, this objection is a bit far-fetched, since no sexual act with another man is involved, nor need there be any lust entailed. Others consider the so-called one flesh principle as to be opposed to AID, but simply because the conception was not born of sexual intercourse between husband and wife does not mean they are not "one flesh" in their marriage. In fact, the "one flesh" is possible without sexual intercourse; it refers to the intimacy of marriage, not just to sexual intercourse (Gen. 2:24).

Still others object that in AID the baby is not really the husband's child, only the wife's. But if this is pressed it would also be an argument against adoption, where the child is neither the husband's or the wife's.

Finally, some object because of the use of an autosexual act in obtaining the sperm necessary for the insemination. However, if obtaining the sperm is done in the context of a marital relation, the objection loses its force. First of all, inside a marriage the act need not be autosexual; it can be mutual. Second, as long as the act is done without lustful intentions toward a woman other than one's wife, the objection loses its force. Masturbation is wrong as a form of lust and when it is done outside of a marital relationship. It is also unnecessary since there are other alternatives, such as abstinence and marriage.

In short, whatever social, psychological, and legal arguments can be urged, and these should be considered, there seems to be no moral reason against either AIH or AID from a biblical perspective. Of course, a childless couple may want to choose to remain that way or to adopt, but there is no moral duty to do so. They may also choose pregnancy of the wife through artificial insemination.

The morality of artificial insemination within the bounds of marriage does not automatically extend to the unmarried. For example, the Bible does not recommend a believer marrying an unbeliever (1 Cor. 7:39), yet it forbids divorcing an unbelieving spouse (v. 12). Likewise, one-parent families may be necessitated by death or other circumstances. But they are less than ideal under any circumstance, and should not be promoted by artificial insemination. Hence, lesbian or bachelor motherhood by artificial insemination is not God's ideal for a home. Children need a father and a mother. And while God takes special care of wives who once had a husband (widows) (Deut. 14:29; 1 Tim. 5:9), the Bible repeatedly bemoans fatherlessness (Ps. 10:18; 82:3). Fatherless homes are tragedies to be avoided, not models to be encouraged.

Surrogate motherhood—Even for Christians who accept artificial insemination, surrogate motherhood poses some more difficult problems. In effect, it is a "womb for hire," for the mother carrying the baby is not the wife of the husband. And even though there is no adultery involved, nevertheless there are serious social, legal, and psychological problems to be considered. As notable court cases have dramatized, the maternal instinct is strong, and the biological mother often has a difficult time giving up her child.

Theoretically, surrogate motherhood is only the reverse of artificial insemination and is like an adoption. In this respect there is nothing inherently immoral about it. However, we do not live in a theoretical world. Deep-seated human feelings are involved. Surrogate motherhood carries with it tremendous potential for exploitation of womanhood and the degradation of motherhood. Ethical considerations notwithstanding, wisdom would seem to argue that adoption is a wiser course. And if abortion on demand were not practiced, there would be plenty of babies to adopt.

Certainly, surrogate motherhood for convenience is wrong. Motherhood should not be for hire or rent any more than wifehood should. In this regard, surrogate motherhood is no better than harlotry. God created a place for sex with one's own spouse. And God created a place for having babies; in one's own wife's womb. If we cannot have them there, then maybe we should consider whether it is God's will to have one of our own genetic offspring. Perhaps there are other babies to adopt, or maybe God wants us to help with the care of the fatherless and not to have our own.

In vitro fertilization (IVF)—Although in vitro fertilization is known by the popular expression *test-tube babies,* it is more accurately test-tube conception. Sperm and ovum are united in a Petri dish and later transplanted into a mother's womb. Many babies have already been born of this method where otherwise the couple was unable to have children. It can be done, but here again the question is whether it should be done.

Granted that artificial insemination is permissible, the main question in IVF from a Christian perspective relates to the "wasted" embryos. According to present methods, the majority of embryos are sacrificed in order to get one that will survive. This means that we are knowingly causing the death of many tiny human beings in order to get one to develop. Since the end does not justify this means, in vitro fertilization which wastes embryos is morally wrong. The fact that many naturally fertilized ova spontaneously abort is not relevant, for there is a significant moral difference between a natural death and a homicide. IVF is not a natural death; it is an artificially contrived and unnecessary death. It goes without saying that IVF for the purposes of research and experimentation on humans is doubly wrong.

Of course there is the possibility of perfecting the method so as not to waste human life or to use a natural form whereby a husband's sperm is artificially placed in his wife's womb. But until or unless this kind of thing is done, IVF is morally wrong.

Organ and tissue harvesting—There is an increasing traffic in human organs and tissues created by medical technology and corresponding human demand. Organs from aborted babies are used for transplantation. Brain tissue is utilized in treating Parkinson's disease. Other body fluids have medicinal value. Here again we must be careful not to argue from "can" to "ought." The question is not whether it can be done or is being done, but whether it should be done.

Several principles come to play on the question of harvesting. Certainly if there are legitimate instances of harvesting, it should never be done without informed consent. Then there is the question of human dignity. A human body is not a chemical factory nor an organic pharmaceutical company. Its purpose is not to function as an organ farm but as the body of an immortal person who can worship and glorify God (1 Cor. 6:19–20).

While there is no objection to giving our organs after we are dead, it is contrary to our dignity and mortality to keep bodies alive simply for the purpose of harvesting from them. The only sense in which harvesting is legitimate is in one-time donor gifts by informed consent after death. But growing embryos or keeping bodies alive artificially for this purpose is a denigration of human dignity.

Cryonics—It is possible to deep-freeze human bodies at death with the hope of resuscitating them someday. This could prolong life considerably, especially for those who die of diseases for which we may subsequently find cures. Once more we must not ask if this can be done, but whether it ought to be done. It can and is being done, but should we? The Christian response is negative for several reasons.

There is no evidence that a person can be brought back to life this way. Even if the body can be biologically resuscitated, there is no evidence that the person who occupied it will return. The Bible seems to indicate that when the person leaves the body (Phil. 1:23; 2 Cor. 5:8), only God can bring the person back to his body, and that he will do this at the resurrection (John 5; 1 Cor. 15; Rev. 20). The purpose behind deep-freeze death is a desire to avoid the eventuality of human mortality. But the Bible is clear that God has appointed death (Rom. 5:12; Heb. 9:27) and has limited our lifespan (Ps. 90:10). Attempts to avoid or deny death are not of God (see Gen. 3:4). We should accept the limits of natural life and the eventuality of natural death and not engage in vain attempts to avoid it.

Cloning—"Carbon-copy" human beings are genetically possible. Each cell in the body has the blueprint for that life. Hence, it is theoretically possible to produce an identical twin by nonsexual parenting. Cloning has already been done on some animals. Given the humanistic quest for scientific progress, eventually someone will apply the advanced technology to produce a human clone. From a Christian standpoint, there are serious objections to cloning. First of all, it is playing God, not serving God. It violates the fundamental principle that we are only the custodians of human life, not its creators. It is the ultimate in human presumption and pride, man's technological tower of Babel (Gen. 11:1–2). Second, clones would generate unprecedented psychological and social problems of identity and sibling rivalry. Third, it bypasses the God-ordained means of human propagation, fertilization in a mother's womb. In this sense it is a denial of the sanctity of sex which God has created, hallowed, and ordained (Gen. 1:28; Heb. 13:4). Fourth, it is another way to avoid mortality by having one's identical "twin" live on after one's death, and so on infinitely. So even if it were possible, it would be morally objectionable.

Gene splicing—It is now possible to produce new kinds of biological organisms by splicing the genes of one into another. These laboratory hybrids are already being patented. One such artificially constructed "super bug" (*pseudomonas*) is said to have value in eliminating large oil slicks, since it feeds and multiplies in oil. Many other highly touted uses are in view, including medical cures, higher food production, environmental purification, more useful animals, and even more productive human beings!

Gene splicing has some serious problems. J. Kerby Anderson notes many of these in his excellent book, *Genetic Engineering*. First, there are serious scientific problems including the possibility of escaped organisms, creating new diseases, and creating an imbalance in the delicately arranged micro-world.[13] Second, there are social and legal problems. Anderson comments, "No one would welcome the spread of an infectious disease that destroys car, truck, and airplane lubrication systems."[14]

Finally, there are serious ethical problems. Human gene splicing violates several principles. First, the anticipated benefits (ends) do not justify the means. Gene splicing is another example of the humanistic "end justifies the means" ethic. Second, God made man "in his image."

13. J. Kerby Anderson, *Genetic Engineering: The Ethical Issues* (Grand Rapids: Zondervan, 1982), pp. 87–91.
14. Ibid., p. 92.

Gene splicing is a mixing of the created categories of human and animals. Third, human gene splicing is a classic example of man's desire to be sovereign over creation, rather than being a servant in it. It is a rejection of the Creator and an effort to redesign nature. The creation mandate (Gen. 1:28) did not include destruction or reconstruction of what God created (see chap. 16). It meant service in creation, not sovereignty over it.

An Evaluation of a Christian Biomedical Ethic

Many objections have been raised to a Christian biomedical ethic. Some of them have already emerged in the preceding discussion and been addressed. Here we will summarize the more important ones.

It Holds Back Scientific Progress

It is objected that opposing genetic engineering, cloning, and gene splicing retards scientific progress. However, this objection has serious problems of its own. It assumes that these inventions are really progress, rather than merely changes. Not everything new is morally better. "Scientific progress" is an ambiguous term used to justify almost anything we desire to do. This argument absolutizes scientific progress as the norm by which all else is justified. But science is not morally normative. Science deals with what is, not with what ought to be. The standards for science do not come from within but from beyond. This became painfully evident when German scientists in the Nazi regime engaged in ghastly human "research" at the expense of human respect.

It Lacks Proper Compassion for the Suffering

It is also argued that failing to utilize these advances in science to alleviate human suffering lacks proper concern for human suffering. Why allow some to suffer from Parkinson's disease when the brain tissue from aborted babies can lessen their misery? The end does not justify the means. Extending the life of one person does not justify exterminating the life of another. Evil means are not justified by good ends. Only good means are to be used for good ends.

Respecting human life and dignity is a proper concern. And violating human dignity, sanctity, and responsibility is not the way to show this concern. The humanist's standard for proper compassion is ultimately without justification. He has a moral prescription without a moral Prescriber. He can believe in compassion, but he has no real justification for that belief. If he attempts to justify his moral laws, he finds himself face to face with a moral Lawgiver. But if there is a divine imperative about human life, then the humanist's whole case for utilitarian compassion collapses.

Summary and Conclusion

Biomedical issues clutter the stage of crucial ethical decisions. The conflict in opinion on these issues arises out of two opposed world views, the secular humanist and Christian perspectives. The former denies a Creator, that humans were created, and God-given moral obligations. Humans are merely higher animals with greater intelligence. This intelligence should be used to improve the human species. Hence, secular humanists favor abortion, euthanasia, and genetic engineering to do so.

By contrast with the humanist biomedical ethic, Christians believe that God specially created humans in his own likeness and gave moral imperatives to preserve the dignity and sanctity of human life. Hence, the Christian obligation is to serve God, not to play God. We are not the engineers of life, but merely its custodians. Medical intervention, therefore, should be corrective, not creative. We should repair life, not attempt to reconstruct it. Technology must serve morality, not the reverse.

Select Readings

Anderson, J. Kerby. *Genetic Engineering: The Ethical Issues*. Grand Rapids: Zondervan, 1982.

Anderson, Norman. *Issues of Life and Death*. Downers Grove: Inter-Varsity, 1977.

Ashley, B. M., and K. D. O'Rourke. *Health Care Ethics*. St. Louis: Catholic Health Association of the United States, 1982.

Beauchamp, Tom L., and James F. Childress. *Principles of Biomedical Ethics*. 2d ed. Oxford: Oxford University Press, 1983.

Gish, Duane. *Manipulating Life: Where Does It Stop?* San Diego: Master, 1981.

Lammers, Stephen, and Allen Verhey, eds. *On Moral Medicine*. Grand Rapids: Eerdmans, 1987.

Lester, Lane P., and James C. Hefley. *Cloning: Miracle or Menace?* Wheaton: Tyndale House, 1980.

Mappes, Thomas A., and Jane S. Zembaty. *Biomedical Ethics*. 2d ed. New York: McGraw-Hill, 1986.

Monagle, John F., and David C. Thomasma. *Medical Ethics: A Guide for Health Professionals*. Rockville, Md.: Aspen, 1977.

Ramsey, Paul. *Fabricated Man: The Ethics of Genetic Control*. New Haven, Conn.: Yale University Press, 1970.

11

Capital Punishment

There are three basic views on capital punishment: reconstructionism, which insists on the death sentence for all serious crimes; rehabilitationism, which would not allow it for any crime; and retributionism, which recommends death for some (capital) crimes. Forms of all three views are held by Christians. Since two views share a belief in capital punishment for capital crimes, our discussion will begin with the opposing view, rehabilitationism.

Rehabilitationism: No Capital Punishment for Any Crimes

Proponents of this view include both Christians and non-Christians, those who appeal to the Bible for justification and those who do not. Both types of arguments will be presented. The essence of this position is that the purpose of justice is rehabilitation and not retribution. Justice is remedial, not retributive. We should try to reform the criminal, not punish him, or at least not with capital punishment.

Biblical Arguments for Rehabilitationism

Christian rehabilitationists appeal to Scripture in support of their position, and what follows is a summary of the biblical arguments they use in defending their conclusions. Although their reasoning has wider application to crime in general, it is applied specifically to capital punishment here.

The purpose of justice is to reform, not punish. Ezekiel declared that God takes no pleasure in the death of the wicked but "rather that he should turn from his way and live" (18:23 RSV). God wants to cure the sinner, not kill him.

Capital punishment was abolished with Moses' law. It is argued that capital punishment was part of the Old Testament legalistic system abolished by Christ. In particular, an appeal is made to Jesus' rejection of Moses' "eye for [an] eye" principle (Matt. 5:38). Instead of retribution, Jesus declared, "do not resist an evil person" (v. 39).

Mosaic capital punishment is not practiced today. The Old Testament prescribed capital punishment for some twenty crimes, including breaking the Sabbath, striking one's parents, cursing God, homosexuality, kidnapping—and rebellious children! But no one really believes that all these should still be prosecuted today. Thus none of them should be practiced.

Jesus abolished capital punishment for adultery. One of the crimes deserving of capital punishment in the Old Testament was adultery (Lev. 20:10), but it is argued that Jesus set this aside when he told the woman taken in adultery to "go, and sin no more" (John 8:11 KJV). In 1 Corinthians 5, only excommunication from the church, not execution by the state, was recommended by Paul for the gross case of immorality there.

Cain was not given capital punishment. Even in the Old Testament, capital punishment was not always exacted for capital crimes. Cain killed Abel (Gen. 4) and yet God put a mark upon him and protected his life against anyone who would retaliate against him (v. 15).

David was not given the death sentence. David committed two capital crimes, adultery and murder, and yet was not given capital punishment. As a matter of fact, when he confessed his sin (Ps. 51), he was forgiven (Ps. 32) and even restored to his throne (2 Sam. 18–19).

New Testament love rules out capital punishment. It is argued that the idea that we can love someone's soul while killing his body is inconsistent. As Christians we are enjoined to love even our enemies, and we cannot love them by killing them. Love would constrain us to sacrifice our own life for them (John 15:13), but it would never take their life from them.

The cross was capital punishment for all men. Most Christian rehabilitationists admit that capital punishment was sometimes used in the Old Testament. But they insist that whatever place there may have been for it before Christ came, there is no place for it since. Because sin brings death (Rom. 6:23), and since Christ died for all men (Rom. 5:12–18), it follows that he has already taken capital punishment for all. In view of his suffering the death penalty for all persons, there should be no death penalty for any person.

Moral Arguments for Rehabilitationism

In addition to the biblical arguments, several moral arguments are used to reject capital punishment. Most of them have been used by Christians as well as non-Christians to defend this position.

Capital punishment is unjustly applied. A disproportionate number of minorities are given capital punishment. This being the case, rehabilitationists insist that capital punishment should not be applied at all if it is not applied fairly to all. Otherwise, it is a tyrannical tool to subdue minority groups, a tool to promote racism.

Capital punishment is not a deterrent to crime. It is argued that capital punishment does not really deter crime, for even where it is in effect, capital crimes still continue. In fact, some argue that capital punishment encourages serious crime because it gives state sanction to the violent taking of human life. Thus, by using capital punishment, the state encourages crime rather than deterring it.

Capital punishment is antihumanitarian. We provide shelters and adoption for stray animals; why should we kill wayward humans? It is an inhumane form of punishment. It is cruel and unusual punishment in the extreme.

Criminals should be cured, not killed. Criminals are socially ill and need to be treated, but we cannot cure them by killing them. Patients need a doctor, not a funeral director, and socially sick people need a psychiatrist, not an executioner.

Capital punishment sends unbelievers to hell. Capital punishment is an especially cruel sentence for a Christian to support, for according to the Bible, the unbelievers will be eternally damned (Matt. 25:41–46; 2 Thess. 1:7–9; Rev. 20:11–15). If God is "longsuffering, . . . not willing that any should perish" (2 Pet. 3:9 KJV), then so should we be. To will that an unbeliever be given capital punishment is to will that he go to his eternal doom.

An Evaluation of Rehabilitationism

Since rehabilitationists use both biblical and moral arguments for their view, the response will be divided accordingly. First, a reply to their arguments from the Bible.

An Evaluation of the Biblical Arguments

The primary purpose of justice is not rehabilitation. The primary purpose of justice is not reformation but punishment. This is clear in both Old and New Testaments. God himself punishes sin (Exod. 20:5; Ezek. 18:4, 20), and he demands that proper authorities do it also (Gen. 9:6; Exod. 21:12). The heart of the penal view is manifest in the death of Christ, who was punished as "the just for the unjust" (1 Pet. 3:18). As Paul put it, "The wages of sin is death" (Rom. 6:23).

While it is hoped that those who commit noncapital crimes will reform as the result of their incarceration, this is not its primary purpose. Since capital crimes demand a capital punishment, there is no place for reform, only for a just punishment. And the only just punishment for taking a life is giving a life. Only in this way is justice satisfied.

Capital punishment was prior to Moses' law. The Mosaic law was fulfilled by Christ (Matt. 5:17; Rom. 10:4), but capital punishment was not unique to it. God instituted capital punishment for all men in Noah's day (Gen. 9:6), long before Moses gave the Law to Israel (Exod. 20). Hence, in fulfilling Moses' law for Israel (Heb. 7–8), Jesus did not destroy the moral law for all men (Rom. 2:2–14).

Not only was capital punishment instituted before Moses' law, but it has continued in effect after Moses' time. Paul stated it in principle (Rom. 13:4) and implied it in practice (Acts 25:11). And Jesus stated it in principle (John 19:11) and accepted it in practice when he died on the cross. So capital punishment was not limited to the Mosaic law nor abolished with it.

The Mosaic laws are not in effect today. It is true that few Christians (except reconstructionists) really advocate the position that governments should practice capital punishment for all the religious and moral crimes mentioned in the Old Testament. However, just because one rejects capital punishment for non-capital crimes does not mean capital punishment should not be accepted for capital crimes. In fact, capital punishment was prescribed in the Bible for capital crimes both before and after the time of Moses.

Jesus' response to the adulterous woman did not revoke capital punishment. Jesus' forgiving attitude toward the woman taken in adultery (John 8) is not proof that he rejected capital punishment, and for several reasons. This was not a capital crime and, therefore, even at best it would not prove Jesus rejected capital punishment for murder. Jesus did not reject the law of Moses here, since it demanded at least two witnesses to accuse the woman (Num. 35:30) and there were none willing to accuse her (John 8:11). Jesus' statement to "go, and sin no more" (v. 11 KJV) was not a declaration of the invalidity of capital punishment, but of his forgiveness for her sin.

Cain's punishment implies capital punishment. Cain's murder of Abel is a special case (Gen. 4). There are good reasons why he was not given capital punishment. First of all, who would do it? There was no human government other than the family, and his only brother was dead. Certainly, God would not expect his father or mother to kill their only remaining son. In view of these special circumstances, God personally commuted Cain's death sentence. God has the right to do this because he is the author of life (Deut. 32:39; Job 1:21). But even in God's protection of Cain there is an implication of capital punishment in the "sevenfold vengeance" taken on anyone who would kill Cain (Gen. 4:15). Cain himself seemed to expect capital punishment when he said, "Whoever finds me will kill me" (v. 14).

There were specific reasons why David was not given capital punishment. David committed two sins worthy of death according to Moses' law, murder and adultery. Why then was his life spared? There is no record that anyone pressed charges, and according to the law, there had to be two witnesses (Deut. 17:6). Capital punishment was executed by the government, but Israel was a monarchy, and David was the monarch. In effect, capital punishment of David would have to have been carried out by David.

Perhaps this special circumstance is why God intervened and gave his own sentence through Nathan the prophet. Just as God said, David paid "fourfold," and some of the penalty involved lives. First, the baby of David's adulterous act died. Then David's son Absalom was killed, and David's daughter was defiled as he had defiled another man's wife. And finally, David lost his kingdom. David paid severely for his offenses *(2 Sam. 12–16)*.

Love and capital punishment are not contrary. If love and capital punishment were mutually exclusive, then the sacrifice of Christ was a contradiction. For "God so loved the world that he gave his one and only Son" (John 3:16). Jesus said, "Greater love has no one than this, that he lay down his life for his friends" (John 15:13).

Not only are love and punishment compatible, but the very principle behind capital punishment is the one that made the cross necessary. It is the principle of "a life for a life." The concept behind substitutionary atonement, that it takes life to atone for life (Lev. 17:11), is what makes capital punishment necessary for capital crimes. If there were any other way to satisfy justice and release grace, then surely God would have found it rather than sacrificing his only beloved Son (2 Cor. 5:21; 1 Pet. 3:18). In fact, if capital punishment had not been in effect in the first century, then Jesus could not have died for our sins. Thus capital punishment elevates the value of life rather than lowering it. For the more serious the punishment, the more value we place on the person who was murdered.

The cross didn't abolish capital punishment. It is still commended in the New Testament after the cross (Rom. 13:4; Acts 25:11). As just noted, the cross did not destroy the life-for-a-life principle; it exemplified it perfectly. The cross provided forgiveness of sins, but it did not thereby destroy all the consequences of our sins. Even though Jesus tasted death for every man, nevertheless all men will still die (Rom. 5:12). If a Christian jumps off a high cliff, confessing his sins on the way down will not avert death at the bottom. The truth is that, forgiven or not, there are social and physical consequences of sin. If a Christian commits a capital crime, he can get forgiveness, but he should not expect to avoid the appropriate penalty. And the fitting penalty for taking another life is giving one's own life.

An Evaluation of the Moral Arguments

In addition to the biblical arguments against capital punishment, there are several moral arguments. These too call for comment.

Unequal justice does not negate the need for justice. Several things should be noted in response to the argument against capital punishment on the grounds of its unequal distribution. If justice is applied unequally, then we should work to assure that it is applied equally, not abolish justice altogether. The same thing holds true for capital punishment. We do not argue that all medical treatment should be abolished until everyone has it equally, even though more poor and minority people will die from lack of treatment than others. Why then should capital punishment be abolished until equal numbers of all races are executed?

A disproportionate number of capital punishments is not in itself a proof of inequity any more than a disproportionately high number of minorities in professional basketball is proof of discrimination against majority ethnic groups. This is not to say that one group of people is more sinful than another, but simply that conditions may occasion different social behavior. However understandable and regrettable this may be, a society cannot tolerate violent social behavior, and it must protect its citizens.

Capital punishment affirms human dignity. Punishing a person for his wrong is a compliment, not an insult, to his freedom and dignity. As C. S. Lewis aptly put it, "To be punished, however severely, because we deserved it, because we 'ought to have known better,' is to be treated as a human person made in God's image."[1] The very fact that God places such a high price tag on taking another's life shows what great value he places on human life. Capital punishment, then, is the ulti-

---

1. C. S. Lewis, *God in the Dock*, ed. Walter Hooper (Grand Rapids: Eerdmans, 1970), p. 226.

mate compliment to human dignity; it implies the most affirmative stance possible.

Criminals should be treated as persons, not patients. The working assumption of the view opposing capital punishment is dehumanizing. Prisoners are not patients, they are persons. They are not objects to be manipulated, but human beings to be respected. The criminal is not sick but sinful. It is tyrannical to submit a person to a compulsory cure against his will, an illusory humanitarianism with sinister political implications. It dehumanizes the individual by treating him as a "case" or patient rather than as a responsible person. As Lewis put it, "To be 'cured' against one's will . . . is to be put on a level with those who have not yet reached the age of reason or those who never will; to be classed with infants, imbeciles, and domestic animals."[2] On the other hand, to be punished, however severely, is to be respected as a person created in God's image who knows better and therefore deserves to be punished for his wrongdoing.

Capital punishment does not send people to hell. It is not capital punishment that sends people to hell; their unbelief does (John 3:36). If capital punishment is wrong because unbelievers end in hell as a result, then it could also be argued that capital punishment is right because it sends believers to heaven. Should it then be given only to Christian murderers? If anything, it should be an incentive to belief to know the sure moment of one's death. It certainly eliminates procrastination and encourages sober thinking about life after death.

Reconstructionism: Capital Punishment for All Major Crimes

Reconstructionism is on the opposite end of the spectrum from rehabilitationism. While the latter does not permit capital punishment for any crime, reconstructionism requires it for every major crime. More precisely, reconstructionists believe that capital punishment should be exacted for every nonceremonial crime designated in Moses' law, which included some twenty different offenses.

Classical reconstructionists believe that society should be reconstructed on the basis of Old Testament Mosaic law. Thus, their position is called theonomist because they are governed by the law of God. God's moral law was revealed to Moses and never abrogated. Only ceremonial aspects of the Old Testament law were done away with by Christ. The moral law, however, is eternal since it reflects the very

2. Ibid.

character of God. Jesus said of the Old Testament law and prophets, "I have not come to abolish them but to fulfill them" (Matt. 5:17).

The primary purpose of justice is retribution, not rehabilitation. It is to punish, not to reform. Reconstructionist Greg L. Bahnsen makes this clear in *Theonomy in Christian Ethics* when he contends that "we are to understand the prescription of the death penalty on the basis that such a civic punishment is what the crime *warrants* in God's eyes."[3]

Although they can be numbered differently, there are some twenty-one offenses that called for capital punishment in the Old Testament:

1. Murder (Exod. 21:12)
2. Contemptuous act against a judge (Deut. 17:12)
3. Causing a miscarriage (Exod. 21:22–25)
4. False testimony in a potentially capital crime (Deut. 19:16–19)
5. Negligence by the owner of an ox that kills people (Exod. 21:29)
6. Idolatry (Exod. 22:20)
7. Blasphemy (Lev. 24:15–16)
8. Witchcraft or sorcery (Exod. 22:18)
9. False prophecy (Deut. 18:20)
10. Apostasy (Lev. 20:2)
11. Breaking the sabbath (Exod. 31:14)
12. Homosexuality
13. Bestiality (Lev. 20:15–16)
14. Adultery (Lev. 20:10)
15. Rape (Deut. 22:25)
16. Incest (Lev. 20:11)
17. Cursing parents (Deut. 5:16)
18. Rebellion by children (Exod. 21:15, 17)
19. Kidnaping (Exod. 21:16)
20. Drunkenness by a priest (Lev. 10:8–9)
21. Unanointed individuals touching the holy furnishings in the temple (Num. 4:15)

A careful look at this list reveals several interesting things. Only the first five involve capital offenses, either actually or potentially. The remaining sixteen are for noncapital crimes, even though some of them (rape) could lead to murder and others (rebellion by a son) could prevent murders. The next six (6–11) are for religious offenses, while the next eight (12–19) are for various moral issues. The last two (20–21)

3. Greg L. Bahnsen, *Theonomy in Christian Ethics,* exp. ed. (Phillipsburg, N.J.: Presbyterian and Reformed, 1984), p. 441.

relate to ceremonial duties, though drunkenness is also a moral issue (Prov. 20:1; 23:21). Theonomists argue that these two, because of their ceremonial nature, are not applicable today.[4] But with this exception, they believe that capital punishment is still binding today. They insist that human governments are under divine obligation to implement capital punishment for these offenses. In short, they believe in capital punishment for virtually every major kind of offense, social, religious, or moral.

The Arguments for Reconstructionism

The defense of this Old Testament use of capital punishment boils down to the question of whether the Old Testament law is still binding today. Hence, the reconstructionists' case is basically biblical in nature, though many point to the social consequences of not following what they believe to be God's law for today. Let us examine the most basic reasons in justification of their view.

God's law reflects his unchanging character. The moral law of God is a reflection of the moral character of God. "Be holy, because I am holy," said the Lord (Lev. 11:44). God is just; therefore, he requires justice of us (Ezek. 18:5f.). But if God's law reflects his moral character, and if God's moral character does not change, then God's law given through Moses is still in effect today. It must be, because God has not changed.

The New Testament repeats the Ten Commandments. The very commands given to Moses on Sinai are repeated in the New Testament. Paul states many of them in Romans 13:9. Others appear elsewhere (Eph. 6:2–3). If the Old Testament law is not in effect today, then it is strange that the New Testament repeats these commandments.

The Old Testament was the Bible of the early church. The early Christian church had no New Testament; it was not written until the last half of the first century. When Paul told Christians that "all Scripture is God-breathed and is useful for teaching, . . . and training in righteousness," he was referring to the Old Testament (2 Tim. 3:16). This is clear from verse 15, which refers to the "holy Scriptures" that Timothy learned from his Jewish mother and grandmother (1:5). This being the case, reconstructionists argue that the New Testament church used the Old Testament as its standard for righteousness. And the Old Testament taught that capital punishment should be given for the offenses noted previously.

Jesus said he did not come to abolish the law. Jesus said clearly, "Do not think that I have come to abolish the Law or the Prophets; I

4. Ibid., p. 213.

have not come to abolish them but to fulfill them." He added, "I tell you the truth, until heaven and earth disappear, not the smallest letter, not the least stroke of a pen, will by any means disappear from the Law" (Matt. 5:17–18). On this basis Bahnsen insists that we are bound by the entirety of Old Testament moral law on capital punishment.

Capital punishment is repeated in the New Testament. Furthermore, argue reconstructionists, the New Testament explicitly reaffirms capital punishment in Romans 13:4 where it declares that God has given the sword to human governments. Likewise, both Jesus (John 19:11) and Paul refer to capital punishment (Acts 25:11).

An Evaluation of Reconstructionism

While many Christians have a high view of the profitability of the Old Testament for believers (Rom. 15:4; 1 Cor. 10:11), most do not believe that the Mosaic legislation is still binding on human governments today. There are many reasons for this, but first a response should be made to the arguments given by reconstructionists in favor of capital punishment for everything from breaking the Sabbath to rebellious children.

Not all Moses' law is necessitated by God's character. While all of Moses' law is in accord with God's character, not all of it is necessitated by God's character. God never legislates contrary to his character, but neither does everything flow of necessity from it. God can and has willed different things at different times for different people, all of which are in accord with his nature but not all of which are demanded by it.

Reconstructionists believe that the ceremonial laws of Moses are not binding today. They believe Christ fulfilled the sacrificial and typological system and, therefore, it is unnecessary to bring a lamb to a temple or to abstain from eating pork or shrimp. But if this is so, then there is no reason that God could not will that Old Testament laws about capital punishment could change too.

Furthermore, capital punishment is not a law; it is a penalty or sanction for disobeying a specific law. Hence, one need not argue that God's basic moral principles change when he no longer requires capital punishment for all the offenses listed in the Old Testament.

It is not sufficient to argue that all offenses deserve death (Rom. 1:32; 6:23), for God never gave capital punishment for all offenses, even in the Old Testament. But if God did not require capital punishment for some offenses that deserved death, even in the Old Testament system of law, then there is no reason why he cannot do the same for other offenses in the New Testament. So it is not a question of whether all of these twenty offenses deserve death, but whether God has des-

ignated death as their punishment today. And, as we will see, there is
no evidence that God has designated capital punishment for any but
capital offenses in the New Testament.

Not all of the Ten Commandments are repeated in the New Testament. Reconstructionists err in claiming that the Ten Commandments
of Moses are restated in the New Testament for Christians. First, only
nine of the Ten Commandments are restated in any form in the New
Testament. The command to worship on Saturday is not repeated for
obvious reasons: Jesus rose, appeared to his disciples, ascended into
heaven, and sent the Holy Spirit on Sunday. Thus, the early church
met on the first day of the week (Acts 20:7; 1 Cor. 16:2), not the last
day. So the command to worship on Saturday is no longer binding on
Christians (see Rom. 14:5; Col. 2:16).

Even when one of the basic moral principles embodied in the law of
Moses is restated in the New Testament, it is repeated with a different
promise. For example, when Paul told the children in Ephesians to
"honor your parents" he added a different promise than the one given
to Israel. Israel was promised that they would "live long in the land
[of Palestine] the LORD your God is giving you" (Exod. 20:12). The
Christians at Ephesus were not given Israel's promise of land and
blessing but simply told to honor their parents "that it may go well
with you . . . on the earth" (Eph. 6:3). But if different blessings are
attached to keeping laws in the New Testament, then there is no reason
why different punishments cannot be listed for breaking them. Capital
punishment is not a law but a punishment for breaking a law. Hence,
changing a punishment for a law from the Old Testament times is not
changing any moral law.

Nowhere does the New Testament state, as does the Old Testament,
that capital punishment should be given for adultery. In fact, Paul told
the church at Corinth to have the adulterer excommunicated, not to
have him executed (1 Cor. 5:5). Later, he even told the church to restore
the repentant adulterer to its fellowship. This is a significant change
in penalty from the Old to the New Testament.

The Old Testament is for but not to the church. It is true that the very
early church did not have the entire New Testament. The church began
in A.D. 33, and the first books may not have been written for about
twenty years. They did not need a written New Testament, since they
had living apostles (Acts 2:42; Eph. 2:20) who could perform special
miracles to confirm their divine authority (2 Cor. 12:12; Heb. 2:3–4).

Their use of the Old Testament reveals that they did not believe it
was all written to them but only that it was for them. Paul said, "For
whatever was written in earlier times was written for our instruction"
(Rom. 15:4 NASB). He told the Corinthians the Old Testament was for

Ethical Issues

their example (1 Cor. 10:11). But nowhere is it stated in the New Testament that the whole of Old Testament law is directed to the Christian, to say nothing of civil governments. In fact, as was previously noted, there are some parts of the Mosaic legislation that even reconstructionists admit no longer apply to us today.

Jesus did away with the Old Testament laws. First of all, it is true that Jesus came to fulfill the righteous demands of the Old Testament law (Matt. 5:17–18; see also Rom. 10:2–3). He did not do away with it by destroying it, but rather by fulfilling it.

The New Testament is clear that the law of Moses was superseded by Christ. Paul said that which was written in stone (the Commandments) has faded away (2 Cor. 3:7, 11). The writer of Hebrews declares that "there must also be a change of the law" (7:12). The old covenant was replaced by the new covenant (8:13), just as Jeremiah had predicted (31:31). Paul told the Galatians that "we are no longer under the supervision of the law" since Christ has come (Gal. 3:25). To the Romans he wrote, "we are not under law but under grace" (Rom. 6:15 NASB). And in Colossians he affirms that in view of Christ's death and resurrection God has "canceled the written code, with its regulations" (Col. 2:14).

Just because there are similar moral laws in the New Testament does not mean we are still under the Old Testament. There are also similar traffic laws in Virginia and Texas. But when a citizen of Virginia disobeys one of its traffic laws he has not thereby broken the similar law in Texas. Since God's moral nature does not change from age to age, we should expect that many of the moral laws will be the same. But this does not mean that we are still bound by the Mosaic codification simply because he got them from the same God as did Paul and Peter.

Again there is a confusion here between law and penalty. Even if the basic moral principle embodied in the Mosaic legislation is the same as that expressed in New Testament law for Christians, nevertheless it does not follow that the punishment for breaking it will be the same. And capital punishment is a question of punishment, not a question of moral law as such. For example, it is granted that the moral prohibition against adultery has not changed from age to age. God has always opposed it. The question is whether he has always demanded the same punishment for it in every age. There is no indication that he has. In fact, there is indication that he has not.

Not all Old Testament capital punishments are repeated in the New Testament. It is mistaken to imply that capital punishment is reaffirmed in the New Testament, since all the offenses for which it was demanded in the Old Testament are not in effect in the New Testament.

As was noted earlier, even reconstructionists admit that there are some cases of Old Testament capital punishment that do not apply today. The cases where capital punishment is implied (John 19:11; Acts 25:11; Rom. 13:4) do not include all those offenses in the Old Testament. In fact, it can be argued that all of these were for capital offenses or the equivalent, such as treason. (See Luke 23:2; Acts 17:7.) There is indication that capital punishment was not demanded of some offenses listed in the Old Testament, for example, adultery (1 Cor. 5:5; 2 Cor. 2:6).

A Biblical Critique of Reconstructionism

Many of the critiques of reconstructionism have already been implied in responding to the arguments. The reconstructionist argument for capital punishment is based on the belief that the Old Testament law of Moses is still binding on believers today. In response to this there are many arguments showing that the law of Moses is not binding today.

The distinction between ceremonial and moral categories fails. Nowhere does the Bible divide the law into distinct ceremonial, civil, and moral categories. No such hard-and-fast lines are drawn. Jesus did cleanse all meat (Mark 7:19), and the New Testament writers follow in doing away with the designation of some foods as unclean (Acts 10:15; 1 Tim. 4:3–4). However, the ceremonial aspects of the law are broader than clean and unclean foods. They include regulations on clothes, sacrifices, rituals, and even sanitation (Lev. 11–27). Hence, the cleansing of certain foods cannot be equated with the so-called ceremonial law. Furthermore, the laws against idolatry, immorality, blood, and strangled animals enjoined on Christians (Acts 15:29) were not unique to the Mosaic legislation (see Gen. 9:4).

The law of Moses was a unit. There were civil aspects to the moral law and moral dimensions of the civil law. Indeed, there were moral aspects of the ceremonial law,[5] as is evident from the fact that it was said to reflect God's holiness (Lev. 11:45). Surely God's holiness is not an amoral issue. Nowhere in the Old Testament is there a separation made between the moral and the civil or between the civil and the ceremonial aspects of Moses' law. And nowhere in the New Testament does it declare that only the ceremonial aspects of the law of Moses have been abolished.

The apostles set aside the law. The apostles ruled against the contention that Gentiles must be circumcised and required to "obey the

5. The Westminster Confession (1647) spoke of "ceremonial laws, [as] containing ... divers instructions of moral duties" (19.3).

law of Moses" (Acts 15:5). They insisted only that Christians should "abstain from food sacrificed to idols, from blood, from meat of strangled animals and from sexual immorality" (v. 29). But these were not unique to Moses' law (Gen. 9:4), and they were not all that was required by Moses' law. Hence, the very fact that the apostles did not insist on "anything beyond the [above stated] requirements" (Acts 15:28) proves that they did not believe that Christians were under the law of Moses. Further, the prohibitions the apostles gave to Christians in Acts 15 cannot be considered as rules against purely ceremonial matters, for one of them was against idolatry and another against immorality.

James affirmed the unity of the law. The unity of Moses' law is so strong that James insisted that "whoever keeps the whole law and yet stumbles at just one point is guilty of breaking all of it" (James 2:10). And in the very next verse he quoted the laws against adultery and murder which everyone agrees are moral laws. The law of Moses was considered a unity. So if any of it is done away, then all of it is done away.

Paul said Christians are not under the law. New Testament believers "are not under law, but under grace" (Rom. 6:14). John said, "The law was given through Moses; grace and truth came through Jesus Christ" (John 1:17). Here the law given by Moses is contrasted to the grace brought by Christ. Hence, we cannot be under both.

The Ten Commandments have faded away. Paul told the Corinthians that what "was engraved in letters on stone [the Ten Commandments]" has faded away since Christ (2 Cor. 3:7, 11). It has been replaced by "that which lasts" (v. 11). How was the law of Moses done away with by Christ? He did it "by abolishing in his flesh the law with its commandments and regulations" (Eph. 2:15). The law condemned us, but Christ redeemed us. For "there is now no condemnation for those who are in Christ Jesus" (Rom. 8:1).

Christ is the end of the law. "Christ is the end [*telos*] of the law" for believers (Rom. 10:4). Christ did not simply end the law; rather, he is the End of the Law. He finished it by fulfilling it. He did not do away with the law by destroying it (Matt. 5:17–18) but by completing it. He is the perfect goal of the law because he perfectly kept it (Matt. 3:15; Rom. 8:3–4).

The law was in place only until Christ came. The "law was put in charge to lead us to Christ that we might be justified by faith." But "now that faith has come, we are no longer under the supervision of the law" (Gal. 3:24–25). Here too it is clear that Paul includes the moral law of Moses because he refers to it as what was given at Sinai some 430 years after the promise was confirmed to the patriarchs

(v. 17). And what was given at Sinai were the Ten Commandments which contain the very heart and basis of the moral law. So the whole law of Moses which was given to Israel was taken away by Christ.

The law of Moses was given only to Israel. The Book of Hebrews is emphatic about the fact that "the law was given to the people" of Israel (7:11). And of that law it declares "there must also be a change of the law" (v. 12). By the new covenant "the former regulation is set aside" (v. 18). The old covenant is replaced by the new covenant (8:1–2). And this new one, said the Lord, "will not be like the covenant I made with their forefathers" (8:9). By the very fact of "calling this covenant 'new,' he made the first one obsolete" (8:13). The language could hardly be clearer: the whole covenant given to Israel by Moses, which included moral laws, has been done away with.

We cannot take the law without its curses. Those who believe Christians are still under the law are reminded by Paul, "Cursed is everyone who does not continue to do everything written in the Book of the Law" (Gal. 3:10). That is to say, one cannot take the blessings of the law without its curses (see Deut. 27). According to Paul, with the law it is either all or nothing at all. So on the one hand, if any of the law is binding on Christians, then all of it is. On the other hand, if some of the Mosaic law does not apply to Christians, then none of it does. But Christ has taken the curse of the law for us (Gal. 3:13). So to accept the law of Moses as binding on us is to reject what Christ has done for us (Gal. 3:21).

A Social Critique of Reconstructionism

From a strictly social point of view there are serious problems with reconstructionism. First, it would eliminate our constitutional freedom of religion by establishing one religion as the preferred religion. Thus it would be a violation of the First Amendment of the U.S. Constitution.

Second, it has already been tried and has failed. Calvin's Geneva and the Puritans' early America are cases in point. Baptists had to flee to Rhode Island because they were persecuted by the reconstructionists.

Third, since reconstructionism is government based on religious revelation, the question can always be asked: "Whose revelation?" It is simply bigotry to answer: "Mine!" And it is presumption to respond: "God's." Lest Christians be tempted to say a Christian revelation, we need only be reminded that there is a Muslim revelation too. In a pluralistic world no one's religious revelation is going to be accepted by all others as the basis for government.

Retributionism: Capital Punishment for Some Crimes

The third major view is retributionism, which holds that capital punishment is legitimate for some crimes, namely, capital ones. Since the essence of this position has already emerged in the critique of the other two views, it can be stated more briefly.

Unlike rehabilitationism, retributionism believes that the primary purpose of capital punishment is to punish. Unlike reconstructionism, retributionism does not believe that civil governments today are bound by the Mosaic legislation regarding capital punishment.

Retributionism holds that the criminal is not sick, but sinful. His capital offense is not pathological but is moral. Since he is a rational and morally responsible being, he knows better and therefore deserves to be punished. While capital punishment also protects innocent people from repeated violent crimes, this is not its primary purpose. Furthermore, even though capital punishment will deter crime, at least by that offender, nonetheless, this is not its primary purpose. Its primary purpose is penal, not remedial. Its purpose as such is to punish the guilty rather than protect the innocent.

When God instituted human government and gave it capital authority, it was for the purpose of dealing with capital crimes. God told Noah explicitly:

> From each man, too, I will demand an accounting for the life of his fellow man. Whoever sheds the blood of man, by man shall his blood be shed; for in the image of God has God made man. [Gen. 9:5–6]

When this mandate was later incorporated into the Mosaic law, there were a number of capital crimes spelled out, including murder (Exod. 21:12), avenging a death, causing a miscarriage (Exod. 21:22–23), false testimony in a capital case (Deut. 19:16–19), and owning an ox that killed people (Exod. 21:29). In each case the person who received capital punishment was responsible for the death of an innocent person or persons. In principle this would include treason, since many lives are at stake in treasonous acts. In short, capital punishment is for capital crimes.

When capital punishment is mentioned in the New Testament, it is also in the context of capital crimes. Government has the sword God gave to Noah for capital crimes (Rom. 13:4). Jesus acknowledged Rome's capital authority over his life (John 19:11), but here again the alleged crime was a capital crime, namely, treason (Luke 23:2). Likewise, Paul's alleged crime for which he was willing to receive capital punishment if guilty was treason (Acts 25:11; 17:7).

The Biblical Basis for Capital Punishment

Capital punishment is implied from the very beginning of the Old Testament. It is repeated over and over again throughout the Scriptures, including the New Testament.

The need for capital punishment is implied in man's nature. Human beings, male and female, are created in God's image (Gen. 1:27). They both resemble and represent God on earth. Killing them is an attack on the God who made them. It is a rejection of his sovereignty over human life (Deut. 32:39). For this capital crime God later explicitly declared that he demanded a capital punishment (Gen. 9:6). But such a punishment is implied in the very nature of the crime, even before it is explicitly stated. This becomes obvious in the case of Cain, the first murderer.

Cain deserved and expected capital punishment. There are many indications in the text that when Cain killed his brother Abel, he both expected and deserved capital punishment. God said, "Your brother's blood cries out to me from the ground" (Gen. 4:10). This cry for blood (life) vengeance is a clear indication that justice demanded a life in return. Cain himself plainly expected vengeance on his life when he said, "Whoever finds me will kill me" (v. 14). Even God's pronouncement of protection on Cain implied capital punishment by its reference to "vengeance seven times over" on anyone who later killed Cain (v. 15). Since there was no government nor anyone left (except Cain's father and mother) to execute Cain, God personally commuted Cain's deserved death sentence. Since God is the author of life, he has the right to do it. But the text makes it evident nonetheless that capital punishment was both expected and deserved.

God gave the power of capital punishment to human government. There was capital punishment before the time of Noah, but it was left to relatives to avenge the murderer (Gen. 4:14). By instituting capital punishment, God took justice out of the hands of the families of the deceased and placed the sword in the hands of human government. In this way justice could be more objectively exercised by eliminating the personal revenge factor and the emotional anger. So Noah was not the first to be given the right to capital punishment (Gen. 9:6). This was simply the point at which God instituted human government which was to thereby assume the capital authority that was already being exercised by families.

Capital punishment was incorporated into the Mosaic law. When God enjoined capital punishment on Israel (Exod. 21), it was not the first time he had instituted it. It was implied from the beginning (Gen. 4) and given to human government under Noah for capital crimes

(Gen. 9:6). What Moses' law did was simply to incorporate it and extend it to many other noncapital crimes, including religious and ceremonial ones. Israel was a chosen nation whom God was to rule in a special way (Exod. 19). Hence, as Israel was a theocracy, these additional reasons for capital punishment were not intended for other nations. For example, God never commanded other nations to worship on the Sabbath or to pay tithes to the temple in Jerusalem. Hence, Gentile nations are not condemned for not doing this, even though they are judged for a whole host of sins from pride to injustice (see Obad. 1). Israel, however, is often condemned by God for breaking these special laws. Individuals were even given capital punishment for not keeping the Sabbath (Exod. 31:14).

Under God, Moses did not institute capital punishment for capital crimes; he simply incorporated it into his law. But he did extend capital punishment to noncapital crimes. He did not give capital punishment to the nations in general, but he did apply it to God's chosen nation in special ways.

If capital punishment for capital crimes was not given with the law of Moses, then it did not thereby pass away with the Mosaic law. It abides when that which was unique to Moses' law has passed away (Heb. 7–8).

Capital punishment is reaffirmed in the New Testament. Capital punishment for capital crimes was not given by God simply to Israel, as was the law of Moses (Deut. 4:8; Ps. 147:19–20). It was given to Noah for the whole human race (Gen. 9:6, 9–10). And since God has never abolished this punishment on the race, any more than he has ever abolished his promise to Noah for the whole race never to flood the whole earth (Gen. 9:11), then divinely instituted capital punishment is still in effect for the whole race.

The sword that was divinely given to human government for capital punishment (Gen. 9:6) is explicitly reaffirmed in the New Testament (Rom. 13:4). Jesus acknowledged it before Pilate (John 19:11), as did Paul before the Romans (Acts 25:11). So capital punishment, at least for capital crimes, is stated before the law of Moses and repeated after it. Hence, whatever additions were made in Moses' law regarding capital punishment for other reasons are not binding on the human race today.

An Evaluation of Retributionism—
Negative Criticisms

Many criticisms have been leveled at capital punishment, even for crimes involving the loss of life. Most of these have already been implied in the response to rehabilitationism. Hence, they will be only briefly summarized here.

It is cruel and unusual punishment. If it is, then so is the murder of an innocent person, and justice demands a life for a life. Those who take a life must give their life. What we take, we owe. There is nothing cruel or unusual about this.

It is unfairly applied. Not administering justice for any capital crime is not the answer to injustice for some real crimes. Two wrongs do not make a right. Just because some people die from a lack of proper distribution of medical care does not mean it should be withheld from all. Likewise, just because some people die from an unjust distribution of capital punishment does not mean that justice should be withheld from all.

It does not deter crime. God said it will. When justice is done "all the people will hear and be afraid, and will not be contemptuous again" (Deut. 17:13). One thing is certain, capital punishment will deter that particular violent criminal from ever repeating another crime. If capital punishment does not deter as much other crime as it could, it is probably because it is not exercised widely and speedily enough to be a real threat (Eccles. 8:11).

It is not biblical, at least not today. As we have seen, capital punishment is not biblical today for noncapital crimes. Those were unique to the Mosaic legislation which is no longer binding. But capital punishment for capital crimes was given to human government before Moses' law (Gen. 9:6), and it was reaffirmed after Moses' law (Rom. 13:4; John 19:11; Acts 25:11).

The criminal should be cured, not killed. This is based on the mistaken notion that justice is remedial and not penal. However, the remedial view dehumanizes the criminal by making him into a patient or object to be treated, rather than a person to be respected. It is an illusory humanitarianism that is really antihuman. It has horrendous tyrannical potential in the hands of an elite who can pronounce who is "sick" and must be treated by the state.

Some murderers are not rationally responsible. If this refers to children before they are socially accountable, to imbeciles, or to people who do not have the moral and rational capability to understand their actions, then capital punishment is not an appropriate punishment. Moral responsibility assumes someone is morally responsible. A person cannot be held rationally accountable if he is not rational.

It is contrary to the concept of pardon. First of all, pardon makes no sense in a remedial view of justice. Someone who is sick cannot be pardoned; only a sinner can be forgiven. Hence, the concept of pardon makes sense only in a penal view of justice. All capital crimes deserve death, but not all criminals deserving of death should necessarily die. For that matter, all offenses are worthy of death (Rom. 1:32; 6:23). But even the old law did not demand capital punishment for all offenses. In Genesis 4, God personally commuted the death sentence for Cain. So suspending the deserved death penalty in special cases, especially where there is genuine repentance and restitution, is not without biblical precedent. But the very concept of mercy to the genuinely repentant presupposes the framework of justice which calls for capital justice in capital crimes.

It overlooks those who are insane. No one who is really insane (not in control of his faculties) should be given capital punishment, because he is not morally responsible. However, so-called temporary insanity is often only a fit of rage. And we are responsible for getting angry and for what we do in anger. Being irrational (insane) and acting irrationally (criminally) are two different things. In one sense, all sin is irrational, including capital sins.

An Evaluation of Retributionism— Positive Contributions

In spite of many criticisms, capital punishment for capital crimes has many positive dimensions. Several will be summarized here.

It is based on a high view of man. The retributionist position behind capital punishment presupposes a high view of human freedom and dignity. It is based on the assumption that normal adult human beings are rational and moral beings who know better, who could do otherwise, but yet who chose to do evil anyway, and who therefore deserve to be punished.

It treats the criminal with respect. By punishing someone who deserves it, the state is thereby rendering respect to him. But submitting someone to a compulsory cure against his will is to treat him as an infant, an imbecile, or a domestic animal. Persons who knowingly do wrong deserve to be punished, not to be treated like an object to be manipulated.

It operates on a correct view of justice. As has been noted earlier, the biblical view of justice is penal, not remedial. The primary purpose of justice is moral, not therapeutic. It is ethical and not pathological. This is true whether the crime is incidental or capital. Punishment should be given only because people deserve it.

It does deter crime. All the protests notwithstanding, punishment does deter crime. The Bible says it does (Deut. 17:13), and the facts support it, especially in the case of capital punishment. Dead offenders cannot repeat their crimes. And even common sense dictates that the average person thinks twice about breaking the law if he really believes he will be severely punished.

It protects innocent lives. Capital punishment protects innocent lives in three ways. First, it is a strong advance premium placed upon human life that generates our respect in preserving and protecting life. Second, when it is properly exercised it puts the fear of God into other would-be murderers. Finally, it prevents repeat crimes from capital offenders.

Summary and Conclusion

There are three basic views on capital punishment held by Christians: rehabilitationism, reconstructionism, and retributionism. Rehabilitationism opposes capital punishment for any crime. Reconstructionism insists on capital punishment for all major crimes, whether moral or religious. Retributionism holds that capital punishment is appropriate for some crimes, namely, capital offenses.

Rehabilitationism is based on a remedial (reformatory) view of justice. The criminal is seen as a patient who is sick in need of treatment. The other two views believe that justice is retributive. They view the criminal as a morally responsible person who deserves punishment. Retributionism differs from reconstructionism in that the former does not believe that the offenses calling for capital punishment under Moses' law are still binding today. Rather, retributionism contends that capital punishment is based on the biblically stated principle of a life for a life that is applicable to all persons in all places and all times.

Select Readings

Bahnsen, Greg L. *Theonomy in Christian Ethics.* Exp. ed. Phillipsburg, N.J.: Presbyterian and Reformed, 1984.

Baker, William H. *On Capital Punishment.* Rev. ed. Chicago: Moody, 1985.

————. *Worthy of Death: Capital Punishment—Unpleasant Necessity or Unnecessary Penalty?* Chicago: Moody, 1973.

Davis, John Jefferson. *Evangelical Ethics: Issues Facing the Church Today.* Phillipsburg, N.J.: Presbyterian and Reformed, 1985.

Endres, Michael E. *The Morality of Capital Punishment: Equal Justice for All under the Law?* Mystic, Conn.: Twenty-third Publications, 1985.

Lewis, C. S. *God in the Dock.* Edited by Walter Hooper. Grand Rapids: Eerdmans, 1970.

Moberly, Sir Walter. *The Ethics of Punishment.* Hamden, Conn.: Archon, 1968.

Van den Haag, Ernest. *The Death Penalty: A Debate.* New York: Plenum, 1983.

12

War

What should the Christian's attitude be toward war? Is it ever right to take the life of another person under the command of one's government? Is there a biblical basis for engaging in war? These questions have found varying responses among Christians. Basically, views regarding taking the life of another in war fall into three categories. First, there is *activism,* which holds that the Christian ought to participate in any war engaged in by his government because government is ordained of God. Second, there is *pacifism,* which contends that Christians should never participate in war to the point of killing others because God has commanded men never to take the lives of others. Finally, there is *selectivism,* which argues that Christians should participate in some wars—the just ones. To do otherwise is to refuse to follow the just course commanded by God.

Activism: It Is Always Right to Participate in War

Activism holds that a Christian is duty-bound to obey his government and to participate in every war for which that government enlists his support. Adherents of this position offer two different kinds of arguments in favor of their view, biblical and philosophical (or social). We will begin by examining the biblical data.

The Biblical Argument: Government
Is Ordained of God

Scripture seems emphatic on this point. Government is of God. Whether in the religious or the civil realm, God is the God of order and not of chaos (Gen. 9:6; 2 Cor. 14:33, 40).

Old Testament data on God and government—From the very beginning, Scripture declares that man was to "have dominion over . . . every living thing that moves upon the earth" (Gen. 1:25). Man was to be king over all the earth. After the fall the woman was told, "Your desire shall be for your husband, and he shall rule over you" (Gen. 3:16). When Cain killed Abel it was implied that he failed to realize that he was his "brother's keeper" (Gen. 4:9–10). Finally, when the whole prediluvian civilization had become corrupt "and the earth was filled with violence," God destroyed it and instituted human government. God said to Noah and his family after the flood, "For your lifeblood I will surely require a reckoning . . . ; of every man's brother I will require the life of man." For "whoever sheds the blood of man, by man shall his blood be shed; for God made man in his own image" (Gen. 9:5–6 RSV).

In brief, God ordained human government. Adam was given the crown to reign over the earth. And when evil became rampant, Noah was given the sword to enforce that rule. Government is of God both because order is from God and because disorder must be put down for God. Men have the right from God to take the lives of unruly men who shed innocent blood. Government is invested with divine power.

The sword which was given to Noah was used by Abraham when he engaged in war against the kings who had committed aggression against Abraham's nephew, Lot (Gen. 14). This passage indicates God's approval of wars that protect the innocent from aggressors.

Although the specific form of government changed throughout the Old Testament, there is a reiteration of the principle that government is of God. In the Mosaic theocracy, the powers of government are very explicit: "You shall give life for life, eye for eye, tooth for tooth, hand for hand, foot for foot, burn for burn, wound for wound, stripe for stripe" (Exod. 21:23–25). Even when Israel set up its monarchy contrary to God's plan (1 Sam. 8:7), God nevertheless anointed their choice of a king. God said to Samuel the prophet, "Hearken to their voice, and make them a king" (1 Sam. 8:22). Later Samuel said, "Do you see him whom the LORD has chosen?" (1 Sam. 10:24 RSV). Even before David was king he was commanded to fight against the Philistines who were robbing Israel (1 Sam. 23:1).

As far as the governments of Gentile nations were concerned, the

Old Testament declares that "the Most High is sovereign over the king-doms of men and gives them to anyone he wishes" (Dan. 4:25). And from the rest of Daniel's prophecy, it is clear that God ordained the great Babylonian, Medo-Persian, Grecian, and Roman governments (Dan. 2–7). In fact, the indication is that God has ordained government wherever it is found. And since government is given of God, it would follow that to disobey government is to disobey God. If, therefore, a person's government commands him to go to war, a biblical activism would argue that one must respond in obedience to the Lord, for the Lord has ordained the government with the sword or the power to take lives.

New Testament data on God and government—The New Testament confirms the view of the Old Testament that God has ordained gov-ernment. Jesus declares that we should "give to Caesar what is Cae-sar's" (Matt. 22:21). That civil authority is God-given is further acknowledged by Jesus before Pilate when he says, "You would have no power over me if it were not given to you from above" (John 19:11). Paul admonishes Timothy to pray and give thanks "for kings and all those in authority" (1 Tim. 2:2). Titus is exhorted to "remind the people to be subject to rulers and authorities, to be obedient" (Titus 3:1). Peter is very clear: "Be subject for the Lord's sake to every human institu-tion, whether it be to the emperor as supreme, or to governors as sent by him" (1 Pet. 2:13–14 RSV).

The most extensive passage in the New Testament on the relation of the Christian to government is found in Romans 13:1–7. The first verse makes it clear that all government is divinely established: "Everyone must submit himself to the governing authorities, for there is no authority except that which God has established." Therefore, "he who rebels against the authority is rebelling against what God has instituted, and those who do so will bring judgment on themselves" (vv. 1–2). The further reason given for obeying a ruler is that "he is God's servant to do you good. . . . He is God's servant, an agent of wrath to bring punishment on the wrongdoer" (v. 4).

Paul writes, "This is also why you pay taxes, for the authorities are God's servants, who give their full time to governing" (v. 6). In view of this, the Christian is urged to "pay all of them their dues, taxes to whom taxes are due, revenue to whom revenue is due, respect to whom respect is due, honor to whom honor is due" (v. 7 RSV). What is espe-cially significant about this passage of Scripture is that it is the New Testament's reiteration of the power of government to take a human life. Christians are urged to obey the existing governor or king, "for he does not bear the sword in vain" (v. 4). Government, with its power over life, is ordained of God, and whoever resists his government is resisting God. It would follow from this, according to biblical activists, that one ought to respond to the call of his government to war because God has given the authority of the sword to the governing authorities.

The Philosophical Argument:
Government Is Man's Guardian

Activism is defended by arguments outside the Bible as well. One of the most powerful defenses of this position comes from Plato's dialogue, *Crito*. In it, he offers three explicit reasons (and two more implied ones) why a person should not disobey even a government which is unjustly putting him to death. The scene is the prison where Socrates awaits his death, having been charged with impiety and sentenced to drink the cup of poison. Socrates's young friend Crito urges him to escape and evade the death penalty. In Socrates's reply five reasons are given for obeying an unjust government, even to the point of death.

Government is man's parent. One ought not disobey even an unjust government. "First, because in disobeying it he is disobeying his parent." By this Socrates means that it is under the sponsorship of government that the individual is brought into the world. He is not born into a lawless jungle but comes into this world under the parentage of the state. It is the state which makes his very birth more than barbaric—a birth into a state of civilization rather than anarchy. Just as a parent spends months in preparation and anticipation for a child, many years have likewise been spent in maintaining the state that makes a civilized birth possible, and these years may not be lightly regarded later because one finds himself at odds with the government. If one were to disobey the government, says Socrates, would it not reply, "In the first place did we not bring you into existence? Your father married your mother by our aid and begat you. Say whether you have any objection to urge against those of us who regulate marriage. None, I should reply."[1]

Government is man's educator. Socrates offers another reason for obedience to one's government. "Second, because it is the author of his education." The implication here is that the very education that makes one that which he is (including his knowledge of justice and injustice) was given to him by his government. He is civilized, and not a barbarian, not only by birth, but by training. And both the birth and training were made possible by the government that is now demanding his life. What can one reply against governments which "after birth

---

1. Plato, *Crito,* in *The Dialogues of Plato,* trans. Benjamin Jowett, The Great Books of the Western World, vol. 7 (Chicago: Encyclopaedia Britannica, 1952), p. 217.

regulate the nurture and education of children, in which you also were trained? Were not the laws, which have the charge of education, right in commanding your father to train you in music and gymnastic? Right, I should reply." From this it follows that government could say to us, "Since you were brought into the world and nurtured and educated by us, can you deny in the first place that you are our child and slave, as your fathers were before you?" And if this is true, man is not on equal terms with his government. Man has no more right to strike back at it and revile it than one does to hit one's mother or father. Even if government would destroy us, we have no right to destroy it in return. If one thinks he does have such a right, he has "failed to discover that [his] country is more to be valued and higher and holier far than mother or father or any ancestor."[2] Government is not only prior to the individual citizen, but superior to him as well.

The governed have a duty to obey government. The third reason Socrates gives for a person obeying the government is that "he has made an agreement with [it] that he will duly obey [its] commands." That is, his consent to be governed, given by pledging his allegiance to that government, binds him to its laws. By the very fact that a person makes a given country his country, he has thereby made a tacit covenant to be obedient to its commands. Hence, "when we are punished by [our country], whether with imprisonment or stripes, the punishment is to be endured in silence; and if she lead us to wounds or death in battle, thither we follow as is right."[3] For if one is to accept the privileges of education and protection of his government, then he has thereby implicitly agreed to accept the responsibility to obey his government's laws, submit to its penalties, and even to go to war for it.

The governed is free to leave his government. There are at least two other implied arguments that Socrates uses to contend that one ought not disobey one's government. "Any one who does not like it and the city, may go where he likes, . . . But he who has experience of the manner in which we [rulers] order justice and administer the State, and still remains, has entered into an implied contract that he will do as we command him." Socrates makes it clear, however, that whatever emigrating one is going to do must be done before he is indicted or drafted by his country. To flee in the face of one's responsibilities to his government is "doing only what a miserable slave would do, running away and turning your back upon the compacts and agreements which you made as a citizen."[4] If one is not willing to obey his country,

2. Ibid.
3. Ibid.
4. Ibid.

he should find another country he can obey. If a person assumes the protection and privilege of a country by constant presence there as a citizen, then he or she must not seek exile simply because the country's demands are undesirable.

Without government there would be social chaos. Another reason one should not disobey his government is implied in Socrates's question, "And who would care about a State which has no law?" An unjust law is bad, but no law is even worse. Even a bad monarchy is to be preferred to anarchy. Any government is better than no government at all, and if people were to disobey their government in what they felt was unjust or undesirable, then social chaos would result. If obedience to government were determined individually or subjectively, then no law would be immune from some citizen's disapproval or disobedience, and the result would be chaotic. To borrow a phrase from Scripture, to have no laws that are binding on all citizens would be for "every one to do that which is right in his own eyes." And the result would not be a society, but a social chaos.

Even a government that is closed to its citizens would be better than one open to revolution among its peoples. In these five arguments Plato states the major points used as a basis for activism. A man should always obey his government because it is his guardian. Government—even one that seems to be unjust—should be obeyed to the point of going to war. For without government humans would be no better than savages, living in a state of ignorance and anarchy. Hence, no matter how undesirable one's responsibilities to his government may be, nevertheless he is obligated to obey it as his parent and master.

Contemporary writers have not added many major points to the biblical and classical arguments in favor of activism. One overall argument not explicitly included in the five presented by Plato is that it is a greater evil not to resist an evil aggressor than to fight against him. This is reminiscent of the famous line, "All that is necessary for evil to triumph is for good men to do nothing." If good men will not resist evil men, then evil men will prevail in the world.

Of course, there is a basic problem with the activist's position that pacifists are quick to point out, and that is that in most wars both sides claim to be in the right. Often each country claims the other is the aggressor. The enemy is always wrong, but each country is the "enemy" to the other. At this point the total activist is obliged to admit that both parties (or countries) in a war are not always right. But even when one country is unjustly engaged in war, its citizens are duty-bound to respond to its military draft, for disobedience to government, even an evil one, is a greater evil than obedience to it in an unjust war.

To disobey any government leads to revolution and anarchy, which are greater evils than participating in a war. The complete activist can argue that it would be better to fight on the side of an evil order than to contribute, by disobedience, to disorder and chaos. And if one is in doubt about which government is the best or most just, then he should content himself with obedience to his own government on the ground that it is his guardian and educator. Whether or not his own country is the most just, he can fight for it, believing that the outcome of the war will manifest the triumph of justice.

Pacifism: It Is Never Right to Participate in War

There are many reasons why the pacifist rejects the activist's arguments, and these may serve both as a critique of total activism and as the other side of the dialogue on war which forces the Christian to examine both his Bible and his conscience for guidance. The arguments for pacifism are of two basic types, biblical and social.

The Biblical Argument: War Is Always Wrong

The Christian pacifist's argument against all wars contains many points, but there are a few basic premises underlying all of them. One of these premises is found in the biblical injunction, "You shall not kill" (Exod. 20:13), and another in Jesus' words, "Do not resist one who is evil" (Matt. 5:39).

Killing is always wrong. At the very heart of pacifism is the conviction that intentionally taking another human life is always wrong. Intentionally taking life, especially in war, is basically and radically wrong. The scriptural prohibition, "You shall not kill," includes war, since war is mass murder. Murder is murder whether it is done within one's own society or to people in another society.

Since this conclusion is prima facie at odds with the many cases in Scripture which seem to command war, Christian pacifists must explain why the Bible appears to sometimes command war. Various answers have been given by different pacifists. Some argue that the wars of the Old Testament which God is represented as "commanding" (Josh. 10) were not really commanded by God at all. Rather, they represent a more barbarous state of mankind in which wars were justified by attaching divine sanctions to them. Since this option seems to clearly reject the authority of the Old Testament, it is not a viable alternative for an evangelical Christian. Some pacifists suggest that these wars were unique in that Israel was acting as a theocratic instrument in the hands of God. These were not really Israel's wars at all but God's wars, as is evidenced by the special miracles God performed to win them (see Josh. 6, 10; Ps. 44).

Other pacifists argue that the wars of the Old Testament were not God's perfect will but only his permissive will. That is, God is represented as commanding war in the same secondary and concessive sense that he is said to have commanded Samuel to anoint Saul the king even though God had not chosen Saul but David to be king (1 Sam. 10:1). Wars are commanded by God in the same sense in which Moses commanded divorce—because of the hardness of men's hearts (Matt. 19:8). It is not that God really desires and commands war any more than he likes disobedience or divorce. God has a better way than that and it is obedience and love. God could have accomplished his purposes in Israel and Canaan without war, had they been more obedient to him.

No war as such is ever God's command. What God commands clearly and unequivocally is, "You shall not kill." This command applies to all people, friends or enemies. All men are made in God's image and, therefore, it is wrong to kill them. The Old Testament clearly teaches that one should love his enemies (Lev. 19:18; Isa. 34; Jon. 4), and Jesus reaffirmed this, saying, "Love your enemies and pray for those who persecute you" (Matt. 5:44). War is based in hate and is intrinsically wrong. Taking the life of another person is contrary to the principle of love and is, therefore, fundamentally un-Christian.

Resisting evil with force is wrong. Closely connected with the first basic premise of pacifism, that killing is wrong, is another. Evil should never be resisted with physical force, but rather with the spiritual force of love. Did not Jesus say, "Do not resist one who is evil. But if any one strikes you on the right cheek, turn to him the other also" (Matt. 5:39 rsv)? Did not Christ also teach in this passage that "if any one forces you to go one mile, go with him two miles" (v. 41)? The Christian is not to retaliate or pay back evil with evil, for vengeance belongs to God (Deut. 32:35). Paul wrote, "Beloved, never avenge yourself, but leave it to the wrath of God. . . . No, if your enemy is hungry, feed him; if he is thirsty, give him drink. . . . Do not be overcome by evil, but overcome evil with good" (Rom. 12:19–21). The Christian is to "repay no one evil for evil. . . . If possible, so far as it depends on you, live peaceably with all" (vv. 17–18 rsv).

The story of Jesus driving the money changers from the temple is not incompatible with this position, some pacifists argue, for physical force (the whip) was used only on the animals, not the people. Furthermore, the authority Jesus used was his own and that of Scripture, not that of a strong-armed band of disciples (John 2:15–16). Finally, pacifists argue that the kind of physical force used by Jesus in the temple falls far short of proving that Jesus would sanction using extreme physical force to the point of taking human life.

Jesus' statement, "I have not come to bring peace, but a sword," cannot be used to support war. When Jesus commanded Peter, "Put your sword back into its place; for all who take the sword perish by the sword," he was not defining the purpose but the result of his ministry. He was saying that the effect of allegiance to him would "set a man against his father, and a daughter against her mother" (Matt. 10:35). That is, the effect of Christ's ministry would be to divide families as if by a sword (Luke 12:51), even though this was not the intent of his coming.

Pacifism is committed to the premise that it is essentially wrong to use physical force, at least to the point of taking life, in order to resist evil. This does not mean that the pacifist repudiates all force. It means only that he believes in affirming the greater force of spiritual good in the face of the forces of physical evil. Pacifists believe basically that "we are not contending against flesh and blood but against . . . the spiritual hosts of wickedness in heavenly places" (Eph. 6:12 RSV).

When pressed to the wall by a militant activist asking whether he would kill a would-be murderer of his wife, the consistent pacifist's reply is simple: Why kill a wicked murderer and send him to his eternal doom, when permitting the murderer to kill his believing wife will result in her eternal bliss? The less stringent pacifist (or perhaps one with a non-Christian wife) might argue that wounding or disarming the murderer would be sufficient, but that one should never aim to kill even a murderer.

Another basic premise of pacifism is that there is no real distinction between what one should do as a private citizen and what one should do as a public official. What is wrong for a person to do in his own neighborhood is wrong in any other neighborhood in the world. Putting on a military uniform does not revoke one's moral responsibility. The distinction between person and office is rejected as unbiblical and inconsistent. No one is exonerated from God's command not to kill simply because he has changed his uniform. The command against murder is not abrogated by one's obligation to the state. Only God holds the power of life and death. The powers of the state are social but not capital. The right to take a life belongs only to the Author of life himself (see Job 1:21). No human authority has the right to transcend God's moral law. Indeed, what authority government has is derived from God's moral law.

The Social Arguments: War Is Always Wrong

There are strong social arguments against war. It is not the best way to settle human disputes. A river of human blood flows in the wake of wars down through history. Evils of all kinds result from war: starvation, cruelty, plagues, and death.

War is based on the evil of greed. As far back as Plato's *Republic,* it was recognized by thinking people that the desire for luxury was the basis of warfare. Plato observes, "We need not say yet whether war does good or harm, but only that we have discovered its origin in desires which are the most fruitful source of evils both to individuals and to states."[5] In another place he says, "All wars are made for the sake of getting money."[6] James says, "What causes fights and quarrels among you? . . . You want something but don't get it. You kill and covet, but you cannot have what you want" (James 4:1–2). Paul warns Timothy that "the love of money is the root of all kinds of evil" (1 Tim. 6:10). It is this same creed that is at the heart of war.

War results in many evils. The evils of war are too numerous to be expanded upon here. There is no way to measure the sorrow, pain, and horror of war. One of the most vivid descriptions is in the sixth chapter of the Apocalypse, where John writes, "I looked and there before me was a pale horse! Its rider was named Death, and Hades was following close behind him." They "were given power . . . to kill by sword, famine and plague, and by the wild beasts of the earth" (Rev. 6:8). Such are the evil results of war, to say nothing of rape, cruelty, and other acts of barbarism.

War breeds war. The First World War was advertised as the war to end all wars. But no war up to the present has really made the world free from war. The subdued often rise to retaliate against their oppressors. Many wars never really end; they simply subside. "Cold" wars tend to turn into "hot" wars, and partial wars into full-scale wars. Nothing really provides permanent settlement of hostilities. Rather than bringing people together, war seems to solidify their enmity. War appears to excite the spirit of retaliation and open up the possibility of further conflict. Perhaps it is this sense of futility about war which has led so many to the pacifist's position. Slogans like "Make love, not war" and "Ban the Bomb," as well as the popularity of the antinuclear movement, are evidence of a growing dissatisfaction with war as a means of settling disputes among nations. Even some who are not pacifists by conviction are willing to risk total unilateral disarmament in the hope that it may elicit a similar response from the enemy. "Give peace a chance," they cry out in a desperate attempt to avoid the horrors of war.

In summary, the pacifists argue that war is both unbiblical and

5. Plato, *The Republic* (New York: Oxford University Press, 1967), pp. 61, 62.
6. Ibid., p. 62.

antisocial. It is forbidden by God under the prohibition against murder and it is becoming increasingly repugnant to the human race, which is showing increasing signs of battle fatigue under the continued inhumanities of man to man.

Selectivism: It Is Right to Participate in Some Wars

Not all people are content with the blind patriotism of activism that would kill upon their government's request while shouting, "My country, right or wrong!" Neither is everyone satisfied with a naively passive attitude that would permit a Hitler to attempt genocide without lifting a gun in resistance. Even the otherwise pacifistic Dietrich Bonhoeffer finally concluded that Hitler should have been assassinated. Out of dissatisfaction with the easy solutions of declaring all wars just or unjustifiable, a view is emerging called selectivism, which holds that some wars are justifiable and some are not. This view offers a more satisfactory alternative for a Christian ethic.

Selectivism as a Response to Activism: Some Wars Are Unjust

Both activism and pacifism claim the support of Scripture. Each view represents some truth. The truth of pacifism is that some wars are unjust and Christians ought not participate in these. The truth of activism is that some wars are just and Christians ought to fight in those. Selectivism, then, is committed to the position that one ought to participate only in a just war. In fact, there is a point of agreement (at least theoretically) with all three views. All could assent to the following ethical proposition: One should not participate in an unjust war.

The pacifist, of course, believes that *all* wars are unjust. The activist holds that *no* war is unjust (or at least if there are some unjust wars, then participation in them is not wrong). And the selectivist contends that in principle *some* wars are unjust and others are just. Hence, to support a Christian selectivism one must show both that at least some wars are just in principle, showing that total pacifism is wrong, and that some wars are unjust in principle, thus showing that activism is wrong.

The rejection of total activism is supported by Scripture. The Bible teaches that it is not always right to obey one's government in everything it commands, particularly when its commands contradict the higher moral laws of God. There are clear instances of this in the Bible. The three Hebrew youths disobeyed the king's command to worship an idol (Dan. 3). Daniel broke a law commanding him not to pray to God (Dan. 6). The early apostles disobeyed orders not to preach the gospel of Christ (Acts 4–5). And in a clear case of divinely approved disobedience of civil law, the Hebrew midwives in Egypt disobeyed the command to kill all the male babies born. It is written, "The midwives feared God, and did not do as the king of Egypt commanded them, but let the male children live. . . . So God dealt well with the midwives; and the people multiplied and grew very strong." Further, "because the midwives feared God he gave them families" (Exod. 1:17, 20–21).

This passage clearly teaches that it is wrong to take the life of an innocent human, even if the government "ordained of God" commands it. The government commanding it may be ordained of God, but the morally unjustifiable command is not ordained of God. The parents of Jesus evidenced the same conviction that government has no rights over the life of an innocent human being, since, under God's direction, they fled Herod's attempt to kill the Christ child (Matt. 2:13–14). The inevitable conclusion from these Scriptures is that government is *not* always to be obeyed, especially when its command conflicts with the higher laws of God regarding the taking of innocent human lives. Of course, soldiers of a government engaging in an unjust war are not innocent. Hence, they are liable to attacks on their lives.

Since government is not sovereign in its commands regarding the taking of life, it follows that not all wars waged by one's government are just. Indeed, even within a just war there may be unjust commands given which should be disobeyed. But if there are times when one should not obey his government's command to kill, then total activism is wrong. That is, not all wars nor all acts of war are morally justifiable on the grounds that one is acting in obedience to his government. This was the conclusion of the Nuremberg trials following World War II and was used again during the Viet Nam war in the My Lai incident where babies were shot in their mothers' arms. The moral principle applied in both cases is that no individual member of the armed forces of any country should be excused for engaging in a war crime simply because he has been ordered to commit the act by a superior officer. Evil is evil whether a government commands it or not. The Bible is clear on the point that one should not always obey government.

The Scriptures also teach that not all wars are necessarily evil. That is, contrary to pacifism, some wars are just. Taking life is often clearly commanded by God, both within a nation and between nations. Not all taking of life is murder. Sometimes God delegates the authority to take a human life to other humans. This was clearly the case with the power of capital punishment given to Noah after the flood (Gen. 9:6), that was restated by Moses in the law for Israel (Exod. 21:23), attributed by Paul to the emperor of Rome (Rom. 13:4), and even implied by Jesus before Pilate (John 19:11). It is evident from these passages that every government, even apart from the special theocratic government of Israel, was given divine authority to take the life of one of its citizens guilty of a capital offense.

There is another somewhat neglected statement by Jesus that may lend support to the claim that an individual has the right to wield a sword in his own defense. It is well known that Jesus admonished his disciples not to spread the gospel with the sword (Matt. 26:52). But it is sometimes overlooked that Jesus commanded his disciples to buy a sword (apparently for their own protection). Some pacifists spiritualize this passage. But it is not necessary to interpret this command metaphorically or ironically, as some pacifists do. The fact that the disciples fetched two literal swords in response to Jesus' command would seem to indicate that they took it literally (Luke 22:38). He said to them clearly, "And let him who has no sword sell his mantle and buy one" (Luke 22:36). Since swords were forbidden by Jesus for spreading the gospel, what possible purpose lay behind Jesus' command for the disciples to sell their outer garments and to buy a sword? If swords are excluded by Jesus on religious grounds, we may assume that they are included by Jesus on civil grounds. That is, swords are not valid weapons to fight spiritual battles, but they are legitimate tools for one's civil defense. While Jesus condemned the aggressive use of the sword, he commended its defensive use. While he opposed the use of force on religious grounds, he approved of it on social grounds to protect life.

The story of Abraham's battle against the kings of Genesis 14 lends support to the conclusion that unjust national aggressors should be resisted as well as unjust individual aggressors (see 1 Sam. 23:1–2). Nations as well as individuals can rob and murder. And it is faulty logic to argue that one should resist a murderous individual with the sword but let a murderous country run roughshod over thousands of innocent people.

Further support for the position that defensive military power is sometimes justifiable may be deduced from the life of the apostle Paul. When his life was threatened by unruly men, he appealed to his Roman citizenship and accepted the protection of the Roman army (Acts 22:25–29). On one occasion, certain men dedicated themselves to kill Paul, but he was taken under the protection of a small army of soldiers (Acts 23:23). Paul considered it his right as a citizen to be protected by the army from unjust aggression against his life. His actions clearly demonstrate that he demanded protection as a Roman citizen.

The principle of using military power in self-defense can be extended to a nation as well as to individuals. As pacifists also acknowledge, there is not a double standard of morality in the New Testament, with one rule for the individual and another for the country. After all, countries are made of many individuals. Not all killings or wars are unjust. God sometimes commands that the sword be used to resist evil men. Another support for just wars is evident in the words of John the Baptist. When asked by soldiers who had become believers, "What shall we do?" his answer was not, "Leave the army." Rather, it was in essence, "Be a good soldier." They were simply told, "Don't extort money and don't accuse people falsely—be content with your pay" (Luke 3:14). Surely if it had been wrong to engage in military activity, they would have been told so. The military is not an evil occupation as such. It is really a ministry of God to execute justice on behalf of the government (Rom. 13:4).

Selectivism as a Response to Pacifism: Some Wars Are Just

Christian pacifists appeal to Scripture in support of their position, but in each case the passage is capable of interpretation in another way. In fact, when taken in their proper contexts, these passages do not support the claims of pacifists.

Were commands to kill only concessions? The attempt by pacifists to explain God's commands to kill in the Old Testament as simply divine concessions to human sinfulness is unacceptable. This kind of hermeneutic would undermine the Christian's confidence in all the commands of Scripture. When a command is conditional or cultural, the Scriptures label it as such. For example, Jesus pointed out that Moses had not really commanded divorce but merely allowed it (Matt. 19:8). In point of fact, there is no command to divorce anywhere in Scripture. The passage simply says, "If a man marries a woman who becomes displeasing to him" (Deut. 24:1). This is a concession but not a command to divorce. Even in the Old Testament, God made his view on divorce very clear. " 'I hate divorce,' says the LORD God of Israel" (Mal. 2:16).

The Bible also clearly indicates that God's order to anoint Saul king over Israel was a concession and not God's real desire for Israel (1 Sam. 8:6–9), at least not at that time and in that way. However, when God commanded Israel to exterminate the wicked Canaanites, there is no indication that God really wanted Israel to "make love, not war" with them. In fact, they were past winning; the cup of their iniquity was full (Gen. 15:16). Like a gangrenous leg, they were incurably wicked and God ordered Israel to perform the "amputation" (see also Lev. 18:25–27; Deut. 20:16–17).

Neither is there any indication in the Old Testament that capital punishment was used on murderers simply because the prevailing culture taught this or because the people did not love the murderer enough. On the contrary, the Scriptures state plainly that capital punishment is the very thing that God wanted to be done to such murderers. This is evident from the reason God gave for instituting capital punishment, that "in the image of God has God made man" (Gen. 9:6).

Likewise, the commands to Israel to wage war on Canaan were specifically ordered by God. "He left none remaining, but utterly destroyed all that breathed, as the LORD God of Israel had commanded" (Josh. 10:40 NIV). Before Israel entered Canaan, they were told, "But in the cities of these people that the LORD your God gives you for an inheritance, you shall save nothing that breathes, but you shall utterly destroy them" (Deut. 20:16–17). But with regard to all cities outside of Canaan, they were told, "When you draw near to a city to fight against it, offer terms of peace to it. And if its answer to you is peace and it opens to you, then all the people who are found in it shall do forced labor for you and serve you." But "if it makes no peace with you, but makes war against you, then you shall besiege it; . . . you shall put all the males to the sword, but the women and the little ones, the cattle and everything else in the city, all its spoil, you shall take as booty for yourselves" (Deut. 20:12–14). In this case waging war was conditional, but this was not so with the command of God to wage war on the Canaanites.

From these passages it may be concluded that God not only sanctioned exterminating the Canaanites but also approved other just wars against peoples who would not accept a just peace. In brief, God's command to engage in just warfare cannot be limited to the special theocratic command of God to exterminate the wicked Canaanites. Even in the later monarchies, God is said to have commanded Israel to war against its aggressors (2 Chron. 13:15–16; 20:29). Indeed, throughout the Old and New Testaments, God ordained war as an instrument of justice. Even apostate Israel herself, despite her special covenant relation to God, became the victim of governments raised up by God to defeat her (Dan. 1:1–2). Nebuchadnezzar (Dan. 4:17), Cyrus (Isa. 44:28), and even Nero are described as servants of God empowered with the sword. Paul wrote of the latter, "But if you do wrong, be afraid, for he does not bear the sword in vain; he is the servant of God to execute his wrath on the wrongdoer" (Rom. 13:4). It is evident from these Scriptures that Gentile rulers of both Testaments were given the sword to promote good and resist evil.

Is all taking of life murder? Pacifists argue that one should never take another human life because the Bible says "Thou shalt not kill"

(Exod. 20:13 KJV). But this is a misunderstanding of the passage that is translated correctly by the New International Version: "You shall not murder." All murder involves the taking of life, but not all taking of life is murder. Capital punishment takes life, but it is not murder. In fact, capital punishment is divinely enjoined in the very next chapter of the Bible (Exod. 21:12). Likewise, killing in self-defense is not murder and is approved in the following chapter (Exod. 22:2). War in defense of the innocent is not murder. And a war against an unjust aggressor is not murder (Gen. 14).

The pacifist is not facing squarely all the data of Scripture. Rather, while he clings to the prohibition against murder, he overlooks the verses where God commands taking the lives of wicked men in defense of the innocent. In brief, one cannot justify from Scripture a view that it is never right to take another human life.

Should evil be resisted with physical force? The Sermon on the Mount is the pacifist's stronghold. Did not Jesus say "turn the other cheek" and "do not resist evil"? Yes, but the question is, What did he mean by these statements? It is clear from the total context that Jesus did not mean that we should never use the sword in self-defense or in civil justice. In fact, if one takes this passage too literally, then Jesus is also recommending that we actually pluck out our physical eyes or cut off our hands (Matt. 5:29–30)! Further, the blow on the cheek was probably only a slap on the face with the back of the hand, as indicated by the fact that the normal right-handed person could only use the back of his hand to slap another on the "right cheek" (Matt. 5:39). So Jesus is speaking more of insult than injury. The Greek word is *rapidso*, meaning to "strike with the open hand" or "slap on the cheek."

Indeed, Jesus himself never turned the other cheek to a blow. When he was struck (*rapisma*) in the face (John 18:22), he rebuked those who did it, saying, "If I spoke the truth, why did you strike me?" (v. 23). Finally, the Sermon on the Mount is not pacifistic; it is antiretaliatory. It does not commend a passive attitude, but rather condemns militant activity. Simon, one of Jesus' disciples, was a former Zealot whose compatriots were engaged in guerilla activity against the Romans. Jesus condemned this kind of activity, as well as the desire to get back at those who do evil to us. Rather than return evil for evil, we should return love for hate. But in no way did Jesus demand that we not protect our lives or those of innocent people. Indeed, this would have been against the very law he said he came to fulfill (Matt. 5:17).

Is physical force contrary to love? Pacifists argue that love and war are incompatible. How can we come with the gospel of peace in one hand, they ask, and a gun of war in the other? In response, it is important to note that true love and a just war are not incompatible, for true love will protect the innocent against an evil aggressor. Furthermore, a just war is in the interest of justice. And love and justice are not incompatible. If they were, then they could not both be attributes of God. What greater act of love could one give than to lay down his life for another? One cannot help but be grateful for the thousands of white crosses in Arlington National Cemetery representing those who died that we might be free. Greater love has no young man for his country. To say love and war are inconsistent is itself an inconsistent extending of love to the aggressor but not to the victim. In fact, it is a misunderstanding of love itself. Love sometimes needs to be tough. Only an unbiblical, fuzzy, soft-soap view of love is incompatible with a strong stand for justice and liberty. But the latter sometimes makes war necessary. Consequently, love sometimes necessitates war.

The Basis of Selectivism

The arguments in favor of selectivism can be grouped in two categories, biblical and moral. Since many of the biblical precedents have already been discussed, they need only be summarized here.

The biblical basis of selectivism—There are several instances of morally justified killing in the Bible. Some of these refer specifically to individuals and can be extended to nations, and others refer specifically to a country or countries.

First, there is killing in self-defense that is approved in Exodus 22:2, which says, "If a thief is caught breaking in and is struck so that he dies, the defender is not guilty of bloodshed." Then there is killing in capital punishment mentioned in Genesis 9:6: "Whoever sheds the blood of man, by man shall his blood be shed; for in the image of God has God made man."

There are also divinely approved wars, such as the one Abraham fought against the kings of the Valley (Gen. 14). When they took aggressive action and "carried off Abram's nephew Lot and his possessions" (v. 12), Abraham "attack[ed] them and he routed them. . . . He recovered all the goods and brought back his relative Lot and his possessions" (vv. 15–16). After this Abraham was blessed by Melchizedek, who said, "Blessed be Abram by God Most High, Creator of heaven and earth. And blessed be God Most High, who delivered your enemies into your hand" (vv. 19–20). Thus, Abraham's military activity in defense of the innocent was clearly blessed by God.

This divinely sanctioned war is an especially important case because it occurred before Israel was established as a theocracy (Exod. 19). Hence, it cannot be argued that this war is a special case of a theocratic war such as God commanded Joshua to wage in exterminating the wicked Canaanites (Josh. 10). (It can be justifiably argued that what applied *uniquely* to Israel as God's chosen instrument is not normative for any other nation since then.)

The New Testament reaffirms that the sword is still a divinely appointed means of human justice. Paul wrote to the Romans, "But if you do wrong, be afraid, for [the one in authority] does not bear the sword in vain" (Rom. 13:4).

John the Baptist sanctioned the role of the military when he was asked by soldiers what they should do after they had become believers. He did not tell them to leave the army but simply to be good soldiers (Luke 3:14).

Jesus recognized that Pilate had God-given authority over his life. When Pilate said to him, "Don't you realize I have power either to free you or to crucify you?" he replied, "You would have no power over me if it were not given to you from above" (John 19:10–11).

The apostle Paul showed both his acceptance of the government's right to kill and his acceptance of the military. He said to Caesar's court, "If . . . I am guilty of doing anything deserving death, I do not refuse to die" (Acts 25:11). But when his life was threatened by militant Jews, he demanded and got the protection of the Roman army as a Roman citizen (Acts 23).

The moral basis of selectivism—The moral arguments for selectivism emerge naturally out of the arguments against activism and pacifism. They may be stated briefly.

In an evil world force will always be necessary to restrain evil persons. Ideally, killings by police and military should not be necessary, but this is not an ideal world—it is an evil world. Ideally, we should not need locks on our doors or prisons. But it is simply unrealistic to presume we can get along without them in this wicked world.

It is evil not to resist evil; it is morally wrong not to defend the innocent. Sometimes only physical force and taking lives are sufficient to accomplish this. All too often in our violent world, hostages are taken and all efforts at negotiation fail. Sometimes military action is the only way to save these innocent lives.

To permit a murder when one could have prevented it is morally wrong. To allow a rape when one could have hindered it is an evil. To watch an act of cruelty toward children without trying to intervene is morally inexcusable. In brief, not resisting evil is a sin of omission, and sins of omission can be just as evil as sins of commission. In biblical language, "Anyone, then, who knows the good he ought to do and doesn't do it, sins" (James 4:17). Any man who does not protect his wife and children against a violent intruder fails them morally. Likewise, any country that can defend its citizens against evil aggressors and does not do it is morally remiss.

Just as the cause of justice demands a life for a life in capital crimes (see chap. 11), the same logic can be extended to the unjust actions of nations. Other nations have a moral duty to take punitive actions against aggressor nations. Hitler is a case in point. It would have been morally remiss for the Allied forces not to invade Germany and subdue the Nazis at the end of World War II. Nothing less would have served the cause of international justice.

The Basis of a Just War

Activism claims that it is always right to obey one's government in war, and pacifism says it is never right to kill. Selectivism, on the other hand, holds that it is only sometimes right to go to war. This leaves one important question: When? What are the criteria of a just war, and who decides? Several criteria of a just war are stated or implied in Scripture.

A war in defense of the innocent is just. It is just to fight a war in defense of the innocent; a war against aggression is a just war. Normally, this means the invader is wrong, unless of course he was first invaded. Genesis 14 is a good case in point. The kings of the Valley had invaded first. Abraham's reinvasion was really in defense of the innocent. The initial aggressor is wrong. However, the invaded country does not have the right to permanently occupy the invading country. It simply has a right to retrieve its citizens and possessions and ensure justice. Two wrongs do not make a right. There is a moral duty to restore the independence of the country that was subdued, in spite of the fact that they were the aggressor. The way Germany and Japan were restored after World War II is an example of what should be done.

Wars fought to execute justice are just. A just war may be punitive in nature. It is sometimes just to take military action against, and even invade, a nation that has assaulted another nation. Hitler was the aggressor in France and other European countries. Thus it was right for the Allied forces to invade Germany in order to subdue the Nazis. Likewise, countries engaged in terrorism against others should receive appropriate military retaliation. The principle behind this kind of penal action is the same one behind capital punishment (see chap. 11)—a life for a life. Justice demands that the punishment fit the crime, whether the criminal is an individual or a nation. Nations engaged in criminal activity against other nations are subject to just retribution for their aggression.

This does not mean that one nation is justified in striking another simply because the other nation is allegedly planning to attack. Preemptive strikes are not necessarily justified, unless perhaps all intelligence information indicates that a devastating first strike is imminent. But even the preemptive blow should be crippling, not devastating. A child who says, "I hit him because he was going to hit me," is wrong. One has the right to duck and defend against the first blow, but not to strike the first blow. Likewise, no nation should strike another in the mere anticipation that the other may strike it first. A country does, however, have the right to shoot down enemy military craft over its country or enemy rockets coming at its land. But a country does not have the right to bomb enemy planes on their own runway simply because they may later be used to attack.

A just war must be fought by a government. God gave the sword to governments, not to individuals (Rom. 13:4). Therefore, individuals within a country cannot engage in just military activity without the approval of their government. The war must be declared by those in power for it to be a just war. Of course, not every war declared by a government is a just war. Only declared wars are just wars. And God has granted this right to use the country's sword only to governments, not to individuals (Gen. 9:6; Rom. 13:4).

This does not mean that individuals cannot protect themselves by means of the sword. As we have seen, even killing in self-defense is justified (Exod. 22:2). However, no unauthorized individual has the right to engage his country in war against another. Nor does an individual (or group) within a government have the right to declare war against its government (see chap. 12). God never gave the sword to the individual to use on his government but to the government to use on the unruly citizen.

A just war must be fought justly. Not every act in a just war is a just act of war. Chemical warfare is inhumane. Torturing or starving prisoners is morally wrong. Intentionally destroying innocent women and children is unjustified. Of course, if a woman or even young child is part of the military, then they can be resisted by whatever force necessary. For example, a child with a hand grenade or bomb tied to him is a legitimate military target. But shooting babies in mothers' arms is not a just act, even in a just war.

The Bible speaks to the matter of just acts of war in Deuteronomy 20:19, where Israel was told, "When you lay siege to a city for a long time, fighting against it to capture it, do not destroy its trees by putting an ax to them, because you can eat their fruit. Do not cut them down." Only trees that did not bear fruit could be used for siege works (v. 20). In other words, they were not to destroy the land's capacity to sustain its people after the battle was over. This would be an inhumane attack upon the people rather than a just attack on the powers in charge.

Some Problems with Selectivism

There are some serious difficulties with the selectivist position on war. Several of them will be briefly noted here.

The problem of nuclear war—Since nuclear war would by its very nature destroy the world's ability to survive after the holocaust, would it not automatically be morally wrong to use nuclear weapons? This poses a serious problem for selectivism, or any view that favors war on any occasion. Several things should be noted in response. First of all, it is a matter of factual dispute whether full-scale nuclear war would irreparably and permanently destroy the world. With proper warning and shelter, much of a population could be salvaged from an all-out nuclear attack. And with proper food storage and equipment, the fading effects of radiation can be survived.[7]

Nuclear war does not have to be that massive. It could be more tactical and limited in scope. This is especially true if a defensive shield or system like the Strategic Defense Initiative ("Star Wars") can be developed to deflect the major impact of an all-out nuclear attack. Furthermore, even if he could, it is not likely that anyone desiring more power would choose to destroy the world over which he wants power. Thus, it is more likely that he would engage in tactical or limited nuclear war.

While the stakes are higher in nuclear war, the principles are the same. Nuclear weapons should be used justly and discriminatingly. They should be directed, for example, at military targets, not civilian populations. Of course, more innocent people may be accidentally killed in nuclear war than by conventional warfare. However, just because the stakes are higher does not mean that the weapons are automatically illegitimate.

If nuclear warfare is ruled unjust, then the unjust will rule. Declaring nuclear weapons unjust makes nuclear blackmail possible. Even the threat of using them by an evil power can make innocent people submit to tyrannical demands.[8] The only realistic way to overcome this is to retain nuclear weapons as a real threat against aggressors. For any tyrant who knows that his opponent will not retaliate with

7. Ernest W. LeFever and E. Stephen Hunt, eds., *The Apocalyptic Premise* (Washington, D.C.: Ethics and Public Policy Center, 1982).

8. Myron S. Augsburger and Dean C. Curry, *Nuclear Arms* (Waco: Word, 1987), pp. 114–24.

similar nuclear force has already won the war. Once nuclear weapons
are outlawed for countries, then only outlaw countries will have them.

The very fact that there is a balance of power among opposing nations with nuclear capabilities is a stabilizing factor for peace. As long
as no one nation has unparalleled power, then it is automatically re-
strained by the realistic expectation that an opposing nation can retaliate in kind. This fact has had a sobering effect on the international
superpowers for nearly half a century now. Once this balance is upset
by unilateral disarmament or by one of the superpowers declaring it
will not use nuclear force, then the real threat of tyranny emerges.
Hence, maintaining a real balance of power, including nuclear power,
is important to world peace.

The problem of who decides—One of the most difficult problems for
selectivism is establishing who has the authority to decide which wars
are just and which are unjust. Would not confusion result if every
individual in a country could make up his mind whether he should
obey a given law? What if everyone could decide which civil or domestic
laws they would obey? The result would be chaotic.

Although selectivism places a heavy responsibility on the individual, nonetheless, this is not undesirable for several reasons. A view is
not wrong because it is difficult. To be sure, both activism and pacifism
are easier positions because the individual does not have to struggle
with the specifics of whether this or that war is just. The activist
believes in advance of looking at the facts that any wars his government declares are just, and the pacifist thinks they are all wrong. Only
the selectivist must struggle to determine whether a given war is just
or unjust.

The selectivist's struggle is not without moral guidelines. The selectivist is not determining which war is just on the basis of his own
subjective feelings. Rather, he is trying to discover which wars are just
on the basis of objective moral principles. So it is not as though the
selectivist is entirely on his own without guidance from God. God has
revealed what is just and what is unjust, and it is the principle of
justice that the selectivist uses to discover whether or not a war to
which his government calls him is just or not. True, the selectivist
must discover the facts of the matter for himself, but he is not left
without values in making his decision based on the facts he has acquired. And he is responsible only for making the best decision in view
of the facts available to him.

If everyone in two countries at war were a conscientious selectivist,
then there would be fewer wars. For the people in the country that is
the aggressor would refuse to fight, making it more difficult for aggressor nations to muster enough support for their unjust aggression.

Unless each individual decides whether a given war is just, then each must simply rely on what the government says is just. This amounts to a "my country right or wrong" approach. This is not patriotism but patriolatry. It is putting the country in the place of God rather than in its rightful place under God.

Summary and Conclusion

There are three basic views on war: activism, pacifism, and selectivism. Activism claims it is always right to go to war in obedience to one's country. Pacifism claims it is never right, and selectivism holds that it is sometimes right—when the war is a just war. As we have seen, activism as such is inadequate because we should disobey government when it commands us to do what is morally wrong. The Hebrew midwives (Exod. 1), the three Hebrew children (Dan. 3), and Daniel (Dan. 6) are biblical examples of divinely approved disobedience of government. Furthermore, total pacifism is also insufficient because it overlooks the clear instances where the Bible commends killings in such circumstances as self-defense (Exod. 22), capital punishment (Gen. 9:6), and defense of the innocent (Gen. 14).

There is, however, truth in both activism and pacifism. The activists are right in pointing out that God has ordained government and given it the sword. They are correct in insisting on human obedience to government, even at times to the point of taking life. However, the pacifists are right that we should pursue peace and try to live peaceably with all men. We should be peacemakers, not warmakers. And we should resort to war only when all efforts at peace fail rather than try peace when all efforts at war fail. Selectivism, therefore, correctly points to the need to put God over government and to encourage obedience to government but preserve the right of conscience to dissent from oppressive commands.

Select Readings

Augsburger, Myron S. *Nuclear Arms: Two Views on World Peace.* Waco: Word, 1987.

Augsburger, Myron S., and Dean C. Curry. *Nuclear Arms.* Waco: Word, 1987.

Augustine, Saint. *City of God* 19.7. In *A Select Library of the Nicene and Post-Nicene Fathers of the Christian Church,* edited by Philip Schaff, vol. 2. Grand Rapids: Eerdmans, 1956.

Clouse, Robert G., ed. *War: Four Christian Views.* Downers Grove: Inter-Varsity, 1981.

Culver, Robert D. *The Peace Mongers*. Wheaton: Tyndale House, 1985.

LeFever, Ernest W., and E. Stephen Hunt, eds. *The Apocalyptic Premise*. Washington, D.C.: Ethics and Public Policy Center, 1982.

Ramsey, Paul. *The Just War: Force and Political Responsibility*. New York: Scribner's, 1968.

————. *Speak Up for Just War or Pacifism*. University Park: Pennsylvania State University Press, 1988.

Vanderhaar, Gerard A. *Christians and Nonviolence in the Nuclear Age*. Mystic, Conn.: Twenty-third Publications, 1982.

13

Civil Disobedience

Should Christians ever disobey their government? If so, when? If not, why not? Is it ever right to revolt against an unjust government or to assassinate a tyrant? These questions are important for Christians in free countries, but are acutely so for believers in oppressed nations.

There are three basic positions on civil disobedience: It is always right, never right, or sometimes right. The first view is *anarchism*; the second is *radical patriotism,* and the third is *biblical submissionism*. Since the first view lacks any Christian justification, our attention will be focused on the latter two.

Radical Patriotism: Civil Disobedience Is Never Right

Radical patriotism is similar to the activism (chap. 12) which argues that all wars are just so long as the government commands one to participate. Here, however, the focus is not on war against another country, but on the citizen's duties to his own country. Should one ever disobey any law of his land? Radical patriotism says no.

An Explanation of Radical Patriotism

"My country, right or wrong!" cries the radical patriot. To the degree that some Christians adopt this stance, they appeal for justification to certain Scriptures. Let's take a look at their arguments.

God-ordained government. God established government after the flood (Gen. 9:6), and he expects this authority to be respected. Paul writes that "there is no authority except that which God has established. The authorities that exist have been established by God" (Rom. 13:1).

God expects obedience to human government. Not only did God establish government, but he expects us to obey it. This is obvious for two reasons. First, we are told to "submit" to it. This implies obedience because "submit" and "obey" are used in parallel in other passages (e.g., 1 Pet. 3:5–6). Second, Paul explicitly enjoins Christians to obey their government when he writes, "Remind the people to be subject to rulers and authorities, to be obedient" (Titus 3:1).

Obedience is necessary even to evil governments. When Paul exhorted the Romans to "submit . . . to the governing authorities" as "God's servant" (Rom. 13:1, 4), Nero was emperor. He killed his mother to ascend to the throne, burned Rome, and even burned Christians alive for street lights. He was a brutal and wicked man, yet Paul called him "God's servant" and asked Christians to obey him. God told Daniel that "the Most High is sovereign over the kingdoms of men and gives them to anyone he wishes" (Dan. 4:32). Sometimes this includes "the lowliest of men" (v. 17). But whomever God establishes is to be obeyed, good or evil. Peter said plainly, "Submit yourselves for the Lord's sake to every authority instituted among men" (1 Pet. 2:13).

On the basis of these and similar Scriptures, the Christian patriot believes that obedience to government is obedience to God. To use Paul's words, the patriot insists that "he who rebels against the authority is rebelling against what God has instituted" (Rom. 13:2). Hence, civil disobedience is never justified.

An Evaluation of Radical Patriotism

There are several objections to the use of these Scriptures to justify unqualified obedience to human government. The foremost reason is that they are not taken in their proper context.

God ordained government, but not its evil. God ordained human government, but does not approve of its evil. There is a hint of this even in the passage in Romans which says the ruler "is God's servant to do you good" (Rom. 13:4). There is no indication here or anywhere else in the Bible that God is pleased with evil governments. In fact, much of the thrust of the Bible, especially the prophets, is to condemn evil governments (see Obad.; Jon. 1; Nah. 2). Isaiah said, "Woe to those who make unjust laws, to those who issue oppressive decrees" (10:1). God appointed government, but does not approve of its evils.

Obedience to government is not unqualified. While it is true that

God demands obedience to human authorities, this obedience is not without some limitations. Peter said to the authorities who commanded him not to preach the gospel, "Judge for yourselves whether it is right in God's sight to obey you rather than God" (Acts 4:19). John spoke of the faithful remnant of the tribulation who would not submit to the idolatrous commands of the Antichrist (Rev. 13). Indeed, as will be seen shortly, there are many divinely approved instances of disobedience to civil authorities (e.g., Exod. 1; Dan. 3, 6). In each case the implication is clear: government should be obeyed as long as it takes its place under God, but not when it takes the place of God.

We need not obey the evils of government. The Bible does enjoin obedience to governments even if they are evil, but it does not demand obedience to the evils of government. Indeed, it forbids doing evil no matter who says so. This is clear from the midwives' refusal to kill innocent babies at the command of Pharaoh (Exod. 1), as well as the unwillingness of the three Hebrew children to worship an idol (Dan. 3). Christians can obey a government that permits evil, but not one that commands them to do an evil. Blind obedience to the evils of government is not patriotic; it is idiotic. Unqualified submission to an oppressive government is not patriotism. It is patriolatry, and patriolatry is idolatry, an ultimate commitment to what is less than ultimate.

Biblical Submissionism: Disobedience to Government Is Sometimes Right

There is general agreement among Christians that there are times when a Christian should engage in civil disobedience. The real problem is where to draw the line, and there are two positions on this. One view holds that government should be disobeyed when it promulgates a law that is contrary to the Word of God. The other view contends that government should be disobeyed only when it commands the Christian to do evil. Both views will be presented and evaluated.

The Antipromulgation Position: Disobedience of Government When It Promulgates Unbiblical Laws

Christians have the right to disobey their government when it promulgates laws or actions that are contrary to the Word of God. (A broader version of this position would say, "When it contradicts the moral law or an individual's conscience." The deist Thomas Jefferson espoused a form of this view.)

Since this is a book on Christian ethics, we will focus here on the Christian form of this viewpoint. It was presented by Samuel Rutherford in his famous *Lex Rex (The Law Is King* [1644]). The late Francis Schaeffer adopted the position in his widely circulated *Christian Manifesto* (1980), which presents the essence of the view.

The power of government is not absolute. Following Rutherford, Francis Schaeffer insisted that "kings then have not an absolute power in their regiment to do what pleases them; but their power is limited by God's Word." In other words, "all men, even the king, are under the law and not above it."[1] The law is king; the king is not the law. Government is under God's law; it is not God's law.

The law is above the government. Schaeffer claimed that "the law is king, and if the king and the government disobey the law they are to be disobeyed."[2] That is to say, the true law is the law of God, and it is not the government but is over the government. The Christian's obedience, then, is to God's law and to government only insofar as it is in accordance with God's law.

Governments which rule contrary to God's law are tyrannical. According to Schaeffer, "the law is founded on the law of God."[3] Hence, "tyranny was defined as ruling without the sanctions of God."[4] In other words, whenever a government rules contrary to God's Word, it has ruled tyrannically. In such cases the Christian should not obey the government.

Citizens should resist a tyrannical government. Not only should citizens disobey a tyrannical government, but they should also actively resist it. Schaeffer declares that "citizens have a moral obligation to resist unjust and tyrannical government."[5] For "when any office commands that which is contrary to the Word of God, those who hold that office abrogate their authority and they are not to be obeyed, and that includes the state."[6]

Resistance takes two forms: protest and force. Citizens should first protest the laws contrary to God's Word. If this fails, then force may be necessary. "Force," according to Schaeffer, "means compulsion or constraint exerted upon a person (or persons) or on an entity such as a state."[7] Force can be used by the local government, or even by a church, against an oppressive state. For "when the state commits illegitimate acts against a corporate body—such as a duly constituted state or local body, or even a church . . . there are two levels of resis-

1. Francis A. Schaeffer, *A Christian Manifesto* (Westchester, Ill.: Crossway, 1981), p. 100.
2. Ibid., p. 99.
3. Ibid.
4. Ibid., p. 100.
5. Ibid., p. 101.
6. Ibid., p. 90.
7. Ibid., p. 106.

tance: remonstration (or protest) and then, if necessary, force employed in self-defense."[8]

A contemporary example of tyranny. Schaeffer believed that disallowing the teaching of creation in the public schools is an example of tyranny. He said emphatically, "If there was ever a clearer example of the lower 'magistrates' being treated with tyranny, it would be hard to find. And this would be a time, if the courts do rule tyrannically, for the state government to protest and refuse to submit."[9] And presumably if the federal government enforced the rule in spite of the protest, it would seem to follow that the people of the state of Arkansas should have used physical force against the federal government that ruled, on January 5, 1982, that creation could not be taught in their public schools. Likewise, all the states should have later rebelled against the Supreme Court when it ruled on June 19, 1987, that no state could insist on teaching creation along with evolution in their public schools.

The Anticompulsion Position: Disobedience of Laws that Compel Us to Do Evil

This position agrees with the antipromulgation position in maintaining that there are times when a Christian should disobey civil laws. They differ only on what those occasions are, and the differences between these two positions on civil disobedience are highlighted in table 13.1.

The difference between the two views can be brought out by a couple of illustrations. According to the antipromulgation position, a citizen should disobey the government when it forbids the teaching of creation in the public schools, because this pronouncement is contrary to the Word of God. This, they claim, limits the freedom of creationists to

TABLE 13.1

Two Views of When
to Disobey Government

Antipromulgation Position	Anticompulsion Position
When it permits evil	When it commands evil
When it promulgates evil laws	When it compels evil actions
When it limits freedom	When it negates freedom
When it is politically oppressive	When it is religiously oppressive

8. Ibid., p. 104.
9. Ibid., p. 110.

express their views, which are based on the Word of God. However, according to the anticompulsion position, the Christian should not disobey this law because it does not compel him to believe or teach that creation is false, nor does it negate his freedom to teach creation outside the public school classrooms. If a government commanded that creation could not be taught anywhere, that would be oppressive and could be disobeyed.

Abortion is another issue that focuses the difference between the two viewpoints. Agreeing that abortion is contrary to the Word of God (see chap. 8), the antipromulgation view insists that a citizen has the right to engage in civil disobedience in order to oppose abortion. Here the antipromulgationists are split between two camps: those favoring such violent actions such as bombing clinics, and others favoring only such nonviolent disobedience as illegal clinic sit-ins.

Anticompulsionists, on the other hand, believe that it is wrong to disobey the law in order to protest abortion. This is because there is a difference between a law that permits abortions and one which commands abortions. We should legally protest unjust laws, but we should not disobey them. It is one thing for a government to allow others to do evil, but it is another thing for it to force an individual to do evil. Only in the latter case is civil disobedience justified.

The Biblical Basis
for the Anticompulsion Position

There are several biblical instances of divinely approved civil disobedience. In each case there are three essential elements: first, a command by divinely appointed authorities that is contrary to the Word of God. Second, an act of disobedience to that command. And finally, some kind of explicit or implicit divine approval of the refusal to obey the authorities.

Refusal to kill innocent babies—In Exodus 1:15–21, Pharaoh commanded that every male Hebrew baby be killed by the midwives. But the Hebrew midwives Shiphrah and Puah "feared God and did not do what the king of Egypt had told them to do; they let the boys live" (v. 17). As a result "God was kind to the midwives and the people increased and became even more numerous. And because the midwives feared God, he gave them families of their own" (vv. 20–21).

Refusal of Pharaoh's command not to worship God—Moses requested of Pharaoh, "Let my people go, so that they may hold a festival to [the LORD] in the desert" (Exod. 5:1). But Pharaoh said, "Who is the LORD, that I should obey him and let Israel go? I do not know the LORD, and I will not let Israel go" (v. 2). But the children of Israel left Egypt with a spectacular display of miraculous interventions on their behalf (Exod. 7–12).

Refusal of prophets to be killed by Queen Jezebel—In 1 Kings 18:4, wicked Queen Jezebel "was killing off the LORD's prophets." In defiance of her orders, the prophet Obadiah "had taken a hundred prophets and hidden them in two caves, . . . and had supplied them with food and water." Although explicit approval of his act is not stated, the whole context and manner of presentation implies that his action was divinely approved (see vv. 13–15), since the government has no right to compel the killing of innocent servants of God.

Refusal to worship an idol—In Daniel 3, the government commanded that everyone in the kingdom "must fall down and worship the image of gold that King Nebuchadnezzar has set up" (Dan. 3:5). But three Hebrew children defiantly replied, "we want you to know, O king, that we will not serve your gods or worship the image of gold you have set up" (v. 18). As a result, God blessed them and miraculously preserved them from the fiery furnace into which they were thrown (3:25–30).

Refusal to pray to the king and not to God—Few biblical stories are more famous than Daniel in the lions' den. It is a classic example of divinely approved civil disobedience. The king had ruled that anyone who prayed "to any god or man [except him] during the next thrity days shall be thrown into the lions' den" (Dan. 6:7). Daniel defied the order when "three times a day he got down on his knees and prayed, giving thanks to his God, just as he had done before" (6:10). Here again God richly blessed the civil disobedience of Daniel who emerged from the lions' den confidently proclaiming, "My God sent his angel, and he shut the mouths of the lions. They have not hurt me because I was found innocent in his sight" (6:22).

Refusal to stop proclaiming the gospel—Although the authorities were religious, not civil, the principles are the same here as in the other cases of divinely approved disobedience. The authorities "commanded [the apostles] not to speak or teach at all in the name of Jesus" (Acts 4:18). But Peter and John replied, "Judge for yourselves whether it is right in God's sight to obey you rather than God" (v. 19). The text goes on to say that "the people were praising God for what had happened" (v. 21), thus indicating God's approval of their refusal to obey this mandate not to preach Christ.

Refusal to worship the Antichrist—During the tribulation period, the faithful remnant of believers will refuse to worship the Antichrist or his image. John said the false prophet "ordered them to set up an image in honor of the beast who was wounded by the sword and yet lived" (Rev. 13:14). But they refused and "overcame him by the blood of the Lamb and by the word of their testimony; they did not love their lives so much as to shrink from death" (Rev. 12:11). God rewarded them with "the crown of life" (Rev. 2:10).

All of these divinely approved cases of civil disobedience follow the same pattern. In each case the believers are compelled to act contrary to their beliefs. God has commanded in his Word that we worship him and not idols, that we not kill innocent people, that we pray only to him, and that we proclaim the gospel. But each civil command given in these illustrations compels believers to act contrary to God's commands. The civil commands do not simply allow others to act contrary to God's law; they force believers to disobey God's law. This is oppressive and should be disobeyed.

How to Disobey Oppressive Laws

The Bible prescribes not only when civil laws should be disobeyed, but also how they should be disobeyed. Here again there are two views that need to be distinguished: one recommends revolt, and the other merely refusal. They are contrasted in table 13.2.

There is a right way and a wrong way to disobey an oppressive government when it compels us to do evil. The biblical pattern is to refuse to obey its compulsive commands, but not to revolt against it. This is evident in all biblical examples just discussed. The midwives, for example, refused to obey Pharaoh's order to kill the male babies, but they did not lead a revolt against Egypt's oppressive government.

Justified civil disobedience should be nonviolent resistance, not violent rebellion. This is true in each biblically approved case of civil disobedience. The midwives do not return violence on Egypt for the violence of Egypt. Nor does Israel start a revolution against Pharaoh's oppression; rather they accept God's salvation from it.

Biblical civil disobedience does not reject the government's punishment, but accepts the penalties for disobeying the law. For example,

TABLE 13.2

Two Views of How
to Disobey Government

Revolt	Refusal
Revolt against it violently	Refuse to obey it nonviolently
Fight it	Flee it
Reject its punishment	Accept its punishment

the three Hebrew children refuse to worship the idol, but they do not refuse to go into the fiery furnace. Likewise, Daniel rejects the order to pray to the king, but accepts the consequent punishment of the lions' den. And the apostles refuse to stop preaching Christ, but accept the consequence of going to prison.

It is legitimate civil disobedience to flee, if possible, from an oppressive government, and not to fight it. Israel fled from Egypt and Obadiah and Elijah fled from wicked Jezebel. But none of them engaged in a war against the government. So whenever a government is tyrannical, a Christian should refuse to obey its compulsive commands to do evil, but should not revolt against it because of its unbiblical commands that permit evil.

This does not mean, of course, that we should not peacefully, legally, and actively work to overcome oppression. It simply means that we should not take the law into our own hands, since "the authorities that exist have been established by God" (Rom. 13:1). And when we cannot accept their command to do evil, then we must either flee or submit to punishment.

An Objection to the Anticompulsion View

Some have argued that the Bible commands us to rescue the innocent. Proverbs 24:11 says, "Rescue those who are being taken away to death." On this basis they insist that it is right to disobey government when innocent lives are at stake, such as the Jews in Nazis Germany or the unborn in societies in which abortion is legal. But there are several serious problems with this position.

First, Proverbs 24:11 does not support civil disobedience to prevent legal abortion. In fact, in this very chapter God enjoins civil obedience on the believers and warns against even associating with lawbreakers (v. 21). Furthermore, those being led away to death (v. 11) are probably victims of lawbreakers, not those being put to death in accordance with the law. There is no indication at all in the text or its context that the command is to interrupt the God-ordained adjudication of the law, even in capital cases.

Second, the comparison between German Jews and the unborn is invalid, since there are significant differences. The Holocaust was mandated by the state, whereas legalized abortion in America is only permitted by the state. The former would allow for civil disobedience but the latter would not. Furthermore, the Jews were unwilling to go to the gas chambers but the mothers (who are responsible for the life in their womb) are willing to have the abortion. Forced abortion is another matter; it would justify civil disobedience. In addition, failure to disobey the law to kill unwilling Jews is tantamount to assisting in

the crime. However, failure to disobey the law that permits abortion
is not assisting in the crime. Finally, the humanity of an adult Jew is
obvious to all, but the full humanity of the unborn is hotly debated.
In legalized abortion both the state and many doctors or aides have
told the mother that the baby is only a "tissue" and not fully or
legally human. These factors make it invalid to argue that because
civil disobedience is justified to save Jews from a Nazi holocaust it
is also right to engage in civil disobedience to prevent willing mothers
from having legal abortions.

Third, the same logic could lead Christians to hinder people going
into Hindu, Buddhist, or Mormon temples so as to prevent them from
committing idolatry. It could also lead us to snatch alcohol and ciga-
rettes out of unbelievers' hands so as to prevent their (and others')
deaths. Likewise, it would justify civil disobedience to hinder a state-
executed capital punishment simply because we believe the person to
be innocent. But this is to presume one's personal belief can override
the God-ordained governmental process of civil justice (Rom. 13:1).

Revolution: The Ultimate Revolt
Against Government

What about revolution? Is it ever justified? If there are just wars,
are there not also some just revolutions? What does the Bible say about
revolutions? Here again there are two basic views: those who favor
some revolutions and those who oppose all revolutions.

Revolutions Are Sometimes Just

The Reformed tradition, springing from John Calvin's teachings,
accepts revolutions against an oppressive government. This view was
stated by Samuel Rutherford and repeated by Francis Schaeffer. Our
own American founders, rooted in the natural-law tradition of John
Locke, also argued for a just revolution.

The Declaration of Independence on revolution—Notice the words
of Thomas Jefferson in the Declaration of Independence in justification of pronouncing our independence from Britain.

> We hold these truths to be self-evident: that all men are created equal;
> that they are endowed by their Creator with certain inalienable rights;
> that they are endowed by their Creator with certain unalienable rights;
> secure these rights, governments are instituted among men, deriving
> their just powers from the consent of the governed; that whenever any
> form of government becomes destructive of these ends, it is the right of
> the people to alter or to abolish it, and to institute new government. . . .

But when a long train of abuses and usurpations, pursuing invariably the same object, evinces a design to reduce them under absolute despotism, it is their right, it is their duty, to throw off such government, and to provide new guards for their future security. Such has been the patient sufferance of these colonies; and such is now the necessity which constrains them to alter their former systems of government.

This declaration manifestly proclaims a belief in just revolutions against unjust governments. The grounds of such revolutions are based in God-given moral rights, such as "life," "liberty," and "happiness." When government "becomes destructive of these ends," then it is "the right of the people to alter or to abolish it." Continued action by such a government to suppress these freedoms, said Jefferson, is an "absolute despotism." Thus Jefferson swore eternal hostility on the altar of God against every form of tyranny over the minds of men. And since Jefferson also believed that "taxation without representation is tyranny," the American revolution was born. But was it biblical? Before responding, let's take a look at another justification of revolution.

Francis Schaeffer on revolution—As has been noted, Schaeffer believed that "when any office commands that which is contrary to the Word of God, those who hold that office abrogate their authority and they are not to be obeyed, and that includes the state."[10] And "if the state deliberately is committed to destroying its ethical commitments to God then resistance is appropriate."[11] For "citizens have a moral obligation to resist unjust and tyrannical government."[12] This means that "when the magistrate acts in such a way that the governing structure of the country is being destroyed . . . he is to be relieved of his power and authority."[13] This relief may be necessary by "force," which means by "compulsion or constraint."[14] And "when the state commits illegitimate acts against a corporate body—such as a duly constituted state or local body, or even a church . . . there are two levels of resistance: remonstration (or protest) and then, if necessary, force employed in self-defense."[15]

This form of just revolution is not based upon "unalienable rights" from the Creator known by "Nature's laws," as Jefferson believed. Rather, it is based upon a government's practice of ruling "contrary to the Word of God." But the net result is the same—revolution against a government one believes to be tyrannical.

10. Ibid., p. 90.
11. Ibid., p. 103.
12. Ibid., p. 101.
13. Ibid.
14. Ibid., p. 106.
15. Ibid., p. 104.

Revolutions Are Always Unjust

Now that we have examined the basis for just revolutions, let us take a look at what the Bible says about revolution. Several points should be made.

God gave the sword to the government to rule, not to the citizens to revolt. The sword was given to Noah to suppress unruly citizens (Gen. 9:6; 6:11). Likewise, Paul told the Romans to submit to Nero because "he is God's servant . . . for he does not bear the sword for nothing" (13:4). Here too it is the government that is to use the sword on the governed, not the citizen who is to use it on the state.

God exhorts against joining revolutionaries. The Scriptures declare explicitly, "Fear the LORD and the king, my son, and do not join with the rebellious" (Prov. 24:21). Since the context of the exhortation deals with fearing God and the king whom he has ordained, it is evident that it is a command not to engage in a rebellion against one's government.

Revolutions are consistently condemned by God. The Bible has many examples of revolutions, but they are consistently condemned by God. Korah led a rebellion against Moses, and the earth opened up to swallow Korah and his followers (Num. 16). Likewise, Absalom's revolution against David backfired, and Absalom was killed (2 Sam. 15). Jeroboam led a revolt of the ten northern tribes against Judah in the south which God severely condemned (1 Kings 12).

The only revolution approved of by God was a theocratic one against wicked queen Athaliah. However, since this was necessary to preserve the only remaining link in the bloodline of Christ, it was a divinely sanctioned special theocratic case, just like the wars against the Canaanites were under Joshua (Josh. 10). Notice that the command to kill her came from God's servant (2 Chron. 23:14) and was blessed by God's word (v. 21). However, this divinely appointed theocratic revolution to preserve the bloodline of the Messiah cannot be legitimately used to justify revolution today, any more than can God's command to slaughter all the Canaanites be used as the basis for killing women and children in a just war today.

Moses was judged for his violent act in Egypt. Exodus tells us that when Moses saw an Egyptian beating a Hebrew and "he saw there was no one around, he struck down the Egyptian and hid him in the sand" (Exod. 2:12 NASB). As a consequence of this violent act, Moses was forced to flee from Egypt and spend forty years in the desert. After that, God used Moses to lead Israel out of Egypt without a revolution (Exod. 12).

Israel did not fight Pharaoh but fled from him. If there was ever justification for a revolution because of oppression, it was the situation of Israel under Pharaoh. However, it was neither recommended or approved by God. Israel did not fight Pharaoh; they fled from him (Exod. 12). True, God miraculously intervened to deliver them, but the lesson is the same: trust God to take care of evil tyrants, but do not rebel against them. God sovereignly set them up, and he will sovereignly take them down (Dan. 4:17).

Jesus exhorted against using the sword. Jesus warned his disciples against the aggressive use of the sword, saying, "put your sword back into its place; for all who take the sword will perish by the sword" (Matt. 26:52). He was not opposed to using a sword in self-defense (Exod. 22:2), but swinging at the servant of an existing authority was another thing (Matt. 26:51).

Jesus spoke against retaliation. If the Sermon on the Mount means anything, then it certainly speaks against retaliation. Jesus said, "You have heard that it was said, 'An eye for an eye, and a tooth for a tooth.' But I say to you, Do not resist one who is evil" (Matt. 5:38–39 RSV). While this sermon does not support total pacifism (see chap. 12), it certainly condemns a revolutionary spirit that desires to take vengeance on an oppressive government. " 'Vengeance is mine; I will repay,' saith the Lord" (Rom. 12:19 KJV).

How to Respond to Oppression

The Bible lays down guidelines for a Christian response to unjust governments. They are summarized in the following pages.

Obey Its Laws under God

The first and foremost responsibility a Christian has to any government, just or unjust, democracy or monarchy, is to obey its laws (Rom. 13:1; Titus 3:1). Peter wrote, "Submit yourselves for the Lord's sake to every authority instituted among men" (1 Pet. 2:13). For "it is God's will that by doing good you should silence the ignorant talk of foolish men" (v. 15). Civil disobedience is a bad testimony for a follower of Christ. Christians should be known as law-abiding citizens, not rebels. The best way to effect lasting change in an unjust government is by being a spiritual example, not by revolution. Only when it takes the place of God should we refuse to obey government, and even then we should not revolt against it.

Pray for Oppressive Governments

Paul urged Christians that "entreaties and prayers, petitions and thanksgivings, be made on behalf of all men, for kings and all who are in authority, in order that we may lead a tranquil and quiet life in all godliness and dignity" (1 Tim. 2:1–2 NASB). One of the most effective ways to change an unjust government is to pray for it. Prayer is the slender nerve by which the muscles of omnipotence are moved. God heard the cries of his oppressed people in times past (Exod. 2:23) and he will hear and answer them again today.

Work Peacefully and Legally to Change It

Politically, there was very little Christians could do to change the Roman government in the New Testament. That is not true for most Christians in the West today. We can not only pray for Caesar, but we can elect him. We can not only resist political evil, but we are free to do political good. And, as James said, "to one who knows the right thing to do, and does not do it, to him it is sin" (James 4:17 NASB). Therefore, to quote Paul, "as we have opportunity, let us do good to all men, and especially to those who are of the household of the faith" (Gal. 6:10). We should fight oppression in our government with the ballot, not the bullet. It should be resisted with good, not with guns.

Disobey Oppressive Commands

As was previously noted, Christians can do something else about oppressive commands—they can disobey them. No human can compel us to disobey God. He is the highest authority, and his Word alone binds our conscience absolutely. This kind of biblical and courageous refusal to do evil will itself have a good effect on evil government. The kings of Babylon were significantly affected by the courageous disobedience of both Daniel and the three Hebrew children (Dan. 3, 6).

Flee Oppressive Governments

Christians do not need to be passive targets of tyranny. We need not be dart boards for despots. When oppressed we should flee to freedom. The prophets fled from Jezebel (1 Kings 18), Israel fled from Egypt (Exod. 12), and even Jesus' family fled from Herod (Matt. 2). So while not using force against unjust governments, we should at least flee their force against us.

Patiently Endure Suffering

Admittedly, fleeing is not always possible, or successful. Sometimes Christians must suffer patiently for Christ's sake. Peter wrote, "Beloved, do not be surprised at the fiery ordeal among you, which comes upon you for your testing, as though some strange thing were happening to you; but to the degree that you share the sufferings of Christ, keep on rejoicing; so that also at the revelation of His glory, you may rejoice with exultation" (1 Pet. 4:12–13 NASB). Sometimes we must simply suffer oppression for Christ, or even martyrdom. John said, "if anyone is to go into captivity, into captivity he will go. . . . This calls for patient endurance and faithfulness on the part of the saints" (Rev. 13:10).

An Evaluation of the Viewpoint Which Rejects Revolution

There are many objections to the viewpoint which rejects all revolutions on biblical grounds. They will be briefly considered at this point.

Scripture Approves of Some Revolutions

For several reasons, the single instance of a God-appointed revolution against Athaliah (2 Chron. 23) cannot be used to support revolutions. This was not a divinely approved human revolution; it was a divinely appointed revolution (v. 14). It was a special case for Israel, the messianic nation, and cannot be applied to other nations. If Athaliah's power had not been usurped, she would have killed Joash, the last remaining heir to the Davidic line leading up to Christ. The Bible speaks consistently against revolution, and the Bible does not contradict itself. Hence, this isolated instance, whatever its special significance, cannot be used to contradict the consistent teaching of the rest of Scripture against revolutions.

Without Revolution Tyranny Reigns

Revolutions are not the only way to fight tyranny. As has been argued, an unjust government can be resisted by prayer, moral example, lawful political action, justified disobedience, flight, and patient suffering when necessary. This objection forgets that God is sovereign over the affairs of government and sets up and takes away whom he will (Dan. 4:17). In brief, we can do many things to resist tyranny, and God can do infinitely more.

If Some Wars Are Just, Why Not Some Revolutions?

Wars and revolutions are not in the same category. Just wars are fought by God-ordained governments to which he gave the sword (Rom. 13:4). But revolutions are fought by citizens, to whom God did not give the sword, against God-ordained governments. God never gave the sword to citizens to use on their government; he gave it to governments to use on rebellious citizens. Just wars are waged against another nation that is aggressing against one's own. Revolutions are against one's own nation. They are, in effect, fatal family feuds. In a revolution we are, as it were, killing off our own kin. In opposing the government God established, one is thereby opposing God, who established it (Rom. 13:2). Just wars, on the other hand, protect one's country against aggression by another and are fought in self-defense.

Revolutions Are Obedience to de Jure Governments

This objection wrongly implies that our divine obligation is not to obey de facto governments. This is wrong for two reasons. Obedience to de facto governments is demanded biblically. Paul said, "the authorities that exist have been established by God" (Rom. 13:1). That is to say, existing governments are divinely appointed. This is precisely what is meant by de facto government. If obedience were not demanded to de facto government, there would be no practical way to maintain law and order in many places in the world, because there is a continual dispute about which government is the real one. The only practical way to avoid anarchy is to demand obedience to the de facto government, since everyone can readily identify it; it is the one in power at the time.

It Means the American Revolution Was Not Just

It is understandable that everyone would like to believe that the revolution in his country was just, even if those in other countries are not. But in all honesty, given the biblical criteria listed here, it is not possible to justify the American Revolution either. What then should American Christians do on the Fourth of July? Can they really celebrate American independence from Britain? In response, a distinction should be made. There is a difference between what is born and how it is born. We are certainly glad for every human being born of fornication or even rape, although we certainly do not approve of the way they got here. Likewise, an American Christian can celebrate what was born of the American Revolution (a great free country) without thereby approving of the way it arrived.

Summary and Conclusion

There are three basic views regarding civil disobedience. Anarchism approves of it any time. Radical patriotism never approves of disobeying government, and biblical submissionism holds that it is sometimes right to do so. While most Christians believe the Bible supports the latter view, there is disagreement about when disobedience is justified.

Antipromulgationists insist on the right to disobey any law that permits actions contrary to God's Word. Anticompulsionists, on the other hand, hold that disobedience is justified only when one is compelled to do an evil.

Even among those who agree that disobedience to government is sometimes called for, there is a difference of opinion concerning how one should disobey. Some believe in revolting against an unjust government, but the biblical view calls for resisting it without rebelling against it. Such resistance is not passive acceptance of injustice in government, but can involve an active spiritual, moral, and political campaign against it.

Select Readings

Aquinas, Thomas. *On Kingship, to the King of Cyprus*. Translated by Gerald B. Phelan. Toronto: The Pontifical Institute of Mediaeval Studies, 1949.

Andrusko, David, ed. *To Rescue the Future*. Toronto: Life Cycle, 1983.

Calvin, John. *Institutes of the Christian Religion*, vol. 1. Reprint. Grand Rapids: Eerdmans, 1957.

Jefferson, Thomas. The Declaration of Independence.

Plato. *Phaedo*. Translated by Hugh Tredennick. In *The Collected Dialogues of Plato*, edited by Edith Hamilton and Huntington Cairns. New York: Pantheon, 1964.

Rutherford, Samuel. *Lex Rex, or the Law and the Prince*. 1644. Reprint. Harrisonburg, Va.: Sprinkle, 1982.

Schaeffer, Francis A. *A Christian Manifesto*. Westchester, Ill.: Crossway, 1981.

Whitehead, John W. *The Second American Revolution*. 2d ed. Westchester, Ill.: Crossway, 1985.

14

Homosexuality

Issues relating to sex can be divided into the categories of homosexuality and heterosexuality. The first will be treated in this chapter and the latter in the next chapter. While most Christians strongly oppose homosexual practices, some have defended them by biblical as well as nonbiblical arguments. Both kinds of support will be examined and evaluated here.

Arguments in Favor of Homosexuality

Homosexual proponents offer two sets of arguments in favor of their activity. Those with a Christian orientation appeal to Scripture as well as to other social and moral factors. First we will examine the biblical arguments.

Biblical Arguments for Homosexuality

The common heterosexual understanding of well-known biblical passages is challenged by homosexuals. Let us examine the chief texts used to defend homosexual practices.

The sin of Sodom was not homosexuality. It is argued that the sin of Sodom and Gomorrah was not homosexuality but inhospitality. This is based on the Canaanite custom that guaranteed the protection of those coming under one's roof. Lot is alleged to have referred to it when he said, "Don't do anything to these men, for they have come under the protection of my roof" (Gen. 19:8). So Lot offered his daughters to satisfy the angry crowd and protect the lives of the visitors who had come under his roof. This sexual appeasement was necessary to save their lives.

Further, it is argued that homosexuality was not envisioned in the request of the men of the city to "know" Lot's friends, since this Hebrew word (*yadha*) simply means "to get acquainted" (Gen. 19:5). It occurs sometimes in the Old Testament, and in the overwhelming number of occurrences it has no sexual connotations whatsoever (see Ps. 139:1). Thus, it is concluded that the sin of Sodom was inhospitality, not homosexuality.

The sin of Sodom was selfishness. The sin of Sodom is spelled out in these words: "Now this was the sin of your sister Sodom: She and her daughters were arrogant, overfed and unconcerned; they did not help the poor and needy" (Ezek. 16:49). No mention is made of homosexuality or related sexual sins. They were condemned simply because they were selfish, not because they were homosexuals.

The Levitical law is no longer applicable. The chief passage in the Old Testament condemning homosexual practices is found in the Levitical law (Lev. 18:22). These same Levitical laws also condemned eating pork and shrimp. However, these ceremonial laws have been done away with (Acts 10:15). This being the case, proponents argued that there is no reason that the laws prohibiting homosexual activity should still be considered binding either.

Barrenness was a curse to Jewish women. According to Jewish belief, barrenness was a curse (Gen. 16:1; 1 Sam. 1:3–8). Children were considered a blessing from the Lord (Ps. 127:3). The blessing of God in the land was dependent on having children (Gen. 15:5). Indeed, the hope of Jewish women was to bear the promised Messiah (Gen. 3:15; cf. 4:1, 25). In view of the emphasis on having children, it is not surprising that the Old Testament law would frown on homosexual activity from which no children come. However, it is reasoned, this in no way condemns homosexual activity as such, nor is it condemned for those not included in this Jewish expectation.

Homosexuality was connected with idolatry. It is also argued that the biblical condemnations used against homosexuality fail to take into account that the purpose of the passages is to prohibit idolatry. Since the temple cult-prostitute was associated with these idolatrous practices, it was condemned along with idolatry (Deut. 23:17). However, proponents insist, homosexuality as such is not thereby condemned, but only homosexuality associated with idolatry, as in the case of the shrine prostitute (1 Kings 14:24).

The Pauline condemnations were private opinions. Most New Testament passages against homosexuality come from the apostle Paul, who was only giving his private opinion (1 Cor. 7:25). In fact, Paul admitted, "I have no command from the Lord" (v. 25) and "I say this (I, not the Lord)" (v. 12). It is in this same book, only a chapter earlier, that Paul gives his condemnation of homosexuals (1 Cor. 6:9). Thus, Paul's opinion on these sexual matters is, by his own confession, not binding.

Paul also condemned long hair on men. According to homosexual proponents, much of what the apostle Paul taught was obviously culturally relative. For example, in 1 Corinthians the apostle also taught that "if a man has long hair, it is a disgrace to him" (11:14). But since this was obviously a culturally relative statement, there is no reason that Paul's statements against homosexuals should be considered to be absolute moral prohibitions.

First Corinthians 6:9 only speaks against offenses. Some homosexuals appeal to the fact that 1 Corinthians 6:9 speaks only against "homosexual offenders," not against homosexuality as such. That is, the passage only condemns offensive homosexual acts, but not homosexual activity per se. This being the case, Paul's apparent condemnation turns out to be an implied approval of unoffensive homosexual acts.

Heterosexuality is unnatural for homosexuals. According to some homosexuals, when Paul spoke against what was "unnatural" in Romans 1:26, he was not declaring that homosexuality was morally wrong, but simply that heterosexual activity was unnatural for homosexuals. Thus, "unnatural" is used in a sociological, not a biological, sense. So it is argued that, rather than condemning homosexual practices, this passage in Romans actually approves of them for homosexuals. Each person should act according to his own sociological tendencies, whether they are heterosexual or homosexual.

Isaiah predicted homosexuals in the kingdom. Isaiah 56:3 declares that eunuchs will be brought into the kingdom of God. The Lord said, "To them I will give within my temple and its walls a memorial and a name better than sons and daughters; I will give them an everlasting name that will not be cut off." This is taken to mean that Isaiah predicted the day of acceptance of homosexuals into God's kingdom, the fulfillment of which some homosexuals now claim is occurring.

David and Jonathan were homosexual. First Samuel 18–20 records the intense love David and Jonathan had for each other. Some see this passage as an indication that they were homosexual, pointing out that it says Jonathan "loved" David (18:3), that Jonathan stripped in David's presence (18:4), that they kissed each other (20:41), and that they "exceeded" (20:41), a term taken to mean ejaculation. David's lack of successful relations with women is also taken to indicate his homosexual tendencies. When all these factors are considered together they show, it is argued, that David and Jonathan were homosexual.

Other Arguments for Homosexuality

In addition to these arguments drawn from the Bible, a number of other reasons are offered in favor of homosexuality. They fall into the general category of social and moral reasons.

There should be no sexual constraints among consenting adults. Many insist that there should be no sexual prohibitions for consenting adults. While admitting that forced sex and sexual abuse of children are wrong, many homosexuals contend that it is a violation of their freedom to prohibit any free sexual expressions. What two persons do sexually and freely is their own moral business. Only coercion of freedom is wrong. Beyond that, a person has the right to do with his body what he desires to do.

The right to privacy protects homosexuality. The Supreme Court articulated a woman's right of privacy over her own body. This constitutional right, it is insisted, also extends to homosexual practices. If a woman has rights over her own sexual processes, so that she can abort the result of conception, then why should not homosexuals have rights over their own sexual processes that do not lead to conception? Privacy is a constitutional right. Therefore, the heterosexual majority have no right to impose their morality on the homosexual minority.

Homosexuals have civil rights too. One of the most often repeated arguments by homosexuals is that homosexuals, like other minority groups, also have civil rights. Simply because the majority of the population chooses to be heterosexual does not justify their passing laws against a homosexual minority. Why should the minority be deprived of their constitutional rights simply because of their sexual preferences? This is discrimination, and discrimination is morally and socially wrong.

Sexual tendencies are inherited. Many homosexuals argue that they cannot change their sex any more than they can change the color of their eyes. Sexual inclinations, they insist, are hereditary, not learned. Hence, a person should no more be condemned for being homosexual than for being short or having red hair. We simply cannot help being what we are by nature, so homosexuals cannot help being what they are.

Morals have changed since ancient times. Even if homosexual practices were condemned in ancient times, it is argued, there is no reason they should be condemned today. Premarital sex was also condemned in times past but is looked upon with favor today. Many other taboos, sexual and nonsexual, were frowned upon in former, more puritanical cultures. However, more recent and more enlightened ones have rejected such restrictions. Likewise, attitudes must change concerning homosexuality as well.

Many other mammals are homosexual too. According to this argument, nature sanctions homosexual activity, for other mammals also practice it. And if homosexual acts are not uncommon among other animals, then there is no reason that they should be thought to be strange among the human species. Homo sapiens is not exempt from other natural behavioral patterns found among fellow mammals.

A Response to the Arguments in Favor of Homosexuality

In response to these arguments in favor of homosexual practices, several criticisms are noteworthy. Let us examine them in the order of the arguments just presented.

A Response to the Biblical Arguments

Each of the foregoing arguments taken from the Bible is based on a misunderstanding or misinterpretation of Scripture. Let us examine them in order.

The sin of Sodom was homosexuality. While it is true that the Hebrew word *know* (*yadha*) does not necessarily mean "to have sex with," nonetheless in the context of the text on Sodom and Gomorrah it clearly has this meaning. This is evident for several reasons. Ten of the twelve times this word is used in Genesis, it refers to sexual intercourse (see Gen. 4:1, 25). It means "to know sexually" in this very chapter when Lot refers to his two daughters not having "known" a man (19:8). The meaning of a word is discovered by the context in which it is used, and the context here is definitely sexual, as is indicated by the reference to the wickedness of the city (chap. 18) and the fact that virgins are offered to appease their sexual passions (19:8). In this context, "know" cannot mean simply "get acquainted with," because it is equated with a "wicked thing" (v. 7). Why offer virgin daughters to appease them if their intent was not sexual? If the men had asked to "know" the virgin daughters, no one would have mistaken their sexual intentions.

The sin of Sodom was not merely inhospitality. The sin of Sodom was not merely selfishness, but also homosexuality. This is made plain by several facts. First of all, as just noted, the context of Genesis 19 reveals that their perversion was sexual. Furthermore, the selfishness mentioned in Ezekiel 16:49 does not exclude homosexuality. In fact, sexual sins are a form of selfishness, a satisfaction of fleshly desires.

The very next verse of Ezekiel (v. 50) indicates that their sin was sexual by calling it an "abomination." This is the same word used to describe homosexual sins in Leviticus 18:22. Another indication that these were sexual perversions is manifest in the very origin and usage of the word *sodomy,* which comes from Sodom. When the sin of Sodom is noted elsewhere in Scripture it is a sexual perversion. Jude even calls their sin "sexual immorality" (v. 7).

The prohibition against homosexuality is moral, not merely ceremonial. Simply because the Mosaic prohibition against homosexuality is mentioned in Leviticus does not mean that it was part of the ceremonial law that has passed away. If this were so, then neither would rape, incest, and bestiality be morally wrong, since they are condemned in the same chapter with homosexual sins (Lev. 18:6–14, 22–23). Homosexual sins among Gentiles, who did not have the ceremonial law, were also condemned by God. It was for this very reason that God brought judgment on the Canaanites (18:1–3, 25). Even in the Levitical law for the Jews there was a difference in punishment for violating the ceremonial law by eating pork or shrimp, which was a few days isolation, and that for homosexuality, which was capital punishment (18:29). Jesus changed the dietary laws of the Old Testament (Mark 7:18; Acts 10:12), but the moral prohibitions against homosexuality are repeated in the New Testament (Rom. 1:26–27; 1 Cor. 6:9; 1 Tim. 1:10; Jude 7).

Barrenness is not why homosexuality is evil. There is no indication in Scripture that homosexuality was considered sinful because no children resulted from it. No place in the Bible is any such connection stated. If homosexuals were punished because they were barren, then why were they put to death (and, thus, could not have any children)? Heterosexual marriage would have been a more appropriate punishment! The same prohibition against homosexuality was not only for Jews but for Gentiles (Lev. 18:24), whose blessings were not dependent on having heirs to inherit the land of Israel. If barrenness were a divine curse, then singleness would be sinful. But both Jesus (Matt. 19:11–12) and Paul (1 Cor. 7:8) hallowed singlehood by precept and practice.

Homosexuality is evil apart from idolatry. Homosexual practices are not condemned in the Bible simply because they were connected with idolatry. This is made evident by several things. Condemnations of homosexuality are often made apart from reference to any explicit idolatrous practice (Lev. 18:22; Rom. 1:26–27). (Adultery was also considered immoral apart from female cult-prostitutes.) When homosexuality is associated with idolatry (such as in temple cult-prostitution), it is not essentially connected. It is only a concomitant but not an equivalent sin. Sexual unfaithfulness is often used as an illustration of idolatry (e.g., Hosea 3:1; 4:12), but it has no necessary connection with it. Idolatry may lead to immorality (Rom. 1:22–27), but they are different sins. Even the Ten Commandments distinguish between idolatry (first table of the Law, Exod. 20:3–4) and sexual sins (second table, Exod. 20:14–17).

Paul's teaching is divinely authoritative. Paul's condemnation against homosexuality is divinely authoritative, even in 1 Corinthians. Actually, Paul's clearest condemnation of homosexuality is in Romans 1, the divine authority of which is not challenged by any Christian accepting the inspiration of Scripture. Paul's apostolic credentials are firmly established in Scripture. He declared in Galatians that his revelations were "not something that man made up" but were "received . . . by revelation from Jesus Christ" (1:12). To the Corinthians Paul affirmed: "The things that mark an apostle—signs, wonders and miracles—were done among you" (2 Cor. 12:12). Even in 1 Corinthians, where Paul's authority is severely challenged by his critics, his divine authority is made evident in three ways. He begins the book by claiming that he has "words taught by the Spirit" (1 Cor. 2:13). He concludes the book by claiming, "What I am writing to you is the Lord's command" (14:29). Even in the disputed seventh chapter where Paul is alleged to be giving his own uninspired opinion, he declares "I too have the Spirit of God" (v. 40). Indeed, when he says "I, not the Lord" he does not mean his words are not from the Lord; this would contradict everything he says elsewhere. Rather, it means that Jesus did not speak directly to this matter while on earth. But Jesus promised his apostles that he would send the Holy Spirit to "guide you into all truth" (John 16:13). And Paul's teaching in Corinthians was a fulfillment of that promise.

Homosexuality is an offense. When 1 Corinthians 6:9 speaks of "homosexual offenders" (NIV) it means the offense of homosexuality, not an offensive act by a homosexual as opposed to an inoffensive one. This is made plain by several factors. "Homosexual" qualifies "offenders," not the reverse. It speaks against a homosexual kind of offense, not an offensive kind of homosexual. If only offensive kinds of homosexual acts were evil, then what about adulterers and idolaters spoken against in the same passage? Are we to conclude that only offensive kinds of adultery and idolatry are evil? No such qualification that only offensive kinds of homosexuality are wrong is made anywhere else in Scripture in the numerous times it is condemned (Lev. 18:22; Rom. 1:26–27; 1 Tim. 1:10; Jude 7).

Homosexuality is not the same as hair length. Nowhere does the Bible classify homosexual sins into purely cultural matters such as hair style. This is not to say that hair styles cannot be associated with

certain morally tainted lifestyles, such as harlots had. It simply means
that the Bible nowhere reduces a homosexual sin to what is purely a
matter of cultural taste. This argument confuses morals with mores
or commands of culture. "What is" is not always what ought to be. By
the same logic there would be no objective moral prohibitions, including those against cruelty, child abuse, rape, or incest. Paul never says
those with long hair will go to hell, but he does declare that no "homosexual offenders . . . will inherit the kingdom of God" (1 Cor. 6:9). Neither did Paul say that hair length was grounds for excommunication
from the church, but he did teach that sexual sins were (1 Cor. 5:1–5).
Paul only said that, given the "nature of things," that "if a man has
long hair, it is a disgrace to him" (1 Cor. 11:14). He did not say it was
a dishonor to God, as he did about homosexuality (Rom. 1:21–27), but
only that it was a disgrace to himself since it made him look like a
woman.

Homosexual sins are contrary to nature. When the Scriptures declare
that homosexual practices are "against nature" (Rom. 1:26 KJV), they
are referring to essential nature, not sociological nature. Hence, this
passage cannot be used to justify homosexuality on the grounds that
heterosexual acts are contrary to the natural inclinations of homosexuals. There are several reasons for this conclusion. Sex is defined biologically in Scripture from the very beginning. In Genesis 1 God
created "male and female" and then told them to "be fruitful and increase in number" (vv. 27–28). This reproduction was only possible if
he was referring to a biological male and female. Sexual orientation
is understood biologically, not sociologically, when God says "for this
reason a man will leave his father and mother and be united to his
wife, and they will become one flesh" (Gen. 2:24). Only a biological
father and mother can produce children, and the reference to "one
flesh" speaks of a physical marriage. The Romans passage says that
"men committed indecent acts with other men," clearly indicating that
this sinful act was homosexual in nature (1:27). What they did was
not natural to them but was "exchanged" for "natural relations" (v. 26).
Their homosexual desires are called "shameful lusts" (v. 26), so it is
very clear that God is condemning sexual sins between those of the
same biological sex.

Isaiah's prediction was about eunuchs. Contrary to the claim of some
homosexuals, Isaiah made no predictions about their being accepted
into the kingdom of God. The prophecy (Isa. 56:3) is about "eunuchs,"
not homosexuals. And eunuchs are asexual, not homosexual. The "eunuchs" spoken of are probably spiritual, not physical. Jesus spoke of
spiritual "eunuchs" who had given up the possibility of marriage for
the sake of the kingdom of God (Matt. 19:11–12). This is a classic

example of reading one's beliefs into the text (eisegesis), rather than reading the meaning out of the text (exegesis), the very thing homosexuals charge heterosexuals with doing with Scripture.

David and Jonathan were not homosexuals. There is no indication in Scripture that David and Jonathan were homosexual. On the contrary, there is strong evidence that they were not. David's attraction to Bathsheba (2 Sam. 11) reveals that his sexual orientation was heterosexual, not homosexual. In fact, judging by the number of wives he had, David seemed to have too much heterosexuality! David's "love" for Jonathan was not sexual (erotic) but a friendship (philic) love. Third, Jonathan did not strip himself of all his clothes in David's presence, but only of his armor and royal robe (1 Sam. 18:4). The "kiss" was a common cultural greeting for men in that day. Further, it did not occur when Jonathan gave David his attire but two and a half chapters later (20:41). Finally, the emotion they expressed was weeping (v. 41), not orgasm. The text says, "They kissed each other and wept together—but David wept the most" (20:41).

A Response to the Other Arguments for Homosexuality

In addition to the biblical arguments used to justify homosexuality, there are also moral, social, and civil ones. The responses here will be examined in the same order in which these were discussed.

Mutual adult consent does not make it right. The argument that whatever adults consent to do is morally justified is obviously wrong, since they can consent to do what is evil. Two adults may consent to rob a bank, kidnap a child, or kill the president. This does not make it right. Even if what they do is only to each other, that does not make it right. For example, consenting to help each other commit suicide would not make it right. Or consenting to mutilate each other's bodies would not justify it either. Mutual consent does not automatically justify an act. This argument wrongly assumes that the individual is the ultimate standard of what is right and wrong and that there are no limitations on human freedom except self-imposed ones. But this is contrary to the fact that we are creatures and not our own creator. And as creatures we have a moral obligation to our Creator who has commanded us not to sexually abuse our bodies.

The right of privacy is not the right to immorality. Our rights to privacy do not extend to unethical activity. For example, we have no right to privately rape or privately kill. Even the U.S. courts have ruled that no one has the right to practice homosexual activity in private. Consistency demands that an immoral activity does not become moral by moving its location. If, for instance, it is wrong to have a public orgy, then it is also wrong to have a private one. Changing the location of an immoral act does not change its violation of a moral law. Of course, the reverse is not true. For example, just because marital sex is good in private does not mean it is good in public. Finally, there is a difference between the morality of performing a private homosexual act and the difficulty of prohibiting it. Whatever the difficulty of enforcing the prohibitions against it, it is still morally wrong.

There are no homosexual rights. Homosexuals have rights as citizens but not as homosexuals. This is evident for several reasons. Homosexual acts are morally wrong, and there is no right to do a wrong. That is moral nonsense. Neither are there any civil rights to do a moral wrong. Homosexuality is morally wrong, and the civil law should not encourage what is morally wrong. Civil law should be based on moral law. Third, it is as meaningless to speak of homosexual rights as it is to speak of rapist's rights, child abuser's rights, or murderer's rights. Rapists have no civil (or moral) right to be rapists, and child molesters have no civil right to be child molesters. Likewise, there are no civil rights to perform homosexual acts. Homosexuality is a moral and civil wrong, and there is no civil right to do a civil wrong. Finally, homosexuals have rights as citizens but not as homosexuals. However, when the practice of homosexuality interferes with the rights of others (as in solicitation of children), then their rights as citizens can be abrogated (by prison).

Homosexual tendencies are not inherited. Homosexual acts cannot be justified on the grounds that they are inherited for several reasons. There is no undisputed scientific evidence to support the contention that homosexual tendencies are genetic. It shows every evidence of being a learned behavior. People are recruited into the movement and taught to perform homosexual acts. Even if there were an inherited tendency toward a homosexual attitude, this would not justify homosexual acts. Some people seem to inherit a tendency toward violence, but this does not justify violent acts. Some people are said to have an inherited tendency toward alcohol abuse, but this does not justify drunkenness. The Bible declares that homosexuality is "unnatural" and comes about only when someone "abandons" his or her natural inclinations (Rom. 1:26–27). The Bible teaches that we all inherit a tendency to sin (Ps. 51:4; Eph. 2:3), but we are still responsible for sinning.

Morality does not change. Basic moral principles do not change; what changes is our understanding of them and our performance of them. To affirm that moral laws themselves change is misinformed for many reasons. It confuses unchanging moral values with changing moral practices. That is, it confuses morals and mores. It confuses an absolute moral command with our relative comprehension of it. My understanding of love has changed over the past fifty years, but love has not changed. Claiming that morals can change confuses facts and values. The reason witches were once killed but no longer are is not because morality has changed but because, as a matter of fact, we no longer believe that witches can kill people by their incantations. If they could, then they should still be punished as murderers. To the degree that moral principles reflect the nature of God, they cannot change, for God cannot change his basic moral character (Mal. 3:6; Heb. 6:18).

Animal behavior is not normative for humans. There are several objections to appealing to animal behavior as a justification for homosexual activity. For the most part, homosexual acts among mammals are casual and temporary, not habitual and lifelong. Thus, the appeal to animal behavior to justify a homosexual lifestyle is unfounded. Judging by the perversion and violence of some human homosexual acts, animals are getting a bad deal in the comparison. Nothing like the human degradation among hard-core homosexuals is known in the animal kingdom. Animal behavior is not normative for human activity. One should not expect that the behavior of brute beasts is exemplary for human conduct. Animals are not rationally and morally responsible creatures. They act from instinct and, hence, are not ethically culpable for their actions. Humans, on the other hand, are created in God's image and are responsible to act in a God-like manner, not like animals.

The Arguments Against Homosexuality

The case against homosexual acts can be made in two ways: biblically and socially. The biblical arguments will be presented first.

Biblical Arguments Against Homosexuality

There are many biblical arguments against homosexuality, both implicit and explicit. The implicit argument is derived from the fact that God ordained heterosexual acts within the bonds of marriage, not homosexual activity. Since this will be treated in the next chapter, it will only be touched upon here.

God ordained heterosexuality, not homosexuality. God ordained heterosexual relationships when he created "male and female" and commanded them to have children (Gen. 1:27–28). Sex was given a family context from the very beginning. God said, "A man [male] will leave father and mother and be united to his wife [female], and they will become one flesh" (Gen. 2:24). Paul makes it clear that "one flesh" implies sexual intercourse (1 Cor. 6:15–17). The writer of Hebrews proclaims that "marriage should be honored by all, and the marriage bed kept pure, for God will judge the adulterer and all the sexually immoral" (Heb. 13:4). Indeed, the Ten Commandments declare: "You shall not commit adultery" and "You shall not covet your neighbor's wife" (Exod. 20:14, 17). These passages make it plain that God ordained sex to be used between a male and female within the bonds of heterosexual marriage.

Canaan was condemned for a homosexual sin. Although the text does not explicitly say so, it appears that Noah's son Ham engaged in a homosexual act with his drunken father. There are several indications in the Bible that this was the case. The phrase *saw his father's nakedness* (Gen. 9:22) is used elsewhere of perverse sexual acts, and the fact that Ham went "inside [Noah's] tent" to see him may indicate sexually perverse intent. It was apparently not an accidental encounter with his nude father. The curse placed on Ham because of this was on Canaan, Ham's son, not on Ham himself (v. 26). This may imply that these same kinds of evil sexual practices between father and son were also engaged in by Canaan as well (v. 24). The fact that Ham's descendants through Canaan were cursed indicated that the severity of the sin was more than an unintentional glance at his nude father. And since they were of the same sex, the evil act involving his naked father was by definition a homosexual one. Finally, the descendants from Canaan on whom the curse fell were characterized by their vile form of homosexuality and bestiality (cf. Lev. 18:22–29).

Sodom and Gomorrah were condemned. The sin of Sodom and Gomorrah was legendary. To this day the very meaning of the word *sodomy* is an indication of the sin that characterized that city. As was indicated earlier, their sin was not simply luxury or inhospitality but homosexuality. The men of the city said plainly to Lot, "Where are the men who came to you tonight? Bring them out so that we can have sex with them" (Gen. 19:5). Lot's attempt to appease their sensual appetites with his virgin daughters failed, and God destroyed the cities. Jude added, "Sodom and Gomorrah and the surrounding towns gave themselves up to sexual immorality and perversion." Hence, the Bible declares that "they serve as an example of those who suffer the punishment of eternal fire" (Jude 7).

The Mosaic law condemned homosexuality. Both sodomy and bestiality were condemned in the Old Testament law. God said, "I am the LORD. Do not lie with a man as one lies with a woman; that is detestable. Do not have sexual relations with an animal and defile yourself with it" (Lev. 18:21–23). He adds, "That is a perversion" (v. 23).

Not only was homosexuality a sin for Jews, but it was for this very reason that God judged the Canaanites. Moses continues, "Do not defile yourself in any of these ways, because this is how the nations that I am going to drive out before you became defiled. Even the land was defiled; so I punished it for its sin, and the land vomited out its inhabitants" (vv. 24–25). The law adds, "Everyone who does any of these detestable things—such persons must be cut off from their people" (v. 29).

It is clear both from the strong language (detestable, defile, perversion, vomited) and the capital punishment exacted that God considered homosexual acts a very serious sin, and His wrath was not limited to Jews but extended also to Gentiles who practiced these perversions.

Homosexual temple prostitutes were condemned. Not only was homosexuality condemned in general, but it was also condemned as part of temple cult practices. Moses wrote, "No Israelite man or woman is to become a shrine prostitute . . . because the LORD your God detests them both" (Deut. 23:17–18). But here again it is to be noted that homosexual acts were not considered sinful because they were connected with idolatry. Rather, God "detests" them for what they are, namely, a perversion of the holy heterosexual marital use of sex he had ordained. This same practice was condemned throughout the Old Testament.

Homosexuality is condemned in Judges. One of the most grotesque and horrifying sins in the Old Testament was provoked by homosexuals. When a man from Gibeah invited a traveler into his home, "some of the wicked men of the city surrounded the house. Pounding on the door, they shouted to the old man who owned the house, 'Bring out the man who came to your house so we can have sex with him' " (Judg. 19:22). The man urged the homosexual crowd: "Don't do such a disgraceful thing" (v. 24). In an attempt to appease them, he offered his virgin daughter and his guest's concubine to them. So the men "raped [the concubine] and abused her throughout the night, and at dawn they let her go" (v. 25). When her master found the concubine limp on the doorstep the next morning, he cut her in twelve pieces and sent one piece to each of the twelve tribes. Everyone who saw it said, "Such a thing has never been seen or done, not since the day the Israelites came up out of Egypt. Think about it! Consider it! Tell us what to do!" (v. 30). It is difficult to imagine a greater perversity growing out of homosexuality than this. But as horrible as the rape and consequent evil that followed, the Levite saw giving his concubine to them as a less "disgraceful thing" than homosexuality (v. 24).

The prophets condemned sodomy. Homosexual acts were condemned throughout the Old Testament. The prophetic writer of Kings (perhaps Jeremiah) speaks over and over of the evil of homosexuality. He wrote, "There were even male shrine prostitutes in the land; the people engaged in all the detestable practices of the nations the LORD had driven out before the Israelites" (1 Kings 14:24). Later, one of Asa's reforms was that "he expelled the male shrine prostitutes from the land" (15:12). Likewise, Jehoshaphat "rid the land of the rest of the male shrine prostitutes who remained there even after the reign of his father Asa" (22:46). When good king Josiah later invoked a revival "he also tore down the quarters of the male shrine prostitutes, which were in the temple of the LORD" (2 Kings 23:7). The prophet Ezekiel spoke out against the sensual sins of Sodom, calling them "detestable things" (Ezek. 16:50). This is the same word used to describe homosexual acts in Leviticus (18:22–23).

Romans 1 condemns homosexuality among pagans. The most descriptive passage on homosexual acts in the Bible is recorded in Romans 1. Paul called it a sin for which "the wrath of God is being revealed from heaven" (v. 18). The descriptions of the sin of homosexuality are virtually unrivaled anywhere in Scripture. It is called a "sinful desire," "sexual impurity," "degrading," "a lie," "shameful lusts," "unnatural," "inflamed . . . lust," "indecent" and a "perversion" (vv. 24–27). As a result of these kinds of wicked practices God "gave them over to a depraved mind." They became "filled with every kind of wickedness, evil, greed and depravity" (v. 29).

The Scriptures vividly describe homosexual acts in these terms: "Even their women exchanged natural relations for unnatural ones. In the same way men also abandoned natural relations with women and were inflamed with lust for one another. Men committed indecent acts with other men, and received in themselves the due penalty for their perversion" (vv. 26–27). Noteworthy are the two words *exchanged* and *abandoned,* both indicating that a free and sinful choice was made to engage in such sinful acts. This refutes the claim that certain persons are born with homosexual tendencies they cannot avoid.

It is also important to observe that homosexual acts are "unnatural" (v. 26). They are contrary to the natural law that God has "written on their hearts" (2:15). Thus, the sin of homosexuality is not simply a violation of biblical ethics; it is a violation of God's natural moral standard for all persons everywhere. For "all who sin apart from the law [of Moses] also perish apart from the law . . . since they show that the requirements of the law are written on their hearts" (2:12–15).

Homosexuals are not in God's kingdom. According to 1 Corinthians 6:9, "Neither the sexually immoral nor idolaters nor adulterers nor male prostitutes nor homosexual offenders . . . will inherit the kingdom of God." It is obvious that the reference here is to unbelievers, since Paul said to the believers at Corinth, "and that is what some of you were" (v. 11). In other words, no believer can be characterized by such a life. Although believers are capable of slipping into any sin, nonetheless no one who continually practices a homosexual lifestyle can be a believer. For "no one who is born of God will continue to sin, because God's seed remains in him; he cannot go on sinning, because he has been born of God" (1 John 3:9).

First Timothy condemns homosexuality. There is a passage in 1 Timothy that condemns homosexuality as well. Paul said the law was made "for murderers, for adulterers and perverts, for slave traders and liars and perjurers—and for whatever else is contrary to sound doctrine" (1 Tim. 1:9–10). The word *perverts* is a broader word for other sexual sins than "adultery." It includes homosexual acts, and is even translated "sodomites" (NKJV) or "homosexual" (NASB). The context in which it is used and the other sins with which it is listed demonstrate the severity of the sin of sodomy.

Jude calls homosexuality a perversion. Jude declares that God judged the angels who sinned, binding them in everlasting chains for the final judgment day. He adds, "In a similar way, Sodom and Gomorrah and the surrounding towns gave themselves up to sexual immorality and perversion. They serve as an example of those who suffer the punishment of eternal fire" (v. 7). And "in the very same way, these dreamers pollute their own bodies, reject[ing] authority" (v. 8). This passage leaves little doubt about both the sexual nature of Sodom's sin or God's attitude toward the homosexual acts they performed.

So from the beginning to the end of the Bible, the sin of Sodom is consistently and repeatedly condemned in the strongest terms. God both describes it in the strongest negative terms and judges it with the most emphatic ways. There is simply no basis for the claim that homosexuality is an acceptable "alternate lifestyle."

Other Arguments Against Homosexuality

. In addition to the repeated biblical condemnations of homosexual practices, there are strong moral and social indications of the wrongness of this deviant sexual practice. The most important of these follow.

Homosexuality is unnatural. Apart from any biblical statement, nature itself reveals that homosexuality is wrong. It is simply contrary to the natural use of one's sexuality. This is obvious for several reasons. No one was born of a homosexual union, and no one was born a homosexual. They became homosexuals somewhere along the line. Homosexual behavior is not a normal behavior. Only a small fraction of the population (about 2 to 4 percent) have this abnormal behavior. Fourth, ex-homosexuals testify that they were recruited to this lifestyle and have since left it for normal heterosexual relations and families. For these reasons it is clear that homosexuality is not a natural condition.

No society accords homosexuality equivalent status. No society, past or present, has ever accorded homosexuals an equivalent status with heterosexuals.[1] Many societies have frowned on it. Those that have accorded a place for homosexuals have done so only for a limited class and for a limited time. Although some American Indian tribes gave it a place, all in all the place was not a desirable one. The Mohaves, for example, interchanged the word for homosexual with the word for coward. This wisdom of the ages should not be regarded lightly, for this virtually universal attitude among societies is not without justification. Every rational society discriminates against socially undesirable elements. Socially deviant behavior is punished, criminals are put in prison, and so on. Rational discrimination is the only wise thing for a society to do, and, as will be shown, homosexuality produces some socially undesirable behavior.

Homosexuality is socially undesirable. Homosexuality is associated with a whole cluster of socially undesirable characteristics. Psychological studies show that there is a disproportionately high degree of egocentricity, superciliousness, narcissism, masochism, and hostility associated with homosexuality. Hitler's storm troopers, for example, had a disproportionately high number of homosexuals. Child molestation cases involve three times as many homosexuals as the general population. Homosexual crimes, some against other homosexuals, are among the most violent committed. These undesirable characteristics are cause for social concern. They counter the claim that homosexual behavior is purely private and, therefore, of no concern to society in general.

No society is sustained by homosexual practices. Society depends for its very existence on healthy and sustained heterosexual relations. Apart from healthy heterosexual relations, there would be no homosexuals. To put it another way, no one was ever born of a homosexual relationship. Heterosexuality is absolutely essential to the continuance of the race. Without it the whole race would become extinct in one generation, and in this sense homosexuality is a threat to the continuance of the human race. It will not suffice to argue that this will never happen since not everyone will practice it, for if it is an acceptable behavior for all, then all could practice it. And if all did practice it, then the race would self-destruct.

Homosexual practices are a threat to lives. One of the most powerful social arguments against homosexual practices is AIDS. There is no question that this deadly disease is spread by homosexual practices. Neither is there any doubt that it is spread from homosexuals to such

    1. Cited in Paul Cameron, "A Case Against Homosexuality," *The Human Life Review* 4, 3 (Summer 1978): 23.

nonhomosexuals as hemophiliacs, users of common needles, medical workers, wives of bisexuals, and others. Predictions are that eventually millions of people will die as a direct or indirect result of homosexual practices that pass on this fatal virus. The disease has reached epidemic proportions. When the physical well-being of society is so threatened, it is necessary for society to protect itself against such life-threatening practices. No rational society would fail to defend itself against other activities that so endangered the lives of its citizens.

Some Objections Considered

Several objections have been leveled against the various arguments counter to homosexuality. These will be briefly considered now.

These arguments produce homophobia. Some object that the case against homosexuality produces an unnatural and unwarranted fear and generates a kind of hysteria against homosexuals, and that it is an overraction based on emotions. However, this objection is not justified. The case against homosexuality is not based on emotions, but on Scripture and on facts and sound reasoning. There is a difference between an appeal to emotions and one based on emotions. Certainly, a strong warning to leave a burning building is an appeal to the emotions, but if the building is ablaze, no one should object, since it is an appeal based on facts. The arguments against the homosexuals' deviant behavior no more deserve to be called productive of homophobia than arguments against stealing should be called productive of kleptophobia. The real question is whether the behavior is morally and socially acceptable, not whether it produces legitimate fear of a socially damaging or dangerous practice.

It discriminates against homosexuals. There are two basic mistakes in this argument. First, it fails to distinguish between homosexuals and homosexuality. Laws against drunk driving do not thereby discriminate against drinkers. One can be opposed to alcoholism without being opposed to alcoholics. We must distinguish between the person and the practice. It is only homosexual behavior that is objectionable, not homosexuals as persons.

Second, this objection incorrectly assumes that all discrimination is wrong. It is a discrimination against discrimination. Actually, the word *discrimination* is a good word. All rational people discriminate. That is why we put a skull and crossbones on poison and warning labels on cigarette packages. We also discriminate against socially disruptive behavior by punishments and imprisonment. It is in this sense that it is legitimate to discriminate against homosexual behavior. Not to discriminate against socially undesirable behavior is as unreasonable as claiming that child abusers or rapists should not be imprisoned since this would be discriminating against them.

It lacks proper Christian love of all persons. This objection assumes wrongly that we cannot love the sinner and yet hate his sin. There is no reason we cannot love an alcoholic but hate alcoholism. Likewise, we can love homosexuals and hate homosexuality. Admittedly, not all Christians consistently practice this distinction. Many reject even their own children when they "come out of the closet." This is a tragic mistake. This is both un-Christian and unhelpful. It is un-Christian because it is not in the spirit of Christ who ministered to publicans and sinners. Nor can one hope to win them by rejecting them.

Of course, if they are professing believers and members of a church, unrepentant practicing homosexuals must be given church discipline (cf. 1 Cor. 5). However, this does not mean that we should not reach out in love as friends and relatives in order to help them. Total rejection of them as persons only drives them farther into their sin. Love reaches out to people, even sinful ones; it does not reject them. Homosexuals need compassion as persons, not condemnation.

Summary and Conclusion

God ordained that sex should be used within the context of a monogamous heterosexual relationship. Homosexual practices are contrary to God's ordained pattern for human beings. In addition, the Bible speaks out explicitly and forcefully against homosexual practices. The Old Testament considered it a capital offense, and the New Testament treats it as grounds for excommunication. Indeed, Paul declared that no homosexual would inherit the kingdom of God. The language of Scripture could scarcely be more emphatic. Homosexual practices are called unnatural, impure, shameful, indecent, perverse, and an abomination.

In addition to the powerful biblical exhortations against homosexuality, there are strong social arguments as well. Indeed no society, past or present, has ever accorded equal status to homosexuals. It is not only psychologically and socially dangerous, but it has become an epidemic threat to the physical lives of millions of people. In view of this, it is necessary for rational societies to protect their citizens against the contaminating influences of such sexually deviant behavior. Nonetheless, as Christians we should love the sinner, even though we hate his sin. Thus we should reach out in love to win them to Christ who loves them and died for them.

Select Readings

Atkins, David. *Homosexuals in the Christian Fellowship.* 2d ed. Grand Rapids: Eerdmans, 1981.

Bahnsen, Greg L. *Homosexuality: A Biblical View:* Grand Rapids: Baker, 1978.

Bailey, D. Sherwin. *Homosexuality and the Western Christian Tradition.* Reprint. Hamden, Conn.: Shoe String, 1975.

Bathelor, Edward, Jr., ed. *Homosexuality and Ethics.* New York: Pilgrim, 1980.

Boswell, John. *Christianity, Social Tolerance, and Homosexuality: Gay People in Western Europe from the Beginning of the Christian Era to the Fourteenth Century.* Chicago: University of Chicago Press, 1980.

Cameron, Paul. "A Case Against Homosexuality." *The Human Life Review* 4, 3 (Summer 1978): 20–49.

Keyson, Edward. *What You Should Know about Homosexuality.* Grand Rapids: Zondervan, 1979.

Ukleja, Philip Michael. "A Theological Critique of the Contemporary Homosexual Movement." Th.D thesis, Dallas Theological Seminary, 1982.

15

Marriage and Divorce

Marriage is the most basic and influential societal unit in the world. It is difficult to overestimate the importance of marriage, yet each year in the United States there are about half as many divorces as marriages. In view of this, it behooves us to consider the biblical basis for marriage and divorce.

A Biblical View of Marriage

Since divorce is the dissolution of a marriage, it is necessary to consider marriage before discussing divorce. Just what is a Christian marriage, and should it ever be dissolved? Christians have more agreement on the nature of marriage than they do on divorce. What follow are the basic elements of a Christian view of marriage.

The Nature of Marriage

Both the nature and length of marriage are important from a Christian perspective. Marriage is a lifelong commitment between a male and a female that involves mutual sexual rights. There are at least three basic elements in the biblical concept of marriage.

Marriage is between a male and a female. A biblical marriage is between a biological male and a biological female. This is clear from the very beginning. God created "male and female" (Gen. 1:27) and commanded them to "be fruitful and increase in number" (v. 28). Natural reproduction is possible only through male and female union. According to the Scriptures, God "formed man of the dust of the ground" (Gen. 2:7). Then "God made a woman from the rib he had taken out of the man" (v. 22). God adds, "For this reason a man will leave his father and mother and be united to his wife, and they will become one flesh" (v. 24).

The use of the terms *husband* and *wife* in the context of "father" and "mother" make it clear that the reference is to a biological male and female. Referring to the creation of Adam and Eve and their marital union, our Lord cited the passage from Genesis saying, "At the beginning the Creator 'made them male and female' " (Matt. 19:4). Then Jesus quoted this very passage about leaving father and mother and cleaving to one's wife (v. 5), thus confirming that marriage is to be between a male and a female. Hence, the so-called homosexual marriages are not biblical marriages at all. Rather, they are illicit sexual relations (see chap. 14). Since they are not really marriages, it follows that the breakup of such a sinful relationship is not really a divorce either. So the first and most basic characteristic of marriage is that it is a union between a male and a female.

Marriage involves sexual union. It is also clear from Scripture that marriage involves sexual union. This is so for many reasons. It is called a union of "one flesh." That marriage includes sex is evident from its use by Paul in 1 Corinthians 6:16 where Paul uses the same phrase to condemn prostitution. God commanded that the "male and female" he created would propagate children (Gen. 1:28). This is possible only by sexual union between biological male and female. After God created them and expelled them from Eden, the Bible says, "Adam lay with his wife Eve, and she became pregnant and gave birth to Cain" (Gen. 4:1). When speaking to the matter of sex in marriage, the apostle Paul wrote clearly:

> But since there is so much immorality, each man should have his own wife, and each woman her own husband. The husband should fulfill his marital duty to his wife, and likewise the wife to her husband. The wife's body does not belong to her alone but also to her husband. In the same way the husband's body does not belong to him alone but also to his wife. [1 Cor. 7:2–4]

In short, marriage involves the right to sexual union between a male and a female. Sexual intercourse before marriage is called fornication (Acts 15:20; 1 Cor. 6:18), and sexual intercourse outside of marriage is called adultery (Exod. 20:14; Matt. 19:9). Under the Old Testament law, those who engaged in premarital intercourse were obligated to marry (Deut. 22:28–29). Sex is sanctified by God for marriage only (1 Cor. 7:2). Hence, the writer of Hebrews declared "marriage should be honored by all, and the marriage bed kept pure, for God will judge the adulterer and all the sexually immoral" (Heb. 13:4).

Although marriage involves sexual rights, it is not limited to sex. Marriage is a companionship (Mal. 2:14), a union that is much more than sexual. It is a social and spiritual as well as a sexual union. Furthermore, the purpose of sex is more than propagation. Sexual relations in marriage are threefold: propagation (Gen. 1:28), unification (Gen. 2:24), and recreation (Prov. 5:18–19).

Marriage involves a covenant before God. Marriage is not only a union between male and female involving conjugal (sexual) rights, but it is a union born of a covenant of mutual promises. This commitment is implied from the very beginning in the concept of leaving parents and cleaving to one's wife. The marital covenant was stated most explicitly by the prophet Malachi when he wrote:

> The Lord has been a witness between you and the wife of your youth, against whom you have dealt treacherously, though she is your companion and your wife by covenant. [Mal. 2:14 NASB]

Proverbs also speaks of marriage as a "covenant" or mutual commitment. It condemns the adulteress "who has left the partner of her youth and ignored the covenant she made before God" (Prov. 2:17).

From these passages it is evident that marriage is not only a covenant, but one of which God is a witness. It was God who instituted marriage, and it is he who witnesses the vows. They are literally made "before God." Jesus said that it is God who literally joins the two together in marriage, adding, "therefore, what God has joined together, let man not separate" (Matt. 19:6).

One further note on the nature of marriage. It is a God-ordained institution for all people, not just for Christians. Marriage is the only social institution that God ordained before the fall of mankind. The Book of Hebrews declares that marriage "should be honored by all [people]" (Heb. 13:4). Thus God has ordained marriage for non-Christians as well as Christians. And he is the witness of all weddings, whether invited or not. Marriage is a sacred occasion whether the couple recognize it or not.

The Duration of Marriage

The Bible is very clear about the duration of marriage: It is a lifelong commitment. It is designed to last for time but not for eternity.

Marriage is a lifelong commitment. The lifelong nature of marriage is entailed in the concept of permanence in marriage to which Jesus referred when he said, "What God has joined together, let man not separate" (Matt. 19:6). It is also stated by Paul when he says, "By law a married woman is bound to her husband as long as he is alive, but if her husband dies, she is released from the law of marriage" (Rom. 7:2). These concepts underlie the time-honored phrase in the marriage ceremony, "till death do us part."

Marriage is not eternal. While marriage is a lifetime covenant before God, it does not extend into eternity. For as Jesus made clear, "at the resurrection people will neither marry nor be given in marriage; they will be like angels in heaven" (Matt. 22:30). Although we will undoubtedly be able to recognize our loved ones in heaven, there will be no marriage in heaven. Furthermore, the fact that widows could remarry (1 Cor. 7:8–9) indicates that their commitment was only until the death of their mate.

Contrary to Mormon teachings about celestial marriage "for time and eternity," the Bible is emphatic about the fact that marriage is only an earthly institution. It is for time but not for all eternity. This conclusion cannot be avoided by claiming that Jesus only denied there would be any marriage ceremonies in heaven but not any marriage relationships. For it was precisely about the marriage relationship in heaven that he was asked when he gave his answer. For they asked him, "at the resurrection whose wife will she be of the seven, since all of them were married to her?" (Matt. 22:28). His answer was: She will not have a marital relationship with any of them, since there will be no marriage relationship in heaven after the resurrection.

The Number of Parties in Marriage

There is another fact about which Christians agree: marriage is monogamous. It is for one man and one wife. Paul said, "Each man [singular] should have his own wife [singular], and each woman her own husband" (1 Cor. 7:2). An elder must be "the husband of but one wife" (1 Tim. 3:2). But monogamy is not merely a New Testament teaching. It was present from the very beginning, when God created one man (Adam) and gave him only one wife (Eve).

If monogamy is God's order for marriage, then why did he seem to approve of polygamy? Many of the great saints of the Old Testament were polygamists, including Abraham, Moses, and David. Indeed, Solomon had seven hundred wives and three hundred concubines (1 Kings 11:3)! In response, it should be noted that the Bible does not approve of every thing it records, at least not explicitly. For example, the Bible records Satan's lie (Gen. 3:4) but certainly does not approve of it. Likewise, it records David's adultery (2 Sam. 11) but does not approve of it.

Contrary to widespread opinion, the Bible does speak strongly against polygamy in both the Old and New Testaments. This is evident from many passages of Scripture. Monogamy was taught by precedent in the Old Testament. God gave Adam only one wife; this set the precedent for the whole race to follow. Monogamy was also taught by precept. God told Moses, "Neither shall [you] multiply wives" (Deut. 17:17 NASB). Thus polygamy was expressly forbidden.

Monogamy was taught as well in the moral prescription against adultery. It is implied in the moral prescription "You shall not covet your neighbor's wife [singular]" (Exod. 20:17). This implies that there was only one lawful wife the neighbor could have. Monogamy was taught by population proportion. Roughly equal numbers of males and females are born. If God designed polygamy, there should be more women than men. Finally, monogamy is taught by punishment. Every polygamist in the Old Testament paid bitterly for his sin. Solomon is the classic example. The Bible declares that "his wives turned his heart after other gods, and his heart was not fully devoted to the LORD his God" (1 Kings 11:4).

The fact that God permitted polygamy no more proves he prescribed it than the fact God permitted divorce indicates that he desired it. What Jesus said of divorce is true also of polygamy; it was "permitted . . . because your hearts were hard. But it was not this way from the beginning" (Matt. 19:8).

Several Christian Views on Divorce

There is general agreement among Christians on the nature of marriage. It is between a male and a female and involves sexual rights. It entails a covenant (vow) before God to be faithful to each other because it is a monogamous relation between one man and one woman. On the other hand, general agreement on divorce is harder to come by among Christians.

Christian Agreement on Divorce

There is no universal agreement among Christians on divorce. Hence, it is difficult to be dogmatic here. However, there are some areas of general agreement among Christians about divorce. At least three can be noted.

Divorce is not God's ideal. It is clear that God did not design divorce. In fact, God said to Malachi, "I hate divorce" (Mal. 2:16). Jesus said God permitted but never intended divorce (Matt. 19:8). God created one man for one woman and desired that they both keep their vows until death. Jesus said emphatically, "What God has joined together, let man not separate" (Matt. 19:6). So whatever divorce is, it is not God's perfect design for marriage. It falls short of the ideal. It is not a norm or a standard. At most, it is less than the best for marriage.

Divorce is not permissible for every cause. Christians are also generally agreed that divorce is not permissible for any cause. Indeed, Jesus was asked this very question: "Is it lawful for a man to divorce his wife for any and every reason?" His answer is an emphatic no. For his response was this: "I say to you, whoever divorces his wife, except for immorality [fornication], and marries another commits adultery" (Matt. 19:9 NASB). Whatever disagreements Christians have about the exception here, it is absolutely clear that he did not believe that one could get a divorce for *any* reason.

Divorce creates problems. Even those who believe divorce is sometimes justifiable for Christians recognize that, whatever problems it may solve, divorce creates problems. Once God's design is forsaken, it is only natural that problems will emerge. Although divorce seems to avert disaster for some, it is not without its problems. There is always a price to pay for the partners, for the children, and in family and societal relations. Divorce leaves scars that are not easily healed.

Christian Disagreement on Divorce

Beyond their agreement on the preceding points, there is little unanimity among Christians on the topic of divorce and remarriage. There are three basic views. It seems best here simply to expound and evaluate each, drawing our conclusions after the arguments for each have been outlined and evaluated in the light of Scripture and good reason.

There are no grounds for divorce. The strict view of divorce claims that there are no biblical grounds for a divorce. We will first examine the reasons given and then evaluate them in the light of Scripture. There are seven primary arguments in favor of the position that divorce is never justified.

1.) Divorce violates God's design for marriage. As has already been shown, God's ideal for marriage is a monogamous lifetime commitment (Matt. 19:6; Rom. 7:2). But divorce violates that covenant. Hence, divorce is never justified.

2.) Divorce breaks a vow made before God. Marriage is a vow before God (Prov. 2:17; Mal. 2:14) for a lifetime. And divorce breaks that vow. But breaking a sacred vow is wrong. The Scriptures declare: "It is better not to vow than to vow and not fulfill it" (Eccles. 5:5).

3.) Jesus condemned all divorce. When Jesus was asked about divorce in Mark (10:1–9), he gave no exceptions. This same position was affirmed by Jesus in Luke 16:18 without any exceptions. The so-called exception in the parallel passage in Matthew (19:1–9; cf. 5:32) does not refer to divorce for adultery but to an annulment for "fornication" before marriage (v. 9). This is in accordance with Matthew's Jewish emphasis and the Jewish law about unchastity before marriage being grounds for annulling the marriage. The term *husband* also referred to an engaged man according to Jewish law (Deut. 22:13–19; Matt. 1:18–25). Furthermore, in Luke Jesus gave no exceptions for divorce but said flatly, "Anyone who divorces his wife and marries another woman commits adultery, and the man who marries a divorced woman commits adultery" (Luke 16:18).

4.) The apostle Paul condemned divorce. Paul exhorted the Corinthians: "I give this command (not I, but the Lord): A wife must not separate from her husband. But if she does, she must remain unmarried or else be reconciled to her husband" (1 Cor. 7:10–11). Even "if a brother has a wife who is not a believer and she is willing to live with him, he must not divorce her." Likewise, "if a woman has a husband who is not a believer and he is willing to live with her, she must not divorce him" (1 Cor. 7:12–13).

5.) Divorce disqualified an elder. One of the qualifications for an elder was that he must be "the husband of but one wife" (1 Tim. 3:2). According to proponents of the strict view on divorce, this means that he could never have been divorced; otherwise he would have been the husband of more than one wife.

6.) One's first partner is the true partner. When the woman of Samaria said to Jesus, "I have no husband," he replied, "You are right when you say you have no husband. The fact is, you have had five husbands, and the man you now have is not your husband" (John 4:17–18). This is taken to imply that one's first spouse is the only true spouse.

7.) Divorce violates a sacred typology. According to Paul, a wife is to her husband what the church is to Christ (Eph. 5:32). Hence, divorce violates that beautiful typology of the heavenly marriage between Christ and his bride the church. That God takes a violation of a sacred type seriously can be witnessed in his punishment of Moses for striking the rock (Christ) twice (Num. 20:9–12).

In summary, there are no grounds for divorce. The "exception" in Matthew 19:9 refers to premarital intercourse (fornication), not to adultery after marriage. Since there are no grounds for divorce, then divorce is sin and remarriage of divorcees is wrong.

There is only one ground for divorce. Many Christians believe that there is only one justified ground for divorce: adultery. Remarriage of divorced persons is not permitted, since they would be living in sin (Matt. 5:32). This they base on several considerations.

1.) Jesus explicitly stated adultery as grounds for divorce. Proponents of this view favor rendering Matthew 19:9 the way the New International Version does:

> I tell you that anyone who divorces his wife, *except for marital unfaithfulness*, and marries another woman commits adultery. [emphasis added]

They point to several factors in favor of this rendering. The Greek word used is *porneia*, which includes illicit sexual relations of married as well as unmarried people (see Acts 15:20; Rom. 1:29). It is used in parallel with the word *adultery* in this very passage, indicating that they have overlapping usages.

2.) Jesus repeated this exception in a parallel passage. Not only did Jesus state adultery as the one ground for divorce when asked, but he stated the same thing in the Sermon on the Mount, saying,

> I tell you that anyone who divorces his wife, *except for marital unfaithfulness*, causes her to become an adulteress, and anyone who marries the divorced woman commits adultery. [Matt. 5:32, emphasis added]

In view of this repeated exception, it is argued that the other reference (in Luke 16:18) where no exception is mentioned must be understood in the light of the clearly stated exception of adultery.

3.) Paul agreed with Jesus' view on divorce. Paul affirmed Jesus' position on divorce for adultery at least implicitly, if not explicitly. He was careful to point to the authority of Christ in these matters by phrases like "not I, but the Lord" (1 Cor. 7:10). And when he said "I, not the Lord," he was not contradicting Christ but merely noting that although Christ never spoke to that particular issue he did, rather, give revelation to Paul (cf. 1 Cor. 2:13; 7:40; 14:37). Furthermore, Paul acknowledged the legitimacy of divorce when he wrote, "If the unbeliever leaves, let him do so. A believing man or woman is not bound [by their marital vows] in such circumstances; God has called us to peace" (1 Cor. 7:15).

In summary, there is only one biblical ground for divorce—adultery. Divorcees cannot remarry or they are living in an adulterous relation. Those who marry divorcees are causing them to sin, since the divorcee is really married to another in God's eyes.

There are many grounds for divorce. "Many" here means two or more. Some proponents of this position hold to only two biblical grounds for divorce: adultery and unbeliever desertion. Others believe that abuse, infectious diseases, and even neglect are also justifications for divorce. The point is simply that all in this group agree that there is not just one basis for a biblical divorce. While not everyone in this camp would agree with all the following arguments, all of these reasons are offered by someone in this camp.

1.) Paul approves of divorce for desertion. When Paul says "if the unbeliever leaves, let him do so" (1 Cor. 7:15), he is speaking of desertion, not adultery. There is no reference to adultery in the passage. It simply states that he or she "leaves." This is desertion by an unbeliever, and Paul says in such cases the faithful remaining partner is not bound by the marriage vows. Although he would like to keep them, the fact of the matter is that he cannot, since the partner has left him. This position that divorce is permissible only for adultery or unbeliever desertion is expressed in the *Westminster Confession,* chapter 24:

> Section V—Adultery or fornication committed after a contract, being detected before marriage, giveth just occasion to the innocent party to dissolve that contract (Matt. 1:18–20). In the case of adultery after marriage, it is lawful for the innocent party to sue out a divorce (Matt. 5:32), and after the divorce to marry another, as if the offending party were dead (Matt. 19:9; Rom. 7:2–3).

> Section VI—Although the corruption of man be such as is apt to study arguments, unduly to put asunder those whom God hath joined together in marriage; yet nothing but adultery, or such willful desertion as can no way be remedied by the Church or civil magistrate, is cause sufficient of dissolving the bond of marriage (Matt. 19:8–9; 1 Cor. 7:15; Matt. 19:6): wherein a public and orderly course of proceeding is to be observed, and the persons concerned in it not left to their own wills and discretion in their own case (Deut. 24:1–4).

2.) The Bible recognizes human frailty. Even though God did not design divorce, he did foresee it and accommodate his plan to it. The very fact that God led Moses to permit divorce (Deut. 24:1–4; cf. Matt. 19:8) shows that God understands that in a fallen world the ideal can not always be realized. In point of fact, when, because of ceremonial contamination, an Israelite could not keep the Passover on the first month, God provided that it could be held on the second month (Num. 9:10–11). Likewise, when God's first choice for lifetime monogamous marriage is not possible, divorce is sometimes necessary.

3.) Even God "divorced" Israel for unfaithfulness. Throughout the Old Testament God "divorced" his people for alienation of affection. They went after idols and God divorced them. God said through Jeremiah, "I gave faithless Israel her certificate of divorce and sent her away because of her adulteries" (Jer. 3:8). Isaiah also wrote of God's divorce of Israel because of her unfaithfulness, saying, "Where is your mother's certificate of divorce with which I sent her away?" (Isa. 50:1). Thus, it is argued that the fact that God divorced Israel because of her unfaithfulness sets the pattern for us.

4.) Marriage is a mutual vow. Unconditional vows should not be broken, but marriage is a mutual vow between two parties, a covenant. As such it is a conditional covenant. Since the relation is mutual, one person's vows are impossible to keep if the other person is unfaithful or leaves. Hence, the innocent party is not bound to his or her vows if the other party leaves (1 Cor 7:15).

5.) Failing to allow divorce is legalistic. Failing to allow for divorce in some circumstances is legalistic. It is the same stance Jesus condemned in the Pharisees who would not allow healing on the Sabbath. Jesus said, "The Sabbath was made for man, not man for the Sabbath" (Mark 2:27). Likewise, marriage was made for man; man was not made for marriage. Hence, the person should be preeminent in the consideration, not simply a prescription about divorce.

6.) Repentance changes the situation. Even though Israel was "divorced" by the Lord (Jer. 3:1), nevertheless she was asked repeatedly to return (vs. 11, 14, 22). This would indicate that repentance can change the status of the guilty parties before the laws on marriage. Hence, even if the original divorce was a sin, God can nonetheless forgive and heal if there is repentance. There is only one unpardonable sin (Matt. 12:32), and it is not divorce.

An Evaluation of the Christian Views on Divorce

Since there is general agreement on the nature of marriage, we will concentrate on the difference regarding divorce. This will be accomplished by evaluating the arguments in favor of the various views.

An Evaluation of the Position Prohibiting Divorce

Those opposed to divorce are correct in affirming that marriage ought never to be dissolved. However, this is a separate question from remarriage. Just because divorce is sinful does not necessarily mean remarriage is not permissible. The two issues are logically distinct.

Marriage is for life. The most commendable and justifiable aspect of the position that there are no grounds for divorce is its emphasis on the permanence of marriage. God intends that marriage be a lifetime monogamous relationship. This is God's standard for Christian marriages, and nothing short of it is right. Divorce breaks God's law for marriage and should never be excused as such. God's ideal for marrige is a lifetime commitment between one man and one woman. The pattern should never be violated, and to do so is wrong.

All the arguments and Bible verses used by the adherents of this position point to this conclusion. God does hate divorce. Jesus did forbid it, and the rest of the Bible concurs. At best, God only permitted divorce but never commanded it. There are no scriptural grounds for divorce, not even adultery. Adultery is a sin, and to say adultery is a justification for divorce is to say that sin justifies divorce. Divorce is a failure to measure up to God's standard no matter what reason. It is an attack upon God's standard, a destruction of his plan for marriage. However, this is logically distinct from the question of whether remarriage is permissible.

Remarriage is another matter. The questions of divorce and remarriage are logically distinct. Just because divorce is always wrong as such does not mean that remarriage is never right. To argue that it does overlooks several important things.

Lifetime marriage is God's ideal, but the ideal is not always possible. We do not live in an ideal world but a real one, even a fallen world. In such a world God's ideal is not always achievable. When it is not, then we must do the next best thing. Just as God allowed the children of Israel to observe the Passover on the second month (when they could not observe the first month because of uncleanness), even so remarriage is not God's ideal either. But it is a realistic accommodation to a less than idealistic world.

Jesus recognized the difference between the ideal and the real when he distinguished between God's command not to divorce and his permission of divorce in the Old Testament. He said, "Moses permitted you to divorce" (Matt. 19:8), but God never intended it that way. For "it was not this way from the beginning." Likewise, while God never commanded remarriage of divorced couples, this does not mean that he never permits it.

Forgiveness can change one's status before God. According to the prophet Jeremiah, God called upon the Israelites whom he had "divorced" to repent and "return" to him (Jer. 3:1, 14). This means that repentance canceled their divorced status. If so, then why cannot repentance cancel the adulterous status of the divorced who remarry? Jesus did say that anyone who was divorced and remarried was living in adultery (Matt. 5:32). But he did not say that divorce was an unpardonable sin. In fact, he said there is only one unpardonable sin, and it is the blasphemy of the Holy Spirit (Matt. 12:32). To make divorce a second unpardonable sin goes beyond Scripture, which affirms that "if we confess our sins, [God] is faithful and just and will forgive us our sins and purify us from all unrighteousness" (1 John 1:9).

Jesus condemned those who exalted some laws at the expense of lives. Even though it was wrong for a Jew to work on the Sabbath, Jesus approved of working to get one's ox out of the ditch on the Sabbath (Luke 14:5). He declared that "the Sabbath was made for man, not man for the Sabbath" (Mark 2:27). Likewise, divorce laws were made for man, not man for divorce laws. The person is more important than the precept. Divorce precepts were made to help persons, not hurt them. When legalistic emphasis is placed on the divorce law at the expense of showing mercy to the divorced, then we find ourselves in the same legalism Jesus repeatedly condemned in the Pharisees.

Often forgotten in the matter of divorce is the fact that some laws are higher than other laws (see chap. 7). There are greater virtues, like love and mercy (John 15:13; 1 Cor. 13:13). When these come in conflict, we are obligated to the higher moral law and not held responsible for not keeping the lower one. For example, if it is necessary to disobey government to protect lives (Exod. 1) or to avoid idolatry (Dan. 3), then God does not hold us responsible for failure to keep his command to obey government (Rom. 13:1; Titus 3:1; 1 Pet. 2:13). Likewise, even though divorce as such is wrong, there may be occasions when a greater responsibility overrides this law.

For example, suppose that both individuals in a couple with children were each once married to someone else by whom they had no children, and that both of those previous partners are now married to someone else by whom they have children. Would not confession of their sins and a legal divorce from their first partner be in order so that they can be legally married to their present partner and continue their present family? They cannot go back to their first partners; those partners are now remarried and have children. It is unmerciful to break up this marriage and leave the children without parents or take them away from their parents. However, if one carries the position prohibiting divorce through logically, this is exactly what would have to be done. Someone might cry "purely hypothetical," but this very counseling situation happened to a young pastor I know very well. A recognition that there is a gradation of moral laws or a hierarchy of responsibility can make it possible to easily handle such problems. A dogged legalism will have disastrous results on human lives.

An Evaluation of the Position
Allowing Divorce for Adultery

This position has numerous merits. In fact, it differs from the position prohibiting divorce in only one thing: it claims divorce and remarriage are justified for the innocent party. So, with this one exception, it is to be commended for the same reasons the other view was. With the exception of approving of divorce for adultery, it is right about marriage but wrong about remarriage. The misunderstanding about these two issues revolves around two verses of the Bible.

Misunderstanding of the exception clause—Jesus is quoted twice in Matthew as saying divorce is wrong "except for fornication (*porneia*)" (Matt. 5:32; 19:8). Proponents of the position allowing divorce only for adultery take this to refer to sexual unfaithfulness *after* marriage by one of the partners. This interpretation, however, is not supported by either the context, parallel passages, or the customs of the day.

There is a different word for adultery used in the New Testament. It is the Greek word *moikeia*. If Matthew had meant adultery (illicit sex involving a married person) he could have used this word, not "fornication" (*porneia*). Matthew used the word *moikeia* when describing adultery (Matt. 15:19) and the verb form *moikeuo* ("to commit adultery") several times (Matt. 5:27–28; 19:18). Other New Testament writers regularly use the words *moikeia* and *moikeuo* to describe adultery (e.g., Mark 7:21; Luke 16:18; John 8:4; Rom. 2:22; James 2:11; Rev. 2:22). The two words *fornication* (*porneia*) and *adultery* (*moikeia*) are repeatedly used in distinction from each other in the same passage. For example, Jesus said, "for out of the heart come . . . adultery, fornication" (Matt. 15:19 NASB; see also Mark 7:21; Gal. 5:19).

Only Matthew mentions the exception for fornication. The parallel passage in Mark (10:11) says simply, "Anyone who divorces his wife and marries another woman commits adultery against her." And Luke (16:18) likewise reads, "Anyone who divorces his wife and marries another woman commits adultery." If there were an exception that applied to their audiences, surely they would have mentioned it.

Matthew's Jewish background and emphasis would understandably lead him to emphasize the Jewish exception for premarital fornication. The law of Moses said, "If a man takes a wife and, after lying with her . . . did not find proof of her virginity, . . . she shall be brought to the door of her father's house and there the men of her town shall stone her to death" (Deut. 22:13–21). However, if her parents can bring "proof of her virginity" and "display the cloth [stained bed sheet] before the elders of the town," then "she shall continue to be his wife; he must not divorce her as long as he lives" (vv. 14, 17, 19). With this custom in mind, it is perfectly understandable why Matthew would want to explain for the Jews in his audience this justifiable premarital exception.

Misunderstanding of the "cause adultery" statement—According to both those totally opposed to divorce and those allowing divorce for adultery, those who are divorced, or divorced for adultery, cannot remarry or else they commit adultery. This is based on Jesus' statements that "anyone who divorces his wife and marries another woman commits adultery against her" (Mark 10:11) and "a man who marries a divorced woman commits adultery" (Luke 16:18; cf. Matt. 19:8). Matthew 5:32 says "anyone who divorces his wife except for the cause of unchastity, *makes her commit adultery*" (NASB, emphasis added). The implication here is that, as far as God is concerned, the original partner is the true spouse. So in God's eyes the "divorced" person is still married. Hence, living with another is adultery, since it is sexual intercourse with a married person.

While it must be acknowledged that this seems to be a valid inference from the passage with respect to God's ideal for marriage, nonetheless it is wrong to assume that this eliminates all remarriage for several reasons.

First, Jesus obviously does not mean that the innocent party is really committing adultery, for it is his or her partner who has committed adultery. God is simply treating the innocent party as if he or she has committed adultery. In like manner, 1 John 1:10 says, "If we say we have not sinned, we make [God] out to be a liar." But it is clear that we cannot actually make God to be a liar. By claiming sinlessness, we treat God as if he were a liar. Thus, since divorce violates God's ideal for marriage, even the innocent party is treated as if he or she were an adulterer, even though he or she is not.

Second, as all admit, the death of one partner would make remarriage valid. For in such a case the other party would not be committing adultery by remarrying.

Third, as the Westminster Confession argued, there are other situations than divorce that are "as if the *offending party were dead*" (emphasis added). Desertion, for example, is the virtual equivalent of death.

Fourth, as noted, forgiveness by confession cancels the state of sin status of the divorcee (Jer. 3:1, 14). The only reason they are living in sin after a divorce is that the divorce was a sin. And as long as they do not confess the sin of the divorce, they are still living in sin. But if they do confess their sin God will forgive it like any other sin (1 John 1:9).

An Evaluation of the Position
Allowing Divorce for Many Reasons

Although, as we have already seen, there is no justification for divorce as such, nevertheless, the position that permits divorce for many reasons has a great deal of merit. Its value is not in the grounds it allows for the dissolution of a marriage, but in its arguments in favor of encouraging a remarriage. That is, they cannot be used to justify divorce; whatever value they have can only be used to justify remarriage. At best, they are not arguments in favor of breaking an old marriage, but simply reasons for making a new marriage. Some of the reasons deserve repetition.

Marriage is a mutual vow. Since marriage is a mutual vow, it is both impossible and unnecessary for only one person to keep a vow when the other person has irrevocably broken it. We do not mean that a believer should not seek reconciliation. On the contrary, as long as it is possible to make the first marriage function, the believer has a responsibility to do so. Following the example of Hosea, we should even forgive and receive back an adulterous partner (Hos. 3). On the other hand, if the other person is dead (or the equivalent) or has remarried, then there is obviously no possibility of reconciliation. In such cases, the other party is not bound by the wedding vows, since they were vows to another person to whom it is no longer possible to fulfill them.

Frailty should be acknowledged and forgiveness sought. God understands our weaknesses and he forgives our sins. He knew that we would not always be able to keep his commandments. And while he never lowers their demands to our level, he does provide forgiveness for us. Divorce is not an unforgivable sin. The problem is in getting people to recognize that it is a sin. Admittedly, giving "justified" instances for divorce does not help to promote God's ideal for a permanent marriage. On the other hand, neither does ignoring God's forgiveness and installing a second unpardonable sin constitute a helpful ministry to the divorced. At least those favoring divorce for many reasons have some of the right reasons, even if they do use them to prove the wrong point.

Summary and Conclusion

God intends marriage to be a lifetime commitment between one male and one female. While the marriage relationship does not extend into eternity, it is meant to be for all our time together on earth. Divorce as such is never justifiable as such, even for adultery. Adultery is a sin, and God neither approves of sin nor the dissolution of marriage. What he has joined together, he does not want man to put asunder (Matt. 19:6).

However, while divorce is never justifiable, it is sometimes permissible and always forgivable. Hence, those who recognize the sin of the divorce, and their responsibility for it, should be allowed to remarry. But their remarriage should be for life. If they fail again, it would be unwise to allow them to continue to repeat this error. Only those who are inclined to keep their lifetime commitment should be married, to say nothing of remarried. Marriage is a sacred institution and should not be profaned by divorce, especially by repeated divorce. The epidemic proportions which divorce has reached in our society are a sober warning about how the sacredness of marriage has been profaned. Christians should do everything in their power to exalt God's standard of monogamous lifetime marriage.

Select Readings

Adams, Jay E. *Marriage, Divorce and Remarriage.* Phillipsburg, N.J.: Presbyterian and Reformed, 1980.

Boettner, Loraine. *Divorce.* Phillipsburg, N.J.: Presbyterian and Reformed, 1974.

Duty, Guy. *Divorce and Remarriage.* Minneapolis: Bethany Fellowship, 1967.

Heth, William A., and Gordon J. Wenham. *Jesus and Divorce.* Nashville: Thomas Nelson, 1984.

Small, Dwight H. *The Right to Remarry.* Old Tappan, N.J.: Revell, 1977.

Steele, Paul E., and Charles C. Ryrie. *Meant to Last.* Wheaton: Victor, 1986.

Stott, John R. W. *Divorce.* Downers Grove: Inter-Varsity, 1971.

16

Ecology

Consider the following scientific data about our environment. Each year a tropical forest the size of Scotland is destroyed on planet Earth. India alone has lost 85 percent of her original forests. Nearly one-half of all forests in developing countries have been cut down in this century. Deforestation is a major cause of modern mass extinction of plant and animal species. Due to deforestation, as many as one million species of plants and animals could become extinct by the end of this century. The use of fluorocarbons is depleting the crucial ozone layer and threatening human health.

In addition to this, chemical wastes have entered the food chain and are found in human body fat. Seventy-seven percent of Americans, and ninety percent of children, are carrying more lead in their bodies than the Environmental Protection Agency says is safe. Ten thousand people die every year from pesticide poisoning and another forty thousand become ill. One-third of all household garbage comes from food packaging material—the average American discards five pounds of trash per day. Since 1960, the U.S. has closed 3,500 landfills and by 1990, one-half of all landfills will be closed.

In view of this dangerous ecological situation, what is the Christian's ethical responsibility to the physical environment in which we live? What are the moral implications of pollution destroying flora and fauna? Is there any ethical obligation to preserve pure water and air? If so, what is it? The answers to these questions vary depending on one's world view. Some atheists like Ayn Rand extol the virtues of technology over nature and show little concern for the natural environment. One of her disciples, Henry Binswanger, even speaks blatantly of "raping" the environment to advance society. At the other end of the spectrum from such humanists are pantheists who virtually worship nature. They oppose drilling for oil offshore, building dams, killing animals for fur, using insecticides, and any other human interventions that disturb the natural environment.

Between the two extremes of the materialist's wastage of nature and the pantheist's worship of it, the Christian believes in the proper respect for and use of natural resources. This respectful utilization of our physical environment grows out of the Christian concept of creation and our divinely appointed obligation to be good stewards of what God has given us.

A Materialistic View of the Environment

Although not all materialists are atheists, most atheists are materialists of some kind. Hence, the philosophical basis of a materialistic view of the environment grows out of an atheistic or secular humanist world view. Such a view is expressed in *Humanist Manifesto I* (1933). After denying a Creator and a distinctive spiritual aspect in human beings, it affirms unbounded optimism in man's ability to solve his own problems:

> Using technology wisely, we can control our environment, conquer poverty, markedly reduce disease, extend our life-span, significantly modify our behavior, alter the course of human evolution and cultural development, unlock vast new powers and provide humankind with unparalleled opportunities for achieving an abundant and meaningful life.[1]

Although humanistic optimism has been dampened over the last generation, the more recent "Secular Humanist Declaration" nevertheless claims that "the scientific method, though imperfect, is still the most reliable way of understanding the world." Thus, "we look to the natural, biological, social, and behavioral sciences for knowledge of the universe and man's place in it."[2]

The essential elements of a secular humanist position on the environment can be briefly outlined. Not all humanists will agree with

1. Paul Kurtz, ed., *Humanist Manifestos I and II* (Buffalo: Prometheus, 1973), p. 14.
2. Paul Kurtz, ed., "A Secular Humanist Declaration," *Free Inquiry* 1 (Winter 1980/81): 5–6.

each point, of course. However, even many who do not claim to be philosophical humanists have adopted some of the tenets of their position into their economic or pragmatic materialism.

Materialistic View of the Environment Explained

Secular humanism embraces a materialistic view of nature. Materialism can be understood in either a philosophical or an economic sense, and both will be included in this discussion. In the latter sense, it often refers to an exploitive form of capitalism. Of course, not all humanists hold this view, but here again even many deists, and some theists, join in affirming economic materialism, at least in practice.

Nature is simply there. One of the characteristics of a materialist's world view is that the existence of nature, with all of its resources, is taken for granted. Historically, for traditional materialists this has meant that the physical world is eternal and uncreated. In support of this an appeal is often made to the first law of thermodynamics, which states that energy can neither be created nor destroyed. This would imply that if energy is uncreated, then there is no Creator, and hence no divine imperative to use it in a particular way.

Energy is unlimited. Another assumption of a materialistic world view is that energy is unlimited. If it cannot be destroyed, then it is indestructible, and if it is indestructible, then we will never run out of it. Energy in some form will always be available for our use. We may run out of certain forms, at least for a time, but human ingenuity will always create new forms to supply human needs. This leads to a third assumption.

Human technology can solve almost any problem. Science can solve virtually any problem. What science cannot solve, governments can. This unbounded optimism flows from a secular humanist's world view. In his book, *The Next Ten Thousand Years,* Adrian Berry declares, "There is no limit to growth, and there is no limit to what developed nations can accomplish."[3] This same unlimited enthusiasm for the success of science is evident in Steve Austin of "Six Million Dollar Man," in the superhuman Mr. Spock of "Star Trek," and earlier in H. G. Wells's novel, *Food of the Gods* (1904), where he projects the discovery of synthetic food that can make ordinary humans grow into giants.

The world suffers mainly from maldistribution. In explaining why much of the world's population suffers, many secular humanists pinpoint the problem in maldistribution of resources. They believe the world is immensely rich and that redistribution of resources could

3. Adrian Berry, *The Next Ten Thousand Years* (New York: Dutton, 1974), p. 59.

solve the problem of need. There is plenty for all, if we could only get it to them. Both resources and means of production are available; proper distribution is all that is lacking.

Global education can correct maldistribution. Secular humanists believe in the limitless ability of humans to solve their own problems. "No deity will save us; we must save ourselves," they boast.[4] The way to salvation is by education. John Stuart Mill went so far as to say that "all would be gained if the whole population were taught to read."[5] Even less optimistic humanists place strong emphasis on public education as the means to attain their humanistic goals. John Dewey, who signed *Humanist Manifesto I,* dedicated himself to this very task.

An Evaluation of the Materialistic View

As a framework for an adequate view of ecology, the secular view is singularly insufficient. This is forcefully stated in David Ehrenfeld's excellent book, *The Arrogance of Humanism* (1978). Ehrenfeld notes that, "Evidence is piled all around us that the religion of humanity is self-destructive and foolish, yet the more it fails the more arrogant and preposterous are the claims of its priests."[6]

The world is not eternal. Materialists often misquote the first law of thermodynamics. It is simply scientifically unfounded to claim that energy cannot be created or destroyed. There is no observational basis for such a declaration. It is not a scientific conclusion but a metaphysical affirmation. More accurately stated, the first law simply says that the amount of actual energy in the universe appears to remain constant. That is to say, we do not observe any new energy coming into existence nor any used energy going out of existence. As far as the evidence goes, there is a fixed amount of energy in the cosmos. Thus the first law makes no statement about the origin of energy in the universe but simply about its constancy.

However, the second law of thermodynamics does speak to the origin of the universe, since it tells us that the amount of usable energy in the universe is decreasing. This means the universe is running out of usable energy. It is winding down. But if it is winding down, then it must have been wound up. To state it another way, if the universe is running down, then it cannot be eternal; it must have been created. And if it was created, then it is reasonable to posit a Creator of it.

---

4. Kurtz, *Humanist Manifestos I and II,* p. 16.

5. As quoted in T. M. Kitwood, *What Is Human?* (Downers Grove: Inter-Varsity, 1970), p. 50.

6. David Ehrenfeld, *The Arrogance of Humanism* (New York: Oxford University Press, 1978), p. 59.

This, of course, is precisely what the Bible does in the first verse when it declares, "In the beginning God created the heavens and the earth."

Energy is not unlimited. Contrary to materialistic belief, energy is not unlimited, at least not usable energy. The second law of thermodynamics informs us of that. In closed isolated systems, such as the whole material universe is by definition, the amount of usable energy is decreasing. Nuclear fission is taking place in stars throughout the universe. Hence, the universe will eventually run out of energy. All its usable energy will be transformed into unusable heat, and the universe will die. Even more quickly than that, the world will run out of precious metals and fossil fuels unless we move quickly to conserve them. The unbounded optimism about our natural resources promulgated by materialists is unfounded in fact.

Technology cannot solve our problems. There are many reasons why human technology and ingenuity cannot solve all our problems. We cannot know and gather in advance all the relevant information to solve our problems. We cannot even know in advance what questions we should ask. Even if we did know all the relevant facts, we still could not make errorless deductions from what we know.[7] In fact, David Ehrenfeld concludes that,

> deep within ourselves we know that our omnipotence is a sham, our knowledge and control of the future is weak and limited, our inventions and discoveries work, if they work at all, in ways that we do not expect, our planning is meaningless, our systems are running amok—in short, that the humanistic assumptions upon which our societies are grounded lack validity.[8]

Maldistribution is not the root problem. To claim that maldistribution is the basic resource problem of the world is empty and tautological. Of course there is an imbalance of distribution. Not everyone who needs the proper resources is getting them. Millions, for example, lack proper food or energy resources. But this is not the problem; it is the result of the problem. The question is: What is the cause of this maldistribution? Here the humanists fail to recognize the sinfulness of man as the cause (James 4:1–2). Human selfishness and greed are at the heart of the problem, but secular humanists are unwilling to acknowledge this realistic and biblical view of human nature.

Education is not the solution. History is ample testimony to the fact that salvation is not attained by education. The Platonic premise that

7. Ibid., pp. 74–75.
8. Ibid., p. 58.

"those who know the good will do the good" is simply contrary to fact. Making a person smarter does not automatically make them better. In fact, sometimes it only makes them more shrewd in concocting evil. The great evil figures in world history have not been more ignorant than average. On the contrary, there have been many evil geniuses, including Stalin, Hitler, and Adolph Eichmann.

This, of course, is not to say that there is no benefit in education. It is simply to point out that education is not the means of salvation, neither morally nor ecologically. As important as overcoming ignorance of the world's ecological crises is, in and of itself this will not solve the problem. Our ecological system will not be transformed until our ethical system is. After all, it is people who are abusing the environment. Hence, we must transform people before we can hope to transform their environment.

A Pantheistic View of the Environment

Materialism does play havoc with the environment. The unfounded belief that energy sources are limitless has led to careless squandering of vital resources. Greed for gain has led to a literal rape of many natural resources. In the name of technology and progress, our seas have become cesspools, our land has become a dump, and our lush forests have become wastelands. In reaction to this destruction, many voices have been raised, and many of these arise out of a pantheistic world view. The widely read *Zen and the Art of Motorcycle Maintenance* (1974) was an early cry against technology. In this same counter-cultural vein, Charles Reich's *Greening of America* (1970) linked technology with capitalism and insisted that "Modern society makes war on nature. A competitive market uses nature as a commodity to be exploited—turned into profit. Technology sees nature as an element to be conquered, regulated, controlled. . . ."[9]

Pantheistic View of the Environment Explained

A pantheistic approach to the environment is distinctively anti-materialistic and mistakenly anti-Christian. Characteristic of the pantheists' misunderstanding of the Christian view is Ian McHarg, who claims that "the Biblical creation story of the first chapter of Genesis . . . not only fails to correspond to reality as we observe it, but its insistence upon dominion and subjugation of nature, encourages the most exploitive and destructive instincts in man, rather than those

9. Charles A. Reich, *The Greening of America* (New York: Bantam, 1970), pp. 28–29.

that are deferential and creative."[10] There are several characteristic features of a pantheistic view of ecology. Pantheism is the belief that God is all and all is God. As in the case of animistic religions, nature is a manifestation of the sacred or divine. Devotees therefore revere nature, for nature is divine. It is really Nature with a capital *N*. This attitude is exemplified in animistic religions which see a sacred *mana* or soul in all things, including material things. The native Koyukons of Alaska, for example, believe that "natural entities are endowed with spirits and with spiritually based power." Hence, "knowledge of these spirits is considered essential for success in harvesting natural resources and living harmoniously within the environmental community."[11]

Nature is a living organism. Not only is nature a manifestation of God, but it is alive. The soul or life force that permeates it is one great living organism. This view finds popular expression in George Lucas's *Star Wars* series in which Yoda, the tiny creaturely Zen master, declares:

> My ally is the Force. And a powerful ally it is. Life creates it and makes it grow. Its energy surrounds us and binds us. . . . Feel the Force around you. Here . . . between you and me and the tree and that rock.[12]

Everything is alive with a living force or energy that binds nature into a living organism.

Living species are manifestations of God. God is manifest in nature with great diversity. Each living species is a manifestation of God. Hence it is necessary to preserve the multiplicity of species that exist. In fact, species preservation is an ethical obligation. Thus, when human technology in the form of a dam threatens the tiny two-inch snail darter (a fish), then building the dam must be opposed. For when a species becomes extinct, we have lost one of the manifestations of God. New Age writer Mark Satin proposes the ethical precept of "maximization of environmental quality—including the maximization of the well-being of all creatures."[13]

Humans are one with nature. Satin acknowledges that "North American Indian spirituality has inspired many of us and has a lot to teach us." He cites the Shoshone medicine man Rolling Thunder with approval:

10. Ian McHarg, *Design with Nature* (Garden City, N.Y.: Natural History Press, 1969), p. 26.

11. Richard K. Nelson, *Make Prayers to the Raven: A Koyukon View of the Northern Forest* (Chicago: University of Chicago Press, 1983), p. 228.

12. Donald F. Glut, *The Empire Strikes Back* (New York: Ballantine, 1980), p. 123.

13. Mark Satin, *New Age Politics* (New York: Dell, 1979), p. 105.

Rolling Thunder's way is to work externally, to sharpen the senses, to
embrace the world. . . . Through interaction with his environment [he]
learns about the natural world and then comes to understand his own
nature. He becomes one with nature. He becomes one with nature, one
with himself, one with the Great Spirit.[14]

Since humans are one with nature and their environment, they should
live in harmony with it and work cooperatively with it.

We are not kings over but servants of nature. In spite of the fact that
humans are, with all of nature, a manifestation of God, Satin says
"we would find it hard to think of our selves as 'kings' of the universe."[15] We do not have dominion over it, but rather are servants of
it. It is not our domain or possession. Hence, we should have "species
modesty." We should learn from other species. For example, whales,
dolphins, and porpoises have shown a better survival rate than humans have today. Thus, Satin asks, "what kind of interpersonal relations, ethics, philosophy has led to their survival over the last
15-million-year period? What is this mysterious business that they can
do and we can't?"[16]

An Evaluation of a Pantheistic View of Ecology

There are obviously many desirable aspects of a pantheistic view of
the environment, especially when compared with a materialistic view.
Nature is neither a free pond to fish empty nor a woods to hunt dead.
Nor is it an open mine to rob of all its treasures. On the other hand,
neither is nature a god to deify. Herein lie several important critiques
of a pantheistic view of the environment.

Nature is not divine. The heart of the problem with the pantheistic
view of the environment lies not so much in what it recommends doing
about the environment, but rather in why it recommends it. Nature
should be respected, but not because it is divine. The pantheist's spir-
itualistic view of nature is as extreme in one direction as is the humanist's materialistic view in the other. Nature is neither a machine
nor a god, neither mere matter in motion nor a living soul. It is a
wonderful and beautiful creation of God.

The pantheist confuses creation and manifestation. Nature is from
God but it is not out of God. It is a reflection of God, but it is not God
any more than our reflection in a pond is us. Nature is made by God
and for God, but not out of God. Nature is not God-stuff. It is as dif-

14. Ibid., p. 113.
15. Ibid., p. 107.
16. Ibid.

ferent from God as a painting is from a painter or as a sculpture is from a sculptor. Of course God is in nature like an author is in his book; it has come from his head and his ideas are manifest in it. But God is no more his creation than an author is his book.

Nature is not alive. Nature is not a living organism. It contains a multiplicity of living organisms, but it also contains nonliving matter. There is a qualitative difference between living and nonliving things. Life is characterized by specified complexity.[17] Crystals are specified but not complex. Random polymers are complex but not specified. In all of nature only living things are both specified and complex.

There is no scientific evidence that matter is alive. Matter is energy, and its energy is intelligently organized by its Creator. But matter is not alive. It is dead, inanimate stuff. While it is good (Gen. 1:31) and reflects its Creator, matter is neither alive nor divine. It is not animated by any sacred or life-force. As a consequence, any ecology based on such a view is without proper foundation.

Species are not manifestations of God. Since nature is not divine, neither are the species that are a part of nature. Thus, while species preservation can be justified on other grounds, they are not to be preserved at all costs because they are divine. This is species deification, not species preservation. As creations of God, all living species reflect the hand of their Creator, but there is an absolute difference between the creature and the Creator. The Creator is eternal and infinite; all living creatures are temporal and finite. Since species are not God, it follows that when a species becomes extinct, we do not lose part of God. God exists independently of all creatures. The whole of creation, living and nonliving, could become extinct and God would still be.

Humans are not one with nature. Pantheists confuse harmony and identity. Humans live in harmony with nature, or else they do not live. They either cooperate with nature, or their bodies soon become a material part of it by death. But there is a real difference between cooperating with nature and being part of the very corpus of nature. To be sure, human beings share a physical body with the rest of God's material living things, but humans are different from other living things in two important ways. First, our body is not their body. We have different bodies. Second, we have human souls; the rest of living things do not. Humans are created in God's image; no other living thing is (Gen. 1:27). Thus, while there is a unity of human beings and nature, there is no identity between them.

Kings can be servants. Pantheistic ecology presents a false dichotomy between dominion and service. A good sovereign serves his people

17. Leslie Orgel, *The Origins of Life* (New York: Wiley, 1973), p. 139.

well. In fact, the Christian concept of ruling is serving well. Jesus was the perfect example of this (Mark 10:45; Phil. 2:5–8). Thus, it is an unwarranted assumption to suppose that dominion must mean destruction. God did give Adam dominion over creation (Gen. 1:28), but he also commanded Adam to till the earth, and keep the garden. This entails cultivation and care. The earth is God's garden and man is God's gardener. The earth is the Lord's (Ps. 24:1) and we are his earth-keepers.

A Christian View of the Environment

Of all the great religious and philosophical systems, none gives greater dignity to the material creation than does the Judeo-Christian tradition. Both Testaments of Scripture support the contention that the physical universe is good and that it reflects the glory of its Creator (Ps. 19:1; 1 Tim. 4:4). There are several elements of a Christian view of the environment and human responsibility in it.

An Explanation of a Christian Basis for Ecology

Like everything else, Christian ecology flows out of Christian theology. Our view of the world flows out of our world view. Since biblical Christianity has a theistic world view, it will be distinct from both materialism and pantheism. Pantheism claims that God is all. Materialism believes there is no God at all. But Christians believe that God created all. Hence, a Christian view of the environment grows out of the doctrine of creation. As such it has several important elements.

The world is a creation of God. Traditional materialists hold that the world is an endless process of generation. Pantheists believe it is an eternal emanation. But theists hold to a temporal creation of the world. The universe has a beginning. "In the beginning God created the heavens and the earth" (Gen. 1:1). Atheists think the world emerged *ex materia* (out of matter). Pantheists believe the world arose *ex deo* (out of God). By contrast, Christians hold to creation *ex nihilo* (out of nothing).

The doctrine of creation has several important implications for ecology. While the world is not God, as pantheists say, neither is it ours, as materialists imply. Arising from this are two important aspects of a Christian ecology: divine ownership and human stewardship. As the hymn writer put it, "This is my Father's world." God owns it, and man is supposed to keep it.

The world is a possession of God. "The earth is the Lord's and everything in it" (Ps. 24:1). God made it, and he owns it. God is the owner of the garden, and man is the keeper of it. The Lord said to Job, "Everything under heaven belongs to me" (Job 41:11). God owns all the land, the trees, the animals, and the minerals. The Lord declared, "Every animal of the forest is mine, and the cattle on a thousand hills . . . for the world is mine, and all that is in it" (Ps. 50:10, 12). God owns the environment; humans merely occupy it. Hence, God's ownership is the basis for our stewardship.

The world is a reflection of God. Contrary to the Greek mind, the Old Testament affirms the essential goodness of the material creation. The physical world is not an evil to be rejected; it is a good to be enjoyed. The material world is not a manifestation of evil but a reflection of the glory of God. After nearly every day of creation, the record says that "God saw that it was good" (see Gen. 1:4, 10, 12, 18, 21, 25). On the final day "God saw everything that he had made, and, behold, it was very good" (1:31). Man is said to be the very best of the material creation because he is made in the "image of God."

Not only is the natural world called essentially good, but it is also said to reflect the glory of God. The psalmist wrote, "The heavens are telling the glory of God: and the firmament proclaims his handiwork" (Ps. 19:1 RSV). Again, "When I look at thy heavens, the work of thy fingers, the moon and the stars which thou hast established; what is man that thou art mindful of him" (Ps. 8:3–4 RSV). Creation reflects the glory of the Creator, according to the Old Testament. Nature is the reflection of God. God is everywhere manifest; he is in the light and darkness, on the land and in the sea, in the height and in the deep (cf. Ps. 139:7–12). The observing eye can see evidences of God everywhere. According to the New Testament, "ever since the creation of the world his invisible nature, namely, his eternal power and deity, has been clearly perceived in the things that have been made" (Rom. 1:20).

The world is sustained and operated by God. According to the Bible, God is not only the originating cause of the world, but he is also the sustaining cause of it. In fact, Christ is "sustaining all things by his powerful word" (Heb. 1:3). For by him "all things hold together" (Col. 1:17). God not only brought all things to be, but he causes them to continue to be. In short, God is active not only in the origin of the universe, but also in the operation of it. The psalmist wrote,

He makes springs pour water into the ravines; it flows between the mountains. They give water to all the beasts of the field; . . . He makes grass grow for the cattle, and plants for man to cultivate—bringing forth food from the earth (Ps. 104:10–14).

The Bible does not support a deistic or impersonal view of nature. God's hand is seen in the storms, the thunder, and the rain (Ps. 77:17–18). He causes the wind and the darkness (Amos 4:13). God is active in and through all of creation, "for in him we live and move and have our being" (Acts 17:28). Since God is the upholder and operator of the natural world necessary to sustain life, ecological interference with his operation is a creaturely presumption with serious ethical implications.

The world is under covenant with God. When Noah emerged from the ark after God had destroyed the world by water, God made a covenant with "all living creatures" (Gen. 9:16). The covenant was not made simply with humans, but with animals and with "every living creature" (v. 12). God said, "This is the sign of the covenant I am making between me and you and every living creature with you, a covenant for all generations to come" (v. 12). When the rainbow appears in the sky, "I will remember my covenant between me and you and all living creatures of every kind. Never again will the waters become a flood to destroy all life" (v. 15). God, the owner of all living things, has made a covenant with them never to destroy them by water again.

It is in this context that we can speak of treating animals with respect. First of all, since every creature is under covenant with God, we have an obligation to preserve each kind God created. Each one is a special creation and has its own special place in God's overall plan. He feeds "the birds of the air" (Matt. 6:26). Although God gave animals for food in this very covenant (Gen. 9:3), nevertheless, humans have no right to abuse animals. In fact, Proverbs says, "A righteous man cares for the needs of his animals, but the kindest acts of the wicked are cruel" (Prov. 12:10). God even notices every sparrow that falls to the ground (Matt. 10:29). Thus we should not only preserve every living thing God has created, but we should also provide for them and protect them.

Mankind is the keeper of the environment. God is the Creator and owner of the world, but man is the keeper. When God created humans in his image, he commanded them: "Be fruitful and increase in number; fill the earth and subdue it. Rule over the fish of the sea and the birds of the air and over every living creature that moves on the ground" (Gen. 1:28). Also, God "took the man and put him in the Garden of Eden to work it and take care of it" (Gen. 2:15). From these verses we can observe at least three basic obligations to our environment: to multiply and fill it; to subdue it and rule over it; and to work in it and take care of it. Let's consider each of these.

The obligation of propagation—All living things multiply "after their kind" (Gen. 1:21). Humans have a duty to do so. God said to

Adam and Eve, "Be fruitful and multiply (*rabah*) and fill (*mala*) the earth" (Gen. 1:28). Thus our first obligation to the natural world is to propagate the human species. Mankind was to fill the earth. Indeed, the Bible says Adam "had a son in his own likeness, in his own image" (Gen. 5:3).

Two things should be noted, however, about the command to propagate. First, it is a command to the race, not necessarily to every individual. Both Jesus (Matt. 19:11–12) and Paul (1 Cor. 7:8) sanctified singlehood for some. Second, it is a command to fill, not to *overfill*, the earth. The imperative is only to populate, not to overpopulate, the world. While there is debate about whether the world is overpopulated now, there is no doubt that the race is threatened with extinction. In short, the human race has done an admirable job at fulfilling this command. Since plants and animals are told to reproduce, and since they are necessary to human existence, there is an implied obligation not to let one kind overrun the other. A balance is needed between plants, animals, and mankind.

The duty of dominion—Mankind was given dominion over the rest of creation. Two words are used to describe this: "subdue" and "rule." "Subdue" (*kabash*) means to tread down or to bring into bondage. It conveys the image of a conqueror placing his foot on the neck of the conquered. It implies some form of control or power over nature. The word *rule* (*radah*) means to trample or to prevail over. The image conveyed is that of a person dominant or victorious. Both taken together leave no doubt that humans are not merely in nature, but are placed over it. They are not simply part of the natural world, but also apart from it. Man is not merely a peasant in creation; he is king over it.

The command to be keeper—In addition to propagation and dominion, the humans have the obligation of preservation. They are to work in the world and care for it. The word *work* or *till* (*abad*) means to serve. Sometimes it even means to be a slave to. The other word, "care" (*shamar*), means to keep, to watch, or to preserve. Both words describe an action taken on behalf of creation, not on behalf of humans as such. Humans are duty-bound to serve and preserve the earth.

To the scripturally uninformed, it would appear that man's duties are contradictory. How can he be king over and yet servant of creation? The answer is exemplified in the Head of the New Creation, Jesus Christ. He was servant in the world, yet sovereign over it. He ruled by serving (Mark 10:45; Phil. 2:5–8). Even leaders in the Christian church are commanded to "rule" the flock of God (Heb. 13:7 KJV). Nonetheless, they are to be "serving as overseers" (1 Pet. 5:2). They rule or take authority not as overlords, but as undershepherds. As Peter put it, "not lording it over those entrusted to you, but being examples to the flock" (v. 3) In this sense there is no contradiction between dominion and service, between having authority over and responsibility in God's creation. Our obligation as king over creation is to serve our subjects well.

An Examination of Some Christian Procedures for Ecology

The Scriptures not only give the general principles of our responsibility for the environment, but also lay down some practical procedures for preserving it. Although Christians are not bound by the Old Testament laws fulfilled in Christ (Rom. 6–7; Gal. 3; Heb. 7–10), nevertheless the Old Testament was written for our instruction and example (Rom. 15:4; 1 Cor. 10:11; 2 Tim. 3:17). Therefore, it is proper to glean from God's instruction to Israel things of benefit for us. Several such commands are relevant for our duty to the environment.

The law of good stewardship—Ecology is good stewardship. God has entrusted the earth and its resources to our care, and we must act responsibly with them. The Scriptures say that "it is required that those who have been given a trust must prove faithful" (1 Cor. 4:2). It is not good stewardship to squander our valuable resources. The earth is God's garden and we are its keeper. He said to Job, "Everything under heaven belongs to me" (Job 41:11). We must not turn God's garden into a desert, nor his seas into cesspools.

The law of Sabbath rest—The weekly Sabbath was not simply for human rest but also for animal rest. God said, "Six days do your work, but on the seventh day do not work, so that your ox and your donkey may rest . . . may be refreshed" (Exod. 23:12). Regular weekly rest is good conservation whether it is for man or beast. Rest is conducive to productivity of life and land.

The law of land resting—An Old Testament law directed specifically at ecological preservation is the law of sabbatical rest for the land. Not only were the people to set aside one day in seven for rest, but they were also not to plow their land so that it could rejuvenate also. Moses declared, "During the seventh year let the land lie unplowed and unused." This rest for the land meant that "the poor among your people may get food from it, and the wild animals may eat what they leave" (Exod. 23:10–11). They were to do the same for their "vineyard . . . and olive grove" (v. 11). These measures assured that the land would not be overused and there would be plenty for both man and animals.

The law of jubilee—God declared that "the world is mine, and all that is in it" (Ps. 50:12). In order to ensure this, he commanded that "the land must not be sold permanently, because the land is mine and you are but aliens and my tenants" (Lev. 25:23). Thus God established the law of jubilee through which every fifty years the land would return to its original owner (v. 28). This prevented the concentration of land possession and exploitation.

The law of harvesting—The children of Israel were commanded: "When you reap the harvest of your land, do not reap to the very edges of your field or gather the gleanings of your harvest" (Lev. 19:9). Likewise, God said, "Do not go over your vineyard a second time or pick up the grapes that have fallen. Leave them for the poor and the alien" (v. 10). This was not only a way to provide for the poor but also the wild animals (cf. Exod. 23:11). Furthermore, it would also be a check on any greedy tendency to rob the land of all its resources. This tendency is at the heart of the ecological crisis.

The laws of sanitation—Pollution of the environment is largely a matter of bad disposal methods. Much of the Book of Leviticus was directed at this very issue. There were laws for cleansing food, hands, and utensils (see Lev. 13–14). There were quarantines for those with infectious diseases (13:9–11). Infected clothing had to be incinerated (13:52). Even infected houses were destroyed (14:43–45). Human waste products had to be buried in the ground. The Law says, "As part of your equipment have something to dig with, and when you relieve yourself, dig a hole and cover up your excrement" (Deut. 23:13). It is interesting to note that all of these methods of sanitation were considered part of holiness, for the very section in Leviticus from which most of them come is prefaced with the words, "I am the LORD who brought you up out of Egypt to be your God; therefore be holy, because I am holy" (Lev. 11:45).

The law of warfare—Even in the exigencies of war, the children of Israel were exhorted to be careful not to disturb the life-preserving environment. God commanded them, "When you lay siege to a city . . . to capture it, do not destroy its trees by putting an ax to them, because you can eat their fruit." He adds, "however, you may cut down trees that you know are not fruit trees and use them to build siege works until the city at war with you falls" (Deut. 20:19–20). Even when war on a city is necessary, it should not be waged on the environment. We cannot defeat a country by destroying its environment.

The law against land greed—God owns the land, not man. He said, "The world is mine, and all that is in it" (Ps. 50:12). God declared to Job, "Everything under heaven belongs to me" (Job 41:11). The psalmist exclaimed, "The earth is the LORD's, and everything in it" (Ps. 24:1). Thus Isaiah condemned land-grabbing greed, declaring, "Woe to you who add house to house and join field to field till no space is left and you live alone in the land" (Isa. 5:8). Why? Because "a ten-acre vineyard will produce only a bath of wine [about six gallons], a homer of seed [about six bushels], only an ephah of grain [one-half bushel]" (v. 10). Land greed destroys the productivity of the land.

An Evaluation of the Christian View of Ecology

Several objections have been leveled at the Christian view of the environment. Most of them boil down to one basic thesis: The Christian concept of subjugation and dominion over the natural world has given rise to wholesale exploitation and pollution of it.

A statement of the charge against Christianity—The most influential work on this topic has been that of Lynn White, Jr., in his short treatise, "The Historical Roots of Our Ecological Crisis." White declares that "Christianity is the most anthropocentric religion the world has even seen. . . . Christianity, in absolute contrast to ancient paganism and Asia's religions . . . insisted that it is God's will that man exploit nature for his proper ends."[18] This exploitation, it is claimed, derives from the command in Genesis 1:28 to "subdue" the world and take "dominion" over it. Indeed, modern science traces its roots to this very passage. When Francis Bacon wrote his famous *Novum Organum* (1620) at the dawn of modern science, he exhorted, "Only let the human race recover that right over nature which belongs to it by divine bequest, and let power be given it."[19]

A Christian response to this criticism—It is true that Christianity is the mother of modern science and that modern technology has emerged from it. However, it is unfair for several reasons to blame the Christian world for our ecological crisis.

Even though the Judeo-Christian concept of creation is at the root of modern science, it is wrong to claim that this gave rise to the exploitation of creation. Even the celebrated statement from Bacon is misunderstood by the critics, for in the very next sentence, after noting that man's rights over nature are of divine origin, Bacon carefully adds, "The exercise thereof will be governed by sound reason and true religion."[20] So he clearly saw the need for divine guidance of and moral restraint upon man's dominion over nature.

It is not the Christian world view that encourages the abuse of nature, but the materialistic view. Those who see nature's resources

18. Lynn White, "The Historical Roots of Our Ecological Crisis," in Wesley Granberg-Michaelson, *Ecology and Life* (Waco: Word, 1988), p. 132.

19. Francis Bacon, *The New Organon,* ed. Fulton H. Anderson (Indianapolis: Bobbs-Merrill, 1960), p. 119.

20. Ibid.

as unlimited and man as the ultimate authority in the use of them are the exploitative ones. As noted earlier, some humanists even speak of "raping" nature. Christianity, by contrast, believes that God is the owner of nature and we are his servants. Our "dominion" is one of faithful stewardship of natural resources. We are over but also in the natural world and are called upon to protect and preserve it. The biblical command to control it does not mean to corrupt it. Our power over nature does not confer the right to pollute it. On the contrary, the Christian has the responsibility to care for and keep the natural world.

While *Christianity* is not responsible for the present ecological crisis, it must be admitted that to a significant degree *Christendom* is. However, as someone noted, Christendom can be defined as a group of dumb Christians. Christians do not always live by Christian principles. To the extent that Christians, like anyone else, are caught up in the spirit of their age, they too are materialistic. Here again, we need to be called back to the truth of Scripture for our true responsibility toward the environment. In this sense, we can be thankful for the helpful rebuke given us by ecological zealots of the New Age. We must remember, however, that it is not the biblical world that is to be blamed for our ecological problems, but rather our failure to live according to it.

Summary and Conclusion

There are three major views regarding the environment, each of which arises from a different world view. The materialistic view sees the environment as a limitless source of energy that has over time produced humans who, by virtue of their higher evolutionary status, are in charge of the world around them. By technology, they can change their environment in ways desirable for their own ends. On the other end of the spectrum are pantheists who believe nature is divine. Hence, it is our obligation to revere the natural world and to protect it against the intrusion of technology. Christianity, in contrast to both, neither believes in technological exploitation nor mystical worship. It holds that God is the Creator and man is the keeper of this magnificent and glorious world which it is our duty to keep and not corrupt, to preserve and not pollute.

There is a strange irony about man's pollution of his world: by polluting our environment, we are poisoning our own food and drink. Thus, we sin not only against the environment, but against ourselves. We sin against the persons who would live in it and against the God who made it both as a revelation of himself and for our good. Even if we destroy ourselves from polluting the environment, the environment will remain in one form or another. We were made to be keepers of the earth, and if we do not keep the earth, then the earth will not keep us. The question we should ask ourselves today is: Am I my earth's keeper? If I am not the earth's keeper, then it is becoming increasingly evident that neither am I my brother's keeper. This is my brother's earth, and if I do not keep it, then it will keep neither him nor me.

Select Readings

DeVos, Peter, et al. *Earthkeeping: Christian Stewardship of Natural Resources.* Edited by Loren Wilkinson. Grand Rapids: Eerdmans, 1980.

Ehrenfeld, David. *The Arrogance of Humanism.* New York: Oxford University Press, 1978.

Granberg-Michaelson, Wesley. *Ecology and Life.* Waco: Word, 1988.

Pirsig, Robert M. *Zen and the Art of Motorcycle Maintenance.* New York: Morrow, 1974.

Reich, Charles A. *The Greening of America.* New York: Bantam, 1970.

Schaeffer, Francis A. *Pollution and the Death of Man: The Christian View of Ecology.* Wheaton: Tyndale House, 1970.

White, Lynn, Jr. "The Historical Roots of Our Ecological Crisis." In *Ecology and Life*, Wesley Granberg-Michaelson. Waco: Word, 1988.

Glossary

Activism—War is always right if engaged in by one's government.

Act-utilitarianism—Each ethical act should be judged by its results.

Active euthanasia—The act of taking a human life for a good purpose in contrast to simply allowing death to occur, as in passive euthanasia (see).

Agapic love—Unselfish love; love with no demand for return.

Anarchy—A state of lawlessness where there is no government.

Antinomianism—There are no ethical rules or norms.

Artificial Insemination by Donor (AID)—Artificially implanting a human sperm from someone other than one's husband for the purpose of conception.

Artificial Insemination by Husband (AIH)—Artificially implanting a husband's sperm into his wife for the purpose of conception.

Bestiality—Having intercourse with animals.

Best-interest Judgment—Judgment made on behalf of an irrational or comatose patient to preserve his life but not to allow other procedures he has not authorized. In contrast to Substitute Judgment (see).

Cloning—Making "carbon-copy" organisms by gene reduplication.

Conjugal Rights—Marital rights, including sexual intercourse.

Cryonics—Popularly known as "deep-freeze" death; the process of freezing the dead with the hope of later reviving them.

311

De Jure Government—The alleged legal or rightful government as opposed to an actual or existing government, known as de facto government.

Deontological ethics—Duty-centered ethics stressing obedience to rules, as opposed to result-centered or utilitarian ethics (see).

Emotivism—Ethical statements are an expression of our feeling but are not really objectively binding.

Erotic love—Selfish or sensual love in contrast with agapic love (see).

Essentialism—An ethical law is willed by God because it is good; it is not good because it is willed by God, as in voluntarism (see).

Fetology—The scientific study of the unborn from conception to birth.

Gene splicing—Grafting characteristic from one animal to another, sometimes producing new kinds of organisms.

Generalism—There are no universal ethical norms, only general ones that admit of exceptions.

Golden Mean—The middle point between extremes, the moderate course.

Graded Absolutism—When two or more universal ethical norms come into unavoidable conflict, our nonculpable duty is to follow the higher one.

Harvesting Organs—Keeping human organisms alive for the purpose of utilizing their organs for research or transplantation.

Hedonism—Pleasure is the essence of life and should be sought for its own sake.

Hierarchicalism—Another term for graded absolutism (see).

Incest—Sexual relations with a close blood relative, especially a family member other than one's spouse.

Infanticide—Intentionally taking an innocent human life after birth.

Informed consent—Properly informing and obtaining voluntary consent before performing a medical procedure.

Intentionalism—The intent is the essence of an act, so that it is right if it is done with good intentions and wrong if it is done with bad intentions.

Intrinsic good—Good in and of itself, as opposed to good only as a means to something else.

In vitro fertilization—Artificially-induced fertilization outside the human womb, popularly known as "test-tube babies."

Jubilee, Law of—Old Testament law (Lev. 25, 27) that provided the land would return to its original owner after fifty years.

Lex Rex—Literally "the Law is King" as opposed to the King is Law; taken from Samuel Rutherford's famous book by that title (1644).

Middle Axioms—Universal ethical principles derived from other universal principles.

Monogamy—A relationship between one husband and one wife, as opposed to polygamy where multiple wives are involved.

Mores—Customs or practices of a culture, whether morally right or not judged as by a prescriptive (see) ethical standard.

Natural passive euthanasia—Allowing someone terminally ill to die naturally without withdrawing food, air, or water from him.

Organ transplants—Replacing defective organs in one person with healthy ones from another who has died.

Pacifism—War is always wrong under all circumstances.

Passive euthanasia—Allowing someone to die without technical or medical intervention to stop it, as opposed to active euthanasia (see).

Patriolatry—Radical patriotism that treats one's country as ultimate or on the level with God.

Personalism—Persons are the essence of moral values, an end in themselves, the only thing with intrinsic good (see).

Positivism—Values are chosen voluntarily as opposed to derived from nature or God; they are decided, not discovered.

Preemptive strike—An attempt of one country to attack its enemy first to disable it.

Prescriptive ethics—Ethical laws are imperative, not descriptive; they are a matter of "ought," not of what "is," as are mores (see).

Principle of Double-effect—An act is good, even though it may also have an evil result, provided that one wills the good result.

Privacy Right—Personal rights of noninterference from others; the rights of persons as private individuals.

Principle of Utility—See Utilitarian Calculus.

Quantitative Utilitarianism—Utilitarian view (see) that defines the greatest good in a quantitative way, measuring how much pleasure over how much pain is likely to result.

Qualitative Utilitarianism—Utilitarian view that measures the greatest good in terms of what kind or quality of pleasure over pain is likely to result.

Quality of Life Principle—Decisions should be made in view of the quality of human life that will result, as opposed to the sanctity of life (see).

Reconstructionism—Old Testament moral laws and punishments are still in effect today, including capital punishment for murder, rape, adultery, fornication, kidnapping, and rebellious children.

Remedial view of justice—Purpose of justice is to reform criminals, not to punish them.

Rule-utilitarianism—Ethical rules are chosen in view of the anticipated results flowing from keeping those rules.

Sadism—Afflicting pain on others for the pleasure of it.

Sanctity of Human Life—Human life is sacred, of great value, and should be protected and preserved.

Secular Humanism—There is no God or God-given moral law; decisions are made situationally in view of humanistic values, such as freedom and toleration.

Selectivism—Only some wars are just; unjust ones should be resisted, even those instituted by one's own government.

Situationism—There are no absolute ethical laws; all decisions are based on changing situations.

Sodomy—Sexual relations with others of the same sex or with animals.

Sperm Banks—Storage of human sperm with a view to later impregnation of human ova to produce a human embryo.

Spontaneous Abortion—A miscarriage: a natural or nonartificially in-duced discharge of a human embryo that cannot survive outside the womb.

Substituted Judgment—A decision regarding treatment or medical proce-dures made for another person unable to make it. Contrasted with Best-Interest Judgment (see).

Teleological Ethics—Ethical decision made in view of the end *(telos)* or re-sults, as opposed to Deontological ethics (see).

Test-tube Babies—Babies conceived outside the womb by in vitro fertiliza-tion (see).

Theocracy—Literally "the rule of God," government directly by God without human authorities.

Theonomists—Literally "God's law," a belief that civil government is obli-gated to abide by God's law as revealed in the Old Testament.

Tyranny—The rule of a tyrant or dictator who has disregard for the rights of human beings.

Unqualified Absolutism—There are many moral absolutes that never ac-tually conflict; all alleged conflicts are only apparent, not real.

Utilitarian Calculus—The formula of anticipated pleasure over pain used by utilitarians (see) to determine which actions are right.

Utilitarianism—The right action is what brings the greatest good to the greatest number in the long run.

Voluntarism—Something is good because God wills it, as opposed to essen-tialism (see) which holds that God wills it because it is good.

Voluntary Euthanasia—The taking of a human life for some good purpose with the person's consent.

Voluntary Sterilization—Medical procedure to render conception impossi-ble, done on either the male or the female organs.

Bibliography

Adams, Jay E. *Marriage, Divorce and Remarriage*. Phillipsburg, N.J.: Presbyterian and Reformed, 1980.

Anderson, J. Kerby. *Genetic Engineering: The Ethical Issues*. Grand Rapids: Zondervan, 1982.

Ashley, B. M., and K. D. O'Rourke. *Health Care Ethics*. St. Louis: Catholic Health Association of the United States, 1982.

Augsburger, Myron S., and Dean C. Curry. *Nuclear Arms*. Waco: Word, 1987.

Augustine, Saint. *On Christian Doctrine*. In *A Select Library of the Nicene and Post-Nicene Fathers of the Christian Church*, vol. 2, edited by Philip Schaff. Grand Rapids: Eerdmans, 1956.

————. *City of God*. In *A Select Library of the Nicene and Post-Nicene Fathers of the Christian Church*, vol. 2, edited by Philip Schaff. Grand Rapids: Eerdmans, 1956.

Austin, John. *The Province of Jurisprudence Determined*. 1832. Reprint. London: Weidenfeld and Nicolson, 1954.

Bacon, Francis. *The New Organon*. Edited by Fulton H. Anderson. Indianapolis: Bobbs-Merrill, 1960.

Bahnsen, Greg L. *By This Standard: The Authority of God's Law Today*. Tyler, Tex.: Institute for Christian Economics, 1985.

————. *Homosexuality: A Biblical View*. Grand Rapids: Baker, 1978.

————. *Theonomy in Christian Ethics*. Exp. ed. Phillipsburg, N.J.: Presbyterian and Reformed, 1984.

Baker, William H. *On Capital Punishment.* Rev. ed. Chicago: Moody, 1985.

————. *Worthy of Death: Capital Punishment—Unpleasant Necessity or Necessary Penalty?* Chicago: Moody, 1983.

Barnhart, Joseph E. "Egoism and Altruism." *Southwestern Journal of Philosophy* 7, 1 (Winter 1976): 101–10.

Beauchamp, Tom L., and James F. Childress. *Principles of Biomedical Ethics.* 2d ed. Oxford: Oxford University Press, 1983.

Bentham, Jeremy. *Introduction to the Principles of Morals and Legislation.* Reprint ed. New York: Hafner, 1965.

Berry, Adrian. *The Next Ten Thousand Years.* New York: Dutton, 1974.

Boettner, Loraine. *Divorce.* Phillipsburg, N.J.: Presbyterian and Reformed, 1974.

Brennan, William. *The Abortion Holocaust: Today's Final Solution.* St. Louis: Landmark, 1983.

Brunner, Emil. *The Divine Imperative.* Philadelphia: Westminster, 1947.

Burtchaell, James Tunstead. *Rachel Weeping: The Case Against Abortion.* San Francisco: Harper and Row, 1984.

Calvin, John. *Institutes of the Christian Religion,* vol. 1. Reprint ed. Grand Rapids: Eerdmans, 1957.

Canright, D. M. "The Law," and "What Law Are Christians Under?" *Baptist Reformation Review* 9:1 (1980): pp. 7–15.

Clouse, Robert G., ed. *War: Four Christian Views.* Downers Grove: Inter-Varsity, 1981.

Coiner, H. G. "Those Divorce and Remarriage Passages." *Concordia Theological Monthly* 39 (June 1968): pp. 367–84.

Culver, Robert. *The Peace Mongers.* Wheaton: Tyndale House, 1985.

Darwin, Charles. *The Origin of Species.* 1859. Reprint. New York: New American Library, 1958.

DeVos, Peter, et al. *Earthkeeping: Christian Stewardship of Natural Resources.* Edited by Loren Wilkinson. Grand Rapids: Eerdmans, 1980.

Doherty, Dennis J. *Divorce and Remarriage.* St. Meinrad, Ind.: Abbey, 1974.

Dostoevsky, Fyodor. *The Brothers Karamazov.* Reprint ed. Chicago: Benton, 1952.

Duty, Guy. *Divorce and Remarriage.* Minneapolis: Bethany Fellowship, 1967.

Ehrenfeld, David. *The Arrogance of Humanism.* New York: Oxford University Press, 1978.

Ellisen, Stanley A. *Divorce and Remarriage in the Church.* Grand Rapids: Zondervan, 1977.

Endres, Michael E. *The Morality of Capital Punishment: Equal Justice under the Law?* Mystic, Conn.: Twenty-third Publications, 1985.

Erickson, Millard J. *Relativism in Contemporary Christian Ethics.* Grand Rapids: Baker, 1974.

Fletcher, Joseph. *Situation Ethics: The New Morality.* Philadelphia: Westminster, 1966.

————. "What Is a Rule? A Situationist's View." In *Norm and Context in Christian Ethics*, edited by Gene H. Outka and Paul Ramsey. New York: Scribner's, 1968.

Fletcher, Joseph, and John Warwick Montgomery. *Situation Ethics: True or False.* Minneapolis: Dimension, 1972.

Geisler, Norman L. *Is Man the Measure?* Grand Rapids: Baker, 1983.

Geisler, Norman L., and J. Kerby Anderson. *Origin Science.* Grand Rapids: Baker, 1987.

Glut, Donald F. *The Empire Strikes Back.* New York: Ballantine, 1980.

Granberg-Michaelson, Wesley. *Ecology and Life.* Waco: Word, 1988.

Heth, William A., and Gordon J. Wenham. *Jesus and Divorce.* Nashville: Thomas Nelson, 1984.

Hitler, Adolf. *Mein Kampf.* London: Hurst and Blackett, 1939.

Hodge, Charles. *Systematic Theology.* Reprint ed. Grand Rapids: Eerdmans, 1952.

Huxley, Julian S. *Essays of a Biologist.* Harmondsworth: Penguin, 1939.

Jackson, Bernard S. "The Ceremonial and the Judicial: Biblical Law as Sign and Symbol." *Journal for the Study of the Old Testament* 30 (1984): pp. 25–50.

Kant, Immanuel. "On a Supposed Right to Tell Lies from Benevolent Motives." In *The Critique of Practical Reason.* 6th ed. Translated by Thomas Kinsmill Abbot. London: Longmans Green, 1963.

Kirk, K. E. *Marriage and Divorce.* London: Centenary, 1933.

Kitwood, T. M. *What Is Human?* Downers Grove: Inter-Varsity, 1970.

Koop, C. Everett. *The Right to Live; the Right to Die.* Wheaton: Tyndale House, 1976.

Krason, Stephen M. *Abortion: Politics, Morality and the Constitution.* New York: University Press of America, 1984.

Kurtz, Paul. *Forbidden Fruit: The Ethics of Humanism.* Buffalo: Prometheus, 1988.

Kurtz, Paul, ed. *Humanist Manifestos I and II.* Buffalo: Prometheus, 1973.

Kurtz, Paul, ed. "A Secular Humanist Declaration." *Free Inquiry* 1, 1 (Winter 1980/81).

Lammers, Stephen E., and Allen Verhey, eds. *On Moral Medicine.* Grand Rapids: Eerdmans, 1987.

LeFever, Ernest W., and E. Stephen Hunt, eds. *The Apocalyptic Premise.* Washington, D.C.: Ethics and Public Policy Center, 1982.

Lewis, C. S. *God in the Dock*. Edited by Walter Hooper. Grand Rapids: Eerdmans, 1970.

Long, Edward Leroy, Jr. *A Survey of Recent Christian Ethics*. New York: Oxford University Press, 1982.

Luther, Martin. *Letters I*. Vol. 48 of *Luther's Works*. Edited and translated by Gottfried G. Krodel. Philadelphia: Fortress, 1963.

Lutzer, Erwin W. *The Morality Gap*. Chicago: Moody, 1972.

————. *The Necessity of Ethical Absolutes*. Grand Rapids: Zondervan, 1981.

McCormick, Richard A., and Paul Ramsey, eds. *Doing Evil to Achieve Good*. Chicago: Loyola University Press, 1978.

MacRory, J. "The Teaching of the New Testament on Divorce." *Irish Theological Quarterly* 6 (1911): pp. 74–91.

Mill, John Stuart. *Utilitarianism*. In *The Utilitarians*. Garden City, N.Y.: Dolphin Books, Doubleday, 1961.

Moore, G. E. *Principia Ethica*. Cambridge: Cambridge University Press, 1962.

Moreland, J. P. "James Rachels and the Active Euthanasia Debate." *Journal of the Evangelical Theological Society* 31, 1 (March 1988): 81–90.

Murray, John. *Divorce*. Grand Rapids: Baker, 1961.

————. *Principles of Conduct*. Grand Rapids: Eerdmans, 1971.

Nathanson, Bernard N. *Aborting America*. Garden City, N.Y.: Doubleday, 1979.

Nelson, Richard K. *Make Prayers to the Raven: A Koyukon View of the Northern Forest*. Chicago: University of Chicago Press, 1983.

Niebuhr, Reinhold. *Moral Man and Immoral Society*. New York: Scribner's, 1932.

Nietzsche, Friedrich. *The Anti-Christ*. Translated by H. L. Mencken. New York: Knopf, 1920.

————. *The Birth of Tragedy and the Genealogy of Morals*. Translated by Francis Golffing. Garden City, N.Y.: Doubleday, 1956.

Olsen, V. Norskov. *The New Testament Logia on Divorce*. Tübingen: J. C. B. Mohr, 1971.

Orgel, Leslie. *The Origins of Life*. New York: Wiley, 1973.

Outka, Gene H., and Paul Ramsey. *Norm and Context in Christian Ethics*. New York: Scribner's, 1968.

Peters, George W. *What God Says about Divorce and Remarriage*. Chicago: Moody, n.d.

Pirsig, Robert M. *Zen and the Art of Motorcycle Maintenance*. New York: Morrow, 1974.

Plato. *The Collected Dialogues of Plato*. Edited by Edith Hamilton and Huntington Cairns. New York: Pantheon, 1964.

————. *The Republic*. New York: Oxford University Press, 1967.

Rachels, James. "Active and Passive Euthanasia." *New England Journal of Medicine* 292 (January 9, 1975): pp. 78–80.

_____. *The End of Life*. Oxford: Oxford University Press, 1986.

Ramsey, Paul. *The Just War: Force and Political Responsibility*. New York: Scribner's, 1968.

_____. *Speak Up for Just War or Pacifism*. University Park: Pennsylvania State University Press, 1988.

Rand, Ayn. *For the New Intellectual*. New York: New American Library, 1961.

Reich, Charles A. *The Greening of America*. New York: Bantam, 1970.

Robinson, John A. T. *Honest to God*. Philadelphia: Westminster, 1963.

Ross, W. David. *Foundations of Ethics*. Oxford: Clarendon, 1951.

Russell, Bertrand. *The Basic Writings of Bertrand Russell*. Edited by Robert E. Egner and Lester E. Denonn. New York: Simon and Schuster, 1961.

Rutherford, Samuel. *Lex Rex, or the Law and the Prince*. 1644. Reprint. Harrisonburg, Va.: Sprinkle, 1982.

Ryrie, Charles C. "The End of the Law." *Bibliotheca Sacra* 124:495 (July–Sept. 1967): pp. 239–47.

Sartre, Jean-Paul. *Being and Nothingness*. Translated by Hazel E. Barnes. New York: Philosophical Library, 1956.

Satin, Mark. *New Age Politics*. New York: Dell, 1979.

Schaeffer, Francis A. *A Christian Manifesto*. Westchester, Ill.: Crossway, 1981.

Singer, Marcus G. *Generalization in Ethics*. New York: Knopf, 1961.

Singer, Peter. *Practical Ethics*. Cambridge: Cambridge University Press, 1979.

Sloyan, Gerard Stephen. "The Bible as the Book of the Church. *Worship* 60 (January 1986): 9–21.

Small, Dwight. *The Right to Remarry*. Old Tappan, N.J.: Revell, 1977.

Soulen, Richard N. "Marriage and Divorce." *Interpretation* 23:4 (October 1969): pp. 439–50.

Steele, Paul E., and Charles C. Ryrie. *Meant to Last*. Wheaton: Victor, 1986.

Storer, Morris B., ed. *Humanist Ethics*. Buffalo: Prometheus, 1980.

Stott, John R. W. *Divorce*. Downers Grove: Inter-Varsity, 1971.

Thielicke, Helmut. *Theological Ethics,* vol. 1. Edited by William H. Lazareth. Philadelphia: Fortress, 1966.

Thompson, Thomas. "A Catholic View on Divorce." *Journal of Ecumenical Studies* 6:1 (1969): pp. 53–67.

Van den Haag, Ernest. *The Death Penalty: A Debate*. New York: Plenum, 1983.

Vanderhaar, Gerard A. *Christians and Nonviolence in the Nuclear Age*. Mystic, Conn.: Twenty-third Publications, 1982.

Vawter, Bruce. "Divorce and the New Testament." *Catholic Biblical Quarterly* 39:4 (Oct. 1977): pp. 528–42.

Warren, Mary Anne. "Severely Disabled Newborn Like Horse with Broken Leg, Philosopher Says." *National Right to Life News*. March 11, 1982.

Wells, H. G. *The Food of the Gods*. In *Seven Science Fiction Novels of H. G. Wells*. New York: Dover, n.d.

Willke, J. C., and Barbara Willke. *Abortion: Questions and Answers*. Cincinnati: Hayes, 1985.

Winnett, Arthur Robert. *Divorce and Remarriage in Anglicanism*. London: Macmillan, 1958.

Index of Subjects

emptive strike, 234; torture in, 234;
unjust, 225
Watergate, 75
Webster v. Reproductive Health
Service, 155
Westminster Confession, 285
Witchcraft, 200, 267

World War I, 224
World War II, 233
Worship: of Antichrist, 245; of idols, 245

Zealot, 230
Zen Buddhism, 299

Index of Authors

Index of Scripture

Genesis

1:1—163, 302
1:4—303
1:10—303
1:12—303
1:18—303
1:21—181, 303, 304
1:21, 27—177
1:25—216, 303
1:27—23, 146, 148, 160, 163, 164, 181, 209, 277, 301
1:27-28—185, 264, 267
1:28—190, 191, 277, 278, 279, 302, 304, 305
1:31—301, 303
2:7—136, 139, 278
2:15—304
2:16-17—22, 164, 168
2:17—182
2:22—278
2:24—264, 267, 275, 279
3—171, 184
3:4—189, 280
3:5—305
3:15—258

3:16—216
3:19—181
4—196, 209, 212
4:1—139, 278
4:1, 25—258, 261
4:9-10—216
4:10—163, 209
4:14—197, 209
4:15—194, 197, 209
6:11—164, 250
7:21-22—139
9:3—304
9:4—205
9:5-6—208, 216
9:6—23, 148, 164, 177, 181, 196, 206, 209, 210, 211, 216, 226, 229, 231, 234, 237, 250
9:6, 9-10—210
9:11—210
9:12—304
9:15—304
9:16—304
9:22—268
9:24—268
9:26—268
11:1-2—190

14—216, 227, 230, 231, 233, 237
14:12—231
14:15-16—231
14:19-20—231
15:5—258
15:16—228
16:1—258
18—261
19—261
19:5—258, 268
19:7—261
19:8—258, 261
20—82, 86
21:8—145
22—31, 90, 94, 108, 117, 120
25:22-23—148
26:7—90

Exodus

1—81, 90, 94, 115, 117, 118, 119, 120, 121, 126, 237, 241, 288
1:15-16—88, 95
1:15-19—26

330